D1519748

ALSO BY JUDITH GIESBERG

Women and the American Civil War: North-South Counterpoints
(Coeditor, with Randall M. Miller)

Sex and the Civil War: Soldiers, Pornography, and the Making of American Morality

Emilie Davis's Civil War: The Diaries of a Free Black Woman in Philadelphia, 1863–1865
(Editor)

Army at Home: Women and the Civil War on the Northern Home Front

Civil War Sisterhood: The U.S. Sanitary Commission and Women's Politics in Transition

LAST SEEN

The Enduring Search by Formerly Enslaved People to Find Their Lost Families

JUDITH GIESBERG

SIMON & SCHUSTER
New York Amsterdam/Antwerp London Toronto Sydney New Delhi

Simon & Schuster
1230 Avenue of the Americas
New York, NY 10020

Copyright © 2025 by Judith Giesberg

All rights reserved, including the right to reproduce this book or portions thereof in any form whatsoever. For information, address Simon & Schuster Subsidiary Rights Department, 1230 Avenue of the Americas, New York, NY 10020.

First Simon & Schuster hardcover edition February 2025

SIMON & SCHUSTER and colophon are registered trademarks of Simon & Schuster, LLC

For information about special discounts for bulk purchases, please contact Simon & Schuster Special Sales at 1-866-506-1949 or business@simonandschuster.com.

The Simon & Schuster Speakers Bureau can bring authors to your live event. For more information or to book an event, contact the Simon & Schuster Speakers Bureau at 1-866-248-3049 or visit our website at www.simonspeakers.com.

Interior design by Kyle Kabel

Images are from the Last Seen Project at https://informationwanted.org

Manufactured in the United States of America

1 3 5 7 9 10 8 6 4 2

Library of Congress Cataloging-in-Publication Data

Names: Giesberg, Judith Ann, author.
Title: Last seen : the enduring search by formerly enslaved people to find their lost families / Judith Giesberg.
Description: First Simon & Schuster hardcover edition. | New York, NY : Simon & Schuster, 2025. | Includes bibliographical references and index. | Summary: "Drawing from an archive of nearly five thousand letters and advertisements, the riveting, dramatic story of formerly enslaved people who spent years searching for family members stolen away during slavery"—Provided by publisher.
Identifiers: LCCN 2024030632 (print) | LCCN 2024030633 (ebook) | ISBN 9781982174323 (hardcover) | ISBN 9781982174330 (paperback) | ISBN 9781982174354 (ebook)
Subjects: LCSH: Freed persons—United States—Biography. | Freed persons—Family relationships—United States—History. | Enslaved persons—Family relationships—United States—History. | African American families—History—19th century. | Family reunification—United States—History—19th century. | African Americans—History—1863–1877.
Classification: LCC E185.2 . G54 2025 (print) | LCC E185.2 (ebook) | DDC 973/.0496073009034—dc23/eng/20241101
LC record available at https://lccn.loc.gov/2024030632
LC ebook record available at https://lccn.loc.gov/2024030633

ISBN 978-1-9821-7432-3
ISBN 978-1-9821-7435-4 (ebook)

For Marisol,
because it is her turn and because I can't
imagine what I would do if I lost her

Contents

A Note on Language

I have preserved the spelling found in the original Information Wanted advertisements in which some formerly enslaved people wrote place and proper names the way they recalled hearing them. I did not include *sic*, but in some cases I have added common spellings in brackets for clarity. When quoting the Federal Writers' Project interviews, I have preserved regional figures of speech, but I used standard English spellings of words. Whereas (mostly white) interviewers were instructed not to do so, many used dialect to capture "Black speech patterns," resulting in transcripts that are confusing and racist. I replaced "dey" with "they," "git" with "get," for example, and "chillum" became "children." I hope that making these changes will draw readers into the experiences of Freedom Generation rather than turn them away.

A THIRTY YEARS' SEARCH.

Mrs. Bashop's Pitiful Quest for Her Daughter, Patience.

THEY WERE SEPARATED AT AN AUCTION SALE OF SLAVES.

The Aged Mother Sought in Many States for Clues of Her Missing Child, but Without Avail—Now She Wants "The World's" Million Readers to Assist in Finding the Girl for Whom She Has Slaved So Long to Discover.

For thirty-three years Mrs. Clara Bashop, of Morristown, N. J., has been searching for her lost daughter, and she is searching still. Tears have often flowed over the woes of Uncle Tom, but her story is sadder and more pathetic than the one Mrs. Stowe so feelingly told.

Mrs. Bashop is tall and slender, and her sad face shows the refinement which the colored women in the aristocratic old families of the South so often possessed. At the Colbath House, in Morristown, where she is in charge of one of the most important departments, she receives the implicit confidence and respect of her employers and of all others who know her.

Mrs. Bashop belonged to Dick Christian, a wealthy country gentleman, who lived near Charles City Court House, Va. But like many other Virginia country gentlemen of those days, Mr. Christian became involved in debt and his slaves were placed on the block. Among them were Mrs. Bashop and her twelve-year-old daughter, Patience.

"She was a bright little girl," said Mrs. Bashop yesterday, "and when we were taken into the market-place to be sold I prayed that wherever we might go we would go together."

But her wish was not fulfilled. She was sold first, and Ben Davis, a professional negro trader, bought her. Then the little girl was placed on the block, and while the weeping mother stood by she was sold to a stranger. Mrs. Bashop fell on her knees before Davis and implored him to buy her daughter from the stranger.

"A Thirty Years' Search" (snippet), New York *World*, October 2, 1892

Introduction

By the time Clara Bashop walked into the office of the New York *World* to describe her search for her daughter, Patience Green, she had relayed the details many times to many different audiences. Freed in Mississippi when the Civil War ended, Clara made her way across the postwar South, searching for the girl, asking ministers for help, and placing advertisements in newspapers. Clara started looking where she last saw her daughter—Richmond, Virginia. Clara's daughter was twelve when they were sold away from each other. She'd be forty-five now, in 1892. Married, maybe. Children of her own.

Thirty-three years after she had last seen her, Clara still hoped to find her Patience.

Clara Bashop was one of thousands of formerly enslaved people who, in the years after slavery ended, took out advertisements in newspapers looking for family members they had lost in the domestic slave trade. That's what brought Clara to the *World*. Ex-slaves searched for sold-away daughters, sons, parents, brothers, sisters, wives, and husbands; described in detail the circumstances of their separation; and recalled the places where loved ones were last seen. Members of Freedom Generation placed these advertisements describing the families they had made in slavery and that they hoped to remake in freedom. This is their story.

Talk of generations is always imprecise. The historian Ira Berlin coined the term "freedom generations" to refer to enslaved people who became free during the Civil War and all of those born afterward.[1] Here, Freedom Generation is used more narrowly to describe men and women who were born enslaved and became free during or just before the U.S. Civil War. Their lives were marked by the great upheaval of the war, and, in the war's aftermath, they carved out new lives for themselves as freed people. The lines between generations are blurry, and experiences overlap. Members of any one generation can never entirely escape the experiences of the previous one. Many members of Freedom Generation, for instance, traveled far, as did their ancestors who had been forced across the Atlantic from Africa—except in their case they were forced into the Mississippi Valley and, beyond that, as far away as Texas. The children of Freedom Generation grew up hearing the stories about sold-away loved ones; they went to school, they learned to read and write, and their parents enlisted their help searching for family. So, while this is a book about those Americans who were born enslaved and lived to tell their stories, it was written for their descendants who continue their search.

The search for family unfolded over many years, as freed people tried to find one another and to memorialize those they could not. As white Americans tired of Reconstruction-era talk about Black equality and civil rights and embraced the Lost Cause mythology about slavery—that the institution was benign, slaveowner and slave were family, slaves were content—they demanded that formerly enslaved people move on. Some African Americans who were born after slavery could also be impatient and even embarrassed with talk of slavery.[2]

Freedom Generation did move on: its members lived out their lives, married or married again, and raised children who would not grow up in slavery. But they continued to live with the ghosts of family members who had been wrenched from them and sent far away. And they kept searching. As they did, the advertisements they published offered a counternarrative to a growing national amnesia about slavery. They resolutely told and retold their family stories, how they fought those who took away their children, and refused to forget mothers and fathers they hardly knew. Clara Bashop never stopped looking for Patience and told her story everywhere she went. Freedom Generation's story is about love and hope—hope that the ads they placed in the papers would bring loved ones back to them, that they would be able someday to remake in freedom what had been unmade in slavery.

✦

The institution of slavery was sustained by a callous assault on enslaved people's families. Enslavers bought and sold people based on financial calculations: how much could they afford, how much could they make, and how long would it take for them to see the return on their investment. Even slaveholders who might have sought to keep enslaved families together prioritized their own families' well-being over those of their slaves, selling "a favorite slave" to pay off a debt or separating a child from their mother to provide financial or emotional support to a daughter on her wedding day or to a son striking out on his own. Some of these sales were local, but many separated enslaved loved ones by hundreds or even thousands of miles through a series of transactions. This buying and selling of human beings is often called America's domestic slave trade. The greater the distance and the more times enslaved people changed hands, the harder it was to keep track of one another.

The term "domestic slave trade" once helped to distinguish it from the tight-packed ships of the transatlantic trade. But from the perspective of survivors, the "numbing privations" of the forced march south were as much a Middle Passage as the one their ancestors had traveled. For this reason, many historians now refer to the transactions that wrenched thousands of people away from their loved ones as the Second Middle Passage.[3]

By 1860, one million enslaved people had been sold from the Upper South to the Deep South. Each of them left behind family. One-quarter of those sold were between the ages of eight and fifteen; these children were often sold without a parent or a sibling.[4] When a child traveled that far from home, to a place where everyone was a stranger and nothing was familiar, they must have felt lost. Many never saw their family again. Enslaved people ran away more often to be close to family members than they did to escape to free states; we know this because when enslavers took out ads looking for runaways, they often had a good idea where to find them—with their spouses, parents, or children.[5] When a child ran away they headed in the direction of their mother or father. But they were not always sure how to get there and sometimes their legs couldn't carry them that far.

When the Civil War began, there were more opportunities for enslaved people to escape to freedom. As the Union Army swept through the South, white civilians fled, taking their possessions, including enslaved people, with them. Enslavers sold slaves deep into the South to distance them from the advancing army. Yet, when the Union Army came, enslaved people abandoned the plantations and sought protection behind army lines. These wartime refugees—about a half million people—came alone and in groups; once behind Union lines, men who enlisted left wives and children to an uncertain fate. Many wound up in army-run "contraband" camps, but these camps provided limited protection from want and recapture. That U.S. Army officials referred to refugees from slavery as "contraband" indicates that they continued to see these people as property, or at least that they were unsure if they were free. In these squalid and overcrowded camps, women and children who had made their way to freedom across the dangerous wartime terrain died of smallpox, starvation, and exposure. Few records were kept of these deaths that families might have used to learn the fate of loved ones.

As people fled slavery, family members lost track of one another. Those who did not escape became free in the same place where they had been enslaved; Clara Bashop was among them. Wherever freedom reached them, and whenever, Freedom Generation sought to find the family that had been taken from them.

There was no federal agency appointed to the task of helping ex-slaves find loved ones—no database of missing persons they could consult. The Bureau of Refugees, Freedmen, and Abandoned Lands, known as the Freedmen's Bureau, oversaw the negotiation of labor contracts between formerly enslaved people and their masters. Bureau agents encouraged freedmen and -women, who in slavery had been denied that right, to marry; once their marriages were recognized by state authorities, so too were their rights to their children. Parents came to the bureau for help having their children released from the apprenticeships that former enslavers continued to hold them in. The bureau as well as a number of private relief agencies opened up schools that filled with ex-slaves of all ages eager to learn to read and write. And, some agents did what they could to help reunite families.

In refugee camps, bureau offices, schools, and churches freed people asked around to see if anyone had news about children, parents, spouses, or anyone from the old master's place who might know where to find them. Sometimes freed people wrote to their former masters for help. "I wish to know what has Ever become of my presus little girl," Violet Lester wrote to the family who had sold her from her daughter, "I left her in goldsborough."[6] *Where was she sold? Did he get to the North safely? Has she remarried? Are they still alive?* In those early days, freed people discovered the limitations of what agents of the federal government could do, even when they were willing to help. But that didn't stop them from asking their questions and continuing to search.

In the absence of a federal commitment to reuniting slavery's separated families, freed people recruited allies from within their own communities. They sought advice from United States Colored Troops (USCT) soldiers and schoolteachers. They repeated the names of loved ones to Black pastors and newspaper editors. They took inspiration from their neighbors. And they left behind an archive of thousands of advertisements printed in Black newspapers documenting their decades-long efforts to rebuild their families after slavery.

✦

From California to New Jersey, Massachusetts to Texas, and everywhere in between, formerly enslaved people took out ads in newspapers searching for what slavery had stolen from them. Under headlines such as "Information Wanted," "Seeking For the Lost," "Do You Know Them?," or, simply, "Dear Editor," they looked for children, parents, siblings, spouses, uncles, aunts, army comrades, and friends. Hundreds of these ads appeared in papers in the first years of freedom, and they continued for decades. Columns of ads could be found in newspapers well into the 1910s, fifty years after emancipation. As late as 1920, the *Chicago Defender* was still publishing ads from formerly enslaved people looking for family lost in slavery.

The ads were a regular feature in African American newspapers, especially Philadelphia's *Christian Recorder* and New Orleans's *Southwestern Christian Advocate*, whose editors were singularly committed to soliciting and publishing them. Both were associated with Black churches, where church and newspaper offices served as clearinghouses for information for Freedom Generation as they searched for their family members. The *Recorder* ran a regular column of ads beginning in 1864 appearing under the heading "Information Wanted," making them easily recognizable to anyone who might have been able to help. Published by Philadelphia's Mother Bethel African Methodist Episcopal Church, the *Christian Recorder* had deep ties to the USCT; during the Civil War the paper printed soldiers' letters from the front and supported their strike for wages equal to white soldiers. Philadelphia was an important training ground for Black soldiers, and recruits traveling through the city circulated the *Recorder* throughout the South. Regimental chaplains took out multiple subscriptions of the paper to support the expansion of literacy and to draw men into the church.[7] A onetime ad cost $1.50 and came with a subscription to the paper; $4 bought an ad that ran for three months, $6 for six months, and for $10, an ad ran for a year. These fees could not have been easy for formerly enslaved people to manage. The editor of the *Christian Recorder*, Rev. Elisha Weaver, appealed to pastors of Black churches throughout the country to read the ads aloud to their congregations. This ensured that each search was broadcast widely and that the ads reached people who could not read the paper or who did not subscribe.

The *Southwestern Christian Advocate* was published by the Methodist Episcopal Church of New Orleans, and, like the *Recorder*, the paper was circulated widely, particularly in Methodist parishes in Louisiana, Mississippi, Arkansas, and Texas.[8] The terms were comparable to those offered in the *Recorder*. Subscribers ran Lost Friends notices for free. Others were charged 50 cents, a smaller onetime fee than paying $2 for an annual subscription. Letters to the *Advocate* appeared under the heading "Lost Friends." A short note appeared at the top of the column directing ministers to read the requests from their pulpits and "report any case where friends are brought together by means of the letters of the *Southwestern*." Freed people sometimes wrote to report they had found their family. "Sir," wrote Naro Gillespie from Egypt, Mississippi, "I feel very thankful for your paper which was the cause of my finding my relatives that I thought were dead. I found them in Sweet Home, Arkansas."[9] The cost of sending a letter to the paper again—and the effort involved—surely dissuaded people from reporting back.

Other papers also ran these ads. Some, like the *Richmond Planet*, were long-lived, but many papers came and went quickly. The *Afro-American Advocate* of Coffeyville, Kansas, for instance, lasted only two years, 1891–1893. The *Chicago Defender* was around for sixty years. The first copies of the *Defender* hit newsstands in 1906; soon after, the paper began publishing ads from formerly enslaved people looking for loved ones lost in slavery.

The advertisements highlight the role newspapers played in supporting Black communities and allow us to see how news and information traveled through and between these communities. The grapevine telegraph from slavery continued in freedom; it overlapped with the newspapers and continued to fill information gaps where there were no papers.

The ads provide narrative accounts of the lived experience of slavery, including everyday resistance. Freed people describe genealogies of slavery, naming kin and giving details about how enslavers and slave traders separated their families. The details allow us to understand how enslaved people survived separation, how family members got word to one another despite great distances and considerable surveillance, and how they managed to maintain hope. Many indicate how the separation occurred, and some offer a rough timeline of events. Sometimes loved ones are described in detail. Including the name of an enslaver could stand in for other details, such as a changed last name or an imprecise location. Memory can be fickle. Age, too, can be its enemy. Written by survivors of traumatic events, the ads that form the basis for this book are imperfect and incomplete, but they are part of an archive of family stories never before told.

◆

The narratives that make up this book were drawn from a unique archive of thousands of advertisements. Most ads were printed in Black newspapers that disappeared long ago. Until recently, these ads containing crucial clues for family genealogists and historians were buried in the storage of local historical societies or on microfilm reels that time forgot. A few early ads date to the 1830s, as fugitives from slavery made their way north and hoped to bring others with them; the latest ads date to the 1920s. They were written by members of Freedom Generation living in all the existing states and territories, and in Great Britain, Sierra Leone, Liberia, and Haiti. Some people writing in search of relatives from Canada likely escaped on the Underground Railroad, as did those writing from Mexico. Isabel Wilkerson described the Great Migration as "the first step that the nation's servant class ever took without asking," but Freedom Generation was on the move even earlier.[10] As they called out the names of their missing loved ones from places far and near to where they had once been enslaved, members of Freedom Generation expressed their great hope that neither time nor distance would matter in their search for family.

I began clipping and saving Information Wanted and Lost Friends ads many years ago as I came across them in the Black newspapers I read via the subscription database at my university library. I knew I had to make the stories told in the ads available to the descendants of the people named in them. Each ad contains information that can help a family find their ancestors. I knew, too, that whatever this archive would look like, it would be free. No one should have to pay to know their family's history. The result was the Last Seen Project website, which my graduate students and I built and which we launched in 2017. We'd dig into the microfilmed copies of African American newspapers that we borrowed through interlibrary loan and see what we found there. We hoped that one day we'd be able to publish one thousand ads.

As I write this book, we have more than 4,500, and people have visited the site more than sixteen million times.

We built a website, informationwanted.org, for family genealogists. We were moved by historian Heather Andrea Williams's description of descendants who "are haunted by the need to know, the desire to find out about those who were lost through sale or through the negligence of history."[11] We workshopped our ideas with African American genealogy groups and returned to debut the website with them when it was nearly ready to go live. The people we met in these groups told us that they wanted to work alongside us, so we arranged to have them transcribe the ads. Once transcribed, each word in each ad can be found via an easy keyword search. Black genealogists wanted to be able to download and post the ads to the family trees they curate on Ancestry.com, a commercial site, and we built in these features. Genealogists regularly report back to tell us when a word has been transcribed incorrectly or a map location is not quite right. Their input drives us to continually update the site to make it easier to use and to invite users to share their family stories.

From time to time, project codirector Dr. Signe Fourmy and I hear from people when they find someone they were looking for. But no bells ring or lights go off when someone finds a family member in one of the ads. Mostly, we don't know how the story ends for people who come to the collection today to find their ancestors, any more than we know how the stories told in the ads ended. When we talk to audiences about the project, the one thing they always want to know is: "Did they find each other?" We call it *the question*.

I always answer *the question* the same way. And no one is ever satisfied with it: "I don't know."

Over time I realized it wasn't enough to say that I didn't know whether people found one another. I wanted a better answer. I wanted to know what it meant for Freedom Generation to look for one another, how they managed it from all the various places where they had become free, who their allies and their detractors were, and what the obstacles, systemic and particular to location, that they faced were as they searched, and also as they lived their lives. What did it mean to be free and yet to feel the tug of those who had been left behind in slavery? To not know if they survived, and if they were also looking?

Each ad opened a door that might allow us to see how a freed person sought answers. So, I decided to follow some of them through those open doors. Each of the ten chapters that follow tells the stories of freed people searching for lost loved ones and working to rebuild their families during a period of dramatic postwar social change.

◆

Each search for family was unique, shaped as it was by the people who were doing the searching and those whom they sought, the places where they lived, and the accuracy of the details both searcher and searchee brought into freedom. The stories included here were chosen because they represent the most common searches found in the archive. Mothers were frequent searchers, as were sons and daughters searching for them. The collection is full and the record long of sisters and brothers looking for one another. Letters from siblings are the most common type, representing about 35 percent of the total. This may reflect their age at emancipation, as the next most common letter writers were children looking for parents (around 25 percent), mostly their mothers. Fathers show up in the archive as both searcher and searchee, but less often.

United States Colored Troops army comrades sought out each other; old soldiers reached out to one another for help with their pensions, perhaps also companionship. Ads appealing for lost wives and husbands appear less frequently than the others, perhaps because their remarriages complicated the search for first husbands and wives.

The most popular stories in the collection are those with happy endings, particularly the reunion of long-lost spouses. The 1903 story "After Forty-Four Years," for example, about Jeff Frierson and Mary Burt finding one another in Shelbyville, Tennessee, reviving the "old love" they had once shared, and marrying in front of their white friends. And an 1884 account, "A Romance of Slavery," out of Missouri about the (re)marriage of Levi and Aggie (their last names were omitted), seventy and sixty years old, respectively, is another favorite. "Everybody in the neighborhood" turned out to hear the old couple's story and to offer Levi and Aggie "many kindnesses." Reunions were crowd-pleasers then as now. Of course, people want stories to end happily. One does not have to buy the Lost Cause narrative about slavery to believe, or to *want* to believe, that Mary and Jeff and Aggie and Levi found one another again.[12] But, concerned that we might be mixing fiction in with nonfiction accounts, Signe and I had a long conversation with our students about whether to exclude stories like these from the collection. To check the urge toward sentimentalism, we decided we'd append a warning message to them instead. Each is tagged "white newspaper." It is our way of alerting readers that those accounts are different from those published in the Black press: they do not represent the experiences of Freedom Generation. The success rate of these advertisements might have been as low as 2 percent. Of the 4,568 advertisements (as of May 14, 2024) that comprise the Last Seen Collection, 105, or 2 percent, are from people who found one another.

Chance meetings of formerly enslaved people were rare.

Tens of thousands of children were taken from their mothers and fathers over the four decades of the Second Middle Passage. There were no nineteenth-century studies on trauma to explain what happened to them throughout their lifetimes. We know more today, for instance, about how trauma changes the way the brain functions and the way memories are formed and that some of these changes can be permanent. Chemical imbalances in the brain cause trauma survivors to continue to feel the effects of stress long afterward, and when they do, young people may miss developmental milestones and older ones age faster.[13] Many advertisements were placed by people who were children when they lost their loved ones. The stories they told in the newspapers are the testimonies of survivors to America's traffic in children. They underscore the central truth that selling children away from their mothers was the rule of American slavery, not the exception. The effects of that traffic followed them long after they became free. Acknowledging that fact can help us to understand how the road Freedom Generation traveled back to their families was littered not only with obvious visible roadblocks, such as political retrenchment and white supremacist violence, but also insidious invisible obstacles that made it harder to hold on to old memories and to make new ones.

Children sold alone had no one with whom they could organize the memories or process the trauma. The letters they wrote to the papers map a geography of loss, of pasts and futures that might have been. They document the "devastating mother loss" that lies "at the heart of the modern Black psyche," as historian Tiya Miles has said.[14] Their stories are difficult to read even today. Because a child who was sold alone or who was left behind at the sale of a parent often had only brief if vivid memories of the last moments spent together with the parent, it's hard to understand how the information in these ads might have helped a child find their mother.

In their ads, these grown-up children recall mothers and fathers whose acts of bravery loom large—large enough to encompass the sons and daughters they left behind. Celebrating the heroism of parents allowed formerly enslaved children to claim courage as their inheritance. They often chose terms that emphasized their small size. Thirty-nine-year-old Mary Delaney, for instance, remembered a mother who was taken from her "when I could but crawl." Lula Montgomery was sold from her parents "when quite a child—a nursing baby." Lula held on to details about her parents and the one memento she had of her mother, the tooth her mother had pulled from her own mouth and "tied it around my neck."[15] Jessie Johnson recalled that he was a "small boy" when his father tried to save him from a slave trader by carrying him across a swollen river and hiding him in a storehouse.[16] Jessie figured he was about fifteen years old at the time—nearly not a boy anymore. When enslaved children described themselves as quite small, the stories that followed served to underscore their own courage as much as they did the actions of their parents—despite being left to go it alone, they ran away, spoke up, and endured the great odds stacked against them. Sometimes simply surviving and remembering were acts of courage.

The truth about America's traffic in children and how, long after the end of slavery, children and their parents and siblings remained separated was an affront to those who believed that Americans were pioneers in developing uniquely child-centered family values. It contradicted the narrative of slavery's happy endings familiar to white audiences. Central to that narrative were the stories of unlikely slave reunions. Mark Twain wrote for *The Atlantic* in 1874 with the "True Story" of Mary Ann Cord's wartime reunion with her son, Henry, one of seven children sold away from her. "De Lord God ob heaven de praise'," Twain concludes the story, in Mary's voice, "I got my own ag'in!"[17] White newspapers perpetuated that narrative. The *Asheville Daily Citizen*, for example, ran an article titled "Found His Mother," about the Christmas Day reunion of John Williams—who was sold away to Mississippi when he was just a boy—with his long-lost mother. "John went along into the house," the story went, "and his mother, upon seeing him, rushed into his arms with many exclamations of joy."[18] Literature aimed at children drove home the point that slavery was a thing of the past, not something that disturbed the present, such as the 1904 children's edition of abolitionist Harriet Beecher Stowe's *Uncle Tom's Cabin* that assured young readers that "there are no slaves now . . . so we need not be sad over it."[19]

We want stories that end in reunion, for families to be made whole. We require that freed people's lives "be made useful or instructive," as author Saidiya Hartman has explained: we demand "a lesson for our future or a hope for history."[20] Today, the desire for Black family reunion remains strong; it explains the proliferation of Black genealogy groups and television shows that cater to them. It drives tourism to the remains of West African slave dungeons. The desire for reunion accounts for the popularity of stories that end happily.

Last Seen: The Enduring Search by Formerly Enslaved People to Find Their Lost Families recounts the story of one generation's work to reimagine and rebuild family against considerable odds. It points to the truth: in spite of efforts that persisted over several generations, few of these searches resulted in happy endings. Still, Freedom Generation's love for their lost family endured—and so did their search.

CHAPTER ONE

Patience and Clara Bashop

Clara Bashop had looked for her children in many places in the years she had been free. In October 1892, she traveled from her home in Morristown, New Jersey, to take her search to the *World*. Surely a newspaper with a name like that, in a place like New York City, could help.

Bashop arrived at the offices of the New York *World* on October 1. Someone noticed her—tall and dignified—walking into the bustling newspaper office on a Saturday and steered her to a reporter's desk instead of to a clerk to whom she might have paid for a short ad describing people and places in the old South, each one a clue that might lead to her daughter, Patience. The reporter was struck by the figure she cut; when Bashop began to talk, the tears "flowed down her face and dropped on the folds of her thick, black veil." Here was a story that would sell papers. "A Thirty Years' Search. Mrs. Bashop's Pitiful Quest for Her Daughter, Patience," read the headline. "Tears have often flowed over the woes of Uncle Tom," but Clara's "story is sadder and more pathetic than the one Mrs. Stowe so feelingly told." Sadder than Eliza's desperate flight across the icy Ohio River with her child in her hands because, unlike the fictional character in *Uncle Tom's Cabin*, Clara Bashop had not managed to save her child.[1] More pathetic because she was a real person, sitting across from the reporter, crying as he wrote down the story she told. A real person who needed the *World*'s help.

"[K]nowing the power of a great newspaper, she came to New York and asked THE WORLD to help her."

Bashop's story was published the next day in the *World* and the *St. Louis Dispatch* and then two days later in the *San Francisco Chronicle*—three major newspapers, spanning the country.[2] This unprecedented coverage gave Clara Bashop an enormous audience for her story of slavery and survival, and it surely raised her hopes for a long-awaited reunion with her daughter. Such a reunion would make good newspaper copy. The reporter for the *World* sprinkled the story with direct quotes from Bashop like "She was a bright little girl," which was sure to touch readers' hearts as they waited for the sequel, to build in anticipation. As was "I would know her the moment I saw her, and I will find her yet."[3]

But for a story focused on a missing person, it was short on crucial details that might have moved readers to come forward with information. The man who purchased Patience is identified only as "the stranger." The name of the person who had purchased Clara is also missing, as are details about how and when she wound up in Mississippi. Some of this information may have been lost in her interview. Of her passage into the lower Mississippi Valley, the *World* said only that "[s]laves changed masters rapidly then, and Mrs. Bashop was sold from one to another, passing into Alabama and Mississippi, being owned at Carrollton, in the latter State, when emancipation came," the endpoint of her "involuntary wanderings."[4]

It may be that the reporter never asked Clara for the names of the men who sold her at each step or that she forgot them. Readers learned that Clara "begged each master to write back to Charles City Court-House, Va.," a request to which "[s]ome complied. Others did not. But no news ever came of the missing girl." By not naming the various men who had bought and sold her, the *World* avoided placing blame for the violence done to Clara Bashop and Patience where it belonged. And, it practically ensured that the piece would have little benefit to Clara. *Who were these masters?* we might have asked. *How did she know that some complied? Did they know where Clara could find her child?*

In keeping "A Thirty Years' Search" so singularly focused on Clara and Patience, the reporter wrote slavery out of the picture. Instead, it became a human-interest story featuring a heartbroken Black mother and a host of hapless and unnamed white characters.

Carrollton, Mississippi, is nearly nine hundred miles from Charles City, Virginia. "Wanderings" did not capture the trauma Clara experienced as she was separated from Patience and then taken farther and farther away from her. Every fall, just after the harvest, enslavers tallied up their account books and decided which of their enslaved people to sell to slave traders. Traders then chained their human property into coffles and began making their way toward New Orleans or Natchez, where they were to be sold again into the cotton fields of Alabama, Mississippi, and Georgia. On foot the trip to New Orleans could take two months; packed into ocean-borne ships or river steamers, less than half that time. Each stage of the voyage was effected through violence, as enslaved people resisted separation from their families and sought to escape the terrifying uncertainties of what awaited them.

Papers like the *World* obscured the truth about the white men who routinely perpetrated violence against enslaved people. Men like Dick Christian and Ben Davis.

"A wealthy country gentleman" is how the *World* reporter described Dick Christian, the man who owned mother and daughter before selling them. Surely a "gentleman" would never have purposely ripped apart a family; only when "Mr. Christian became involved in debt . . . like many other Virginia country gentlemen of those days," did he sell Clara and twelve-year-old Patience to two different men, sending them off to their separate fates and beginning Clara Bashop's thirty-three-year search. Twice described as a "gentleman" and from an "aristocratic" family, Christian was not the villain in the story that the *World* told about Clara Bashop and Patience Green—he was simply an unfortunate victim of "debt," as if, like temporary insanity, such a thing could make otherwise good men do bad things. Enslavers were always in debt, or so they told enslaved people whose resistance they anticipated and hoped to avoid.[5] In 1892, that excuse played well with white audiences uninterested in hearing from ex-slaves about how their children had been taken from them, unless those accounts ended happily. The paper's boasted "Million Readers" were not meant to feel uncomfortable.

Often the slave trader appears as the villain in stories told in white newspapers, but not in this one. In the *World*'s account, as Bashop mounted the auction block, she prayed she would be sold with Patience and wept when the "little girl . . . was sold to a stranger." Dropping to her knees, Bashop begged the man who bought her to buy her daughter. That man, "Ben Davis, a professional negro trader," was so moved by her grief that he offered to buy Patience. "Though hardened by constant sight of such scenes, Davis's heart was touched by the agony of the mother." A slave trader with a heart, Ben Davis nonetheless failed to save the child from "the stranger" who had purchased her. Or, at least that is what he told Clara Bashop, his new property that he needed to secure until he could sell her, and that is what she told the reporter.

The reporter described Clara as "tall and slender" and with a "face [that] shows the refinement which the colored women in the aristocratic old families of the South so often possessed." If the reference to Bashop's "aristocratic" features was meant to imply her mixed race, then the reporter silently acknowledged the routine rape of enslaved women, again without laying blame. As had Stowe in populating *Uncle Tom's Cabin* with light-skinned enslaved people—like Eliza, who was described in the book's opening pages as having a "finely moulded shape; a delicately formed hand and a trim foot and ankle"—the *World* reporter's reference to Clara Bashop's refined features, what writer Caroline Randall Williams has called "rape-colored skin," tapped into white readers' obsession with mixed-race women.[6]

If Bashop's appearance wasn't enough to elicit white readers' sympathies, the author repeated the endorsement of her current employers in Morristown, New Jersey, a bedroom community for wealthy New Yorkers, where Bashop lived and worked at a boardinghouse and where "she was in charge of one of the most important departments." And then there was her motherhood. Clara Bashop's thirty-three-year search for Patience surely was evidence of the universality of mother love, the *World* concluded: that a mother's heart beats just as strong in the "humble bosom of a slave" as in the hearts of the paper's (white) readers.

Although Clara Bashop was a free woman, and had been for more than thirty years, the references to her praying, begging, and weeping collapsed the distance in time and place between late-nineteenth-century New York City and mid-century Virginia, locating Bashop in the same space as the unfortunate Dick Christian, who "became involved in debt" and whose "slaves were placed on the block." Dick Christian was not the villain in this story; in spite of her dignified presentation, though, Clara Bashop was not a victim. She was scarred and traumatized by losing her Patience. In the *World*'s telling of Clara Bashop's separation from her daughter, slavery was scrubbed of meaning; it no longer held the power to explain what happened to Clara, Patience, and millions of other former slaves. It was rather that these things—a man's debt, the auctioning off of human beings, the separation of mother and child—happened *to* people but not because of them.

But of course, separating families was a central fact of slavery. Mothers and daughters, brothers and sisters, wives and husbands were routinely sold away from one another. It was what made possible the settling of the cotton frontier of the Mississippi Valley, from which people like Dick Christian would become rich or lose it all—or both—investing in slavery and slave-produced cotton. *Prime field hands*—that's what people in their late teens and early twenties, like Bashop, were called, because they could pick a lot of cotton in a place like Mississippi and because selling them brought a good price to a Virginia family like the Christians. Of course, people at that age were also very likely to have children, to have claimed for themselves a family within an institution that denied them the privilege. With family came a sense of belonging, and in slavery one *belonged* only to the master. So, while enslavers might condone or tolerate slave families, they saw the ties between family members as loose and easily cut. Slaveholders did not always recognize the market value of children who were too young to work the fields, so often children were not sold with their mothers, fathers, or older siblings.[7] They were sold separately, like Patience.

The reporters at the *World* were not interested in these facts about slavery. Middle-aged Patience was a "lost girl," as the story called her repeatedly, as if she had simply wandered off, and her mother deserved pity for having kept up her search for so long.

The headlines underscored the point. To the New York *World* it was Clara Bashop's thirty-three-year search for Patience, "the Girl for Whom She Has Slaved So Long to Discover," that was slavery. What caused their separation was unclear.

✦

Clara Bashop turned over the rights to her story to a reporter, no doubt white, who wrote it to fit with the popular Lost Cause portrait of slavery. But this is not the way Bashop had explained things in an advertisement she took out in an African American newspaper, the Chicago *Appeal*, several months before. There, appearing at the end of a column of similar ads by ex-slaves that the paper printed for free, Clara Bashop's appeal was stated rather simply:

> Patience Green and John William Harris. I wish to find my daughter Patience Green. I have no trace of her since she was sold at Richmond, Va., 1859. She was then 12 years of age. John William Harris my son went with some servants of Mr. Batts (after the surrender) who lived in Prince George Co. to Washington City. He was 14 years old at that time. Both were of Charles City, C.H., Va., and belonged to Dick Christian, (in name only), by whom they were sold. Information will be gladly received by Mrs. Clara Bashop, Colbath House, Morristown, N.J.[8]

So, although the *World* focused on her search for Patience, Clara Bashop was looking for two children. Of her son, John William Harris, she seems to have picked up a faint trail, learning that the boy left Virginia for Washington, D.C., when the war ended—about six years after Clara was sold into Mississippi. There he would have joined thousands of other ex-slaves, like the "servants of Mr. Batts" of Maryland, who arrived in the nation's capital during the war as refugees; many of them stayed on to fight for political equality. An advertisement like the one Bashop took out in Chicago may have appeared in one of Washington, D.C.'s, several Black newspapers, alerting Harris of his mother's whereabouts and that she was looking for her children. If John William Harris was still in the city, she may have found him.

By the time Clara Bashop's account of slavery and survival had been co-opted by the New York *World* looking for a human-interest story about an old slave woman's faithful search for her daughter, white papers everywhere were publishing similar stories that threw a thick blanket of nostalgia over the history of slavery. The forgetting, the cover-up, began in the stories white newspapers and magazines told about the past, reinforced in public places where statues, plaques, and monuments to enslavers appeared. Many years later, to these was added a flag, associated with this time but really a product of a later one, that flew high over southern capitol buildings. Schools and U.S. military bases were named for men who had raised arms against their country in defense of slavery. By the twentieth century many layers of forgetting lay on top of experiences like Bashop's.

But at first there were words that seemed to be telling the same stories with crucial differences.

Clara Bashop chose her words carefully in the ad she placed in the Chicago *Appeal*. She named both of her children, the man who separated her from them, and the last known places for both Patience and John. She said nothing of Christian's "debt," if that is what made him decide to sell Clara and Patience, nor of her seeking help from her enslavers in finding her children. Nothing about the thirty-three-year search that so captivated the author of the *World* account. Bashop did not use adjectives meant to elicit sympathy or pity. She asked *Appeal* readers to contact her directly if they had information that would be useful to her search. And she added a three-word caveat, a postscript, to the clause identifying the man who had sent her away from her children, who had exercised his legal right as an owner of people to sell them at his convenience. Against this legal right, Clara Bashop asserted a moral and emotional one. Patience and John may have been recognized as the property of Dick Christian, but, she insisted, they had belonged to him "(in name only)."

Clara Bashop's two children did not share her last name, perhaps they never had. Of their whereabouts she knew little, and much of the rest of the family's story is unclear. But about one thing Bashop was very clear. John and Patience belonged to her. They always had.

✦

For every reunion story printed in white newspapers, hundreds of ads ran in Black papers throughout the country. Clara Bashop took out another ad in a Black newspaper in Richmond three years later, listing her address in that city. The paper spelled her name "Baship," but the story was hers. There was Patience Green and John William Harris, unquestionably *hers*. Details about John leaving for Washington at the end of the war. To Clara's original recollection, that John's departure occurred at "the surrender," the ad now read "Lee's surrender," as if associating Bashop's family story with Robert E. Lee added further clarity. And Bashop named Dick Christian in the new ad, a name that connected the fates of Patience, John, and Clara to an extended Virginia family which had at one time held many people in bondage. About Christian, the new ad read "by whom my daughter was sold," repeating a phrase that brought Clara back to that day in Richmond thirty-six years earlier.[9]

Bashop left only the faintest trace in the historical record, and her children left even less. John William Harris wasted no time getting out of Virginia, leaving behind only enough information so that his mother knew he was headed for Washington. No John William Harris matching his description appears in the census in Washington, D.C. When she was twelve, Patience went by the last name Green; by the time her mother came looking for her or word of her in Virginia, she may have gone by a different last name. Many enslaved Virginians carried the name Patience—given to them, perhaps, by enslavers who assigned passive names to people whom they claimed as their property but whose cooperation they could not take for granted. An enslaved child named Patience might be taught to suffer silently. Charity was another name designed to remind enslaved people of their place, as were Fortune and diminutives such as Jack, Sally, Joe, and Betty (instead of John, Sarah, Joseph, and Elizabeth).[10]

"Patience" may have been intended as a prescriptive, but when the name appeared in runaway slave advertisements, it put the lie to the stories enslavers told themselves about the contentment of enslaved people. An enslaver in Farmville, North Carolina, for example, offered a reward for a family of five who ran away in 1818: the husband's name was Adam and the wife's was Patience. The advertisement included the family's likely destination and warned readers not to help them, suggesting that this was not the couple's first attempt to get their family out of slavery. Allusions to suffering and forbearance notwithstanding, Patience and Adam took matters into their own hands.[11]

Slavery was "vastly beneficial" to African Americans, concluded a professor at Columbia University, writing not long after the *World* story, because enslaved people were brought under the "superior intelligence" of whites; slaves "were, in general, entirely contented with their new lot."[12]

Clara Bashop's trauma was compelling not because it was exceptional but because *she* was. And surely there was a happy ending waiting for readers in the next issue of the paper.

Dick Christian left a paper trail that adds a few more details to Bashop's story. Richard Christian appears in the 1860 census in Charles City, Virginia, as owner of nine people: one woman twenty-five years of age, a six-year-old female child, and seven males ranging in age from two to forty-two. Christian employed another eleven enslaved people; the eldest was a sixty-year-old woman and the youngest an eight-month-old girl. He had likely hired these people from their masters.[13] Christian told Clara that he sold her and Patience because he was in debt, but selling people *was* the business of Virginia planters, who had long ago stopped planting much of anything, having turned instead to the big profits to be made in selling people into the cotton frontier.[14] With five enslaved people aged fifteen and younger as his property, Dick Christian looked forward to more such lucrative sales—until war broke out.

Slavery began falling apart in Virginia as soon as the Civil War began. As whites marched off to defend slavery, enslaved people on the Virginia Peninsula fled to freedom by way of Fort Monroe, still under federal control, just down the James River from Charles City Courthouse. Dick Christian enlisted in the Confederate Army in May 1861, leaving the management and security of his slaves to his wife and, perhaps, to other family members living nearby.[15] A few days later, U.S. Army general Benjamin Butler declared enslaved people seeking freedom in U.S. Army camps—like the several hundred already congregated at Fort Monroe—"contraband" of war and refused to return them to their owners. More enslaved people came as word got out. General George McClellan traveled through Charles City in the summer of 1862, turning the plantations along the river's banks into army encampments in an attempt to take Richmond. By then, Clara and Patience were gone, but John still "belonged" to Dick Christian. A number of enslavers with that same last name learned the hard way that their "property" in slaves was not secure.

Eight of William Edmond Christian's enslaved people ran away in one day, on May 1, 1862, early in McClellan's Peninsula Campaign; that was just the beginning of the troubles for Charles City's slaveholders. In August, three of Gideon Christian's slaves followed McClellan's troops as they left the Virginia Peninsula, as did four enslaved people owned by Mary T. Christian, Gideon's wife: John and Peter, both thirty-five years old; Walter, seventeen years old; and, perhaps worst of all for Mary, Albert, thirty-eight and described as a carpenter.[16] It is not clear how these various Christians were related, but one year into the war, they all filed into the county courthouse to report the loss of their slave property to the U.S. Army. Four hundred ninety-two people had left slavery behind in Charles City by 1863; two of them were also named Patience. And when the U.S. Army returned in 1864, under General Ulysses S. Grant, surely more left, maybe even some of Dick Christian's slaves. If so, they began their journey toward freedom years before Clara Bashop, who was far away from the Virginia Peninsula.

By the time Bashop had saved enough money to leave Mississippi for Virginia, to make the nine-hundred-mile journey in reverse, Dick Christian "was dead and the war had swept away old landmarks and old recollections," as the *World* put it. By then, there was little left of the society slaveholders had built. Clara Bashop never got to ask Christian for the name of the man to whom he had sold Patience. Either Clara did not retain or she never adopted the last name Christian as her own, and neither did her children. Their last names—Green and Harris—may link them to previous slaveowners or to the children's fathers. No slaveholders named Green or Harris appear in the Charles City, Virginia, slave schedule, but among the county's free Black population, both surnames were common. Free or enslaved, Patience's father would have been unable to protect his daughter from being sold. Because the status of the child followed that of the mother, Patience was born into slavery, regardless of the status of her father, and because a slave could not be married, the state would not recognize a father's claim to her.

It may be significant that Bashop never mentioned a husband in her ad or to the *World*—if she had one, he may have died, been sold away, or deserted them—but the omission underscores "the turmoil" the law of slavery "had sanctioned over many generations" of Black families, one that freedom could not erase.[17] In this world in which white men had legal claim to the children of Black women and men, Clara Bashop had created a family that included two children and perhaps, at one time, the father of one or the other child. But she never had legal claim to her children, and after slavery, as southern states moved to retroactively legalize the marriages of ex-slaves, the complex and overlapping bonds of affection that slaves had formed with one another were not easily sorted into nuclear family units. In slavery, Bashop's family existed only as long as white men tolerated it.

When freedom came, Bashop, like most freed people, went into the world with nothing of her own. So, she stayed in Mississippi, because "she could not get away." Clara learned to read and write—or perhaps she had "stolen" that knowledge while she was still enslaved. Around 10 percent of enslaved people were literate.[18] Bashop worked her way back to Virginia, then to Kentucky, maybe on some intelligence she'd picked up in Charles City. Then she returned to South Carolina, where, years before, she had been sold for the second time. From there she retraced her own steps into the Second Middle Passage, seeking answers from former enslavers or "professional negro traders" like Ben Davis, who had negotiated Bashop's changing hands from one enslaver to another.

Everywhere in the 1880s and '90s, freed people were pulling up stakes and finding new places to call their own. Some headed far away from the cotton plantations where they had always lived and still labored. Exodusters went to Kansas where, like the Jews in the Book of Exodus, they hoped to find their promised land. Others did not go far at all but instead formed independent Black towns—in Alabama, Mississippi, and Texas, for instance—where they could protect themselves from white violence and where they opened schools, built churches, and started benevolent societies.[19] As they moved, they carved paths that would eventually bring hundreds of thousands out of the South to the North, Midwest, and West. Bashop and the others who traveled these roads built what historian Steven Hahn called a "chain of kin, neighbors, and friends that would guide and support those who followed." Information, too, flowed back and forth along the paths they carved, carried by word of mouth and, as freed people learned to read, via the printed word.[20]

As she retraced her steps, this time with less certainty about where she would find her children, Clara broadcast their names all along the way, enlisting the help of "colored preachers" to spread the word to their congregations, as the *World* had recounted, "in order that one person might tell the story to another and thus spread it throughout the country." The grapevine telegraph is what enslaved people had called the covert means by which they shared news and rumors with one another when doing so could get a slave killed. Now information was shared openly, announced from the pulpits of Black churches and published in Black newspapers, where Clara, among many others, continued her search.

Everywhere Black communities were found, so were Black newspapers—hundreds of them: one scholar described the growth of Black newspapers at this time as an "explosion." By one count, in Mississippi alone, African Americans published 150 newspapers between 1890 and 1910.[21] Many of these papers printed advertisements announcing searches like Bashop's—for children lost in slavery, and for mothers, siblings, fathers, wives, and husbands. In this way, Clara Bashop left behind clues along the roads she traveled, a chain of words and remembrances of John and Patience and the family they had made together. No wonder it is difficult to find Bashop in the records; she seems to have stayed anywhere only long enough to tell her story and place an ad. Then she moved on. How she came to live in New Jersey remains a mystery.

White newspapers told stories of husbands and wives who found each other again and remarried—such as George Harris and Mary J. Brooks, who were separated by sale in Louisiana in 1859 and remarried in California in 1904. "The couple will finish their days in Fresno County at Harris' home, north of town," the story read, "where the large family of thirty-one will be raised in old plantation style."[22] Reunion stories that ended with happy couples raising families, "old plantation style," played well in the white press. The Memphis *Public Ledger* ran them; one on June 28, 1882, appeared under the headline "Romantic Meeting," describing a couple's chance meeting in San Antonio, Texas, and their "reconciliation" after more than twenty years: "The event is a romantic one in the extreme and illustrates the wonderful vicissitudes of human life."[23]

The term "reconciliation" was not incidental. These feel-good vignettes of faithful old slaves meeting and marrying served as metaphors for the reconciliation of North and South as the two former adversaries let go of past grievances and agreed to the Lost Cause version of the past stripped of real facts about slavery. Such as the 1908 *Philadelphia Inquirer* account of Mrs. Louisa Fry of Pleasantville, New Jersey, who, while working at her job as a domestic in Atlantic City, overheard someone mention "an old colored woman in Philadelphia, who claimed to come from the same Virginia village" as she. When Mrs. Fry met the woman, she recognized her as her long-lost mother; inexplicably the paper called Fry's mother "'Aunty' Strong." She claimed to be 106.[24]

The *World*, too, favored slavery stories with happy endings. Like the one the paper published on February 23, 1894, describing the reunion of John Jones with the "long lost mother" from whom he was separated on the "Slave Auction Block." John Jones, who the paper described as "prosperous" and "successful in accumulating the world's goods," found his mother, Parthenia, by writing to the newspapers. "It is hard to appreciate such a condition of affairs in these days of freedom," the paper concluded, "but the facts are incontrovertible."[25] Clara Bashop would not have found it hard to appreciate John's predicament, or Parthenia's; neither would any of those formerly enslaved people whose advertisements appeared alongside hers in the Black press and whose paths she crossed as she searched for her children.

When the *World* devoted a long column to Clara Bashop's search for Patience, they likely anticipated running a follow-up story reporting Clara's reunion, one that could attest to "the power of a great newspaper" and that ended with a well-married and "prosperous" Patience taking in her elderly mother to live with her in her spacious home, where she was raising her own children, "old plantation style," confirming for readers that, however bad slavery had been, it had ended happily.

✦

Three years after Clara Bashop enlisted the help of the *World*, she still had not found her children.[26] She had crossed the country several times, telling the story of her family, and she was not done.

In short, succinct advertisements, members of Freedom Generation continued to tell their stories of love and hope, of families that, against all odds, were made in slavery and that slavery's survivors worked to remake in freedom. Their searches left behind evidence crucial to understanding the experience of people seeking to come out of slavery's long shadow, to the search for family, and of people living out their lives while still holding on to and speaking the truth about the past. Members of Freedom Generation led full lives—in some cases, very long ones, like Mrs. Louisa Fry's mother, for example, or the centenarians interviewed by the Works Progress Administration Federal Writers' Project in the 1930s.[27] And they made new families after slavery while they continued to hold on to those that had been taken from them.

CHAPTER TWO

The Children of Hagar Outlaw

INFORMATION WANTED

Of the children of Hagar Outlaw, who went from Wake Forest. Three of them, (their names being Cherry, Viny, and Mills Outlaw,) were bought by Abram Hester. Noah Outlaw was taken to Alabama by Joseph Turner Hillsborough. John Outlaw was sold to George Vaughan. Eli Outlaw was sold by Joseph Outlaw. He acted as watchman for old David Outlaw. Thomas Rembry Outlaw was taken away by Wm. Outlaw. Julia Outlaw was sold in New Orleans by Dr. Outlaw. I live in Raleigh, and I hope they will think enough of their mother to come and look for her, as she is growing old, and needs help. She will be glad to see them again at her side. The place is healthy, and they can all do well here. As the hand of time steals over me now so rapidly, I wish to see my dear ones once more clasped to their mother's heart as in days of yore. Come to the capital of North Carolina, and you will find your mother there, eagerly awaiting her loved ones.

Hugh Outlaw, if you should find any or all of my children, you will do me an incalculable favor by immediately informing them that their mother still lives.

Hagar Outlaw, "Information Wanted,"
Christian Recorder (Philadelphia, PA), April 7, 1866

Hagar Outlaw spent sixty years in slavery. In that time, she gave birth to at least nine children. One by one, Hagar's children were sold from her. She kept track of them as best she could, and when she became free she got word out to them that "their mother still lives." In a newspaper advertisement in the *Christian Recorder*, she called her children to come to her, naming eight of them, maybe in the order they were sold: Cherry, Viny, and Mills Outlaw; Noah Outlaw; John Outlaw; Eli Outlaw; Thomas Rembry Outlaw; and Julia Outlaw. (One more child, Dolly, was not listed in Hagar's 1866 advertisement.) Her words were urgent—"immediately," "eagerly." Without the comfort of her children or their financial support, an aging freedwoman like Hagar faced an uncertain future. At sixty, Hagar Outlaw did not want to grow old alone.

Hagar's search began in Raleigh, North Carolina, where she placed the advertisement naming her children and some of the men who had bought or sold them. To her children, Outlaw included this message: "Come to the capital of North Carolina, and you will find your mother there, eagerly awaiting her loved ones." "The place is healthy," she added, "and they can do well here."

As she slipped back and forth from third to first person, Hagar Outlaw communicated some of the emotions she felt at a moment when she hoped to be reunited with her children. "I hope they will think enough of their mother to come and look for her, as she is growing old, and needs help," she said. "As the hand of time steals over me now so rapidly, I wish to see my dear ones once more clasped to their mother's heart as in days of yore." She had waited for years to see them. Hagar began her life in freedom by listing her name next to theirs, for all to see the family she had made in slavery.

All of them shared a surname with her former enslaver.

David Outlaw was also in Raleigh, although Hagar Outlaw did not ask for his help in her ad. Lawyer and one-term United States congressman from Bertie County, David Outlaw had been one of North Carolina's biggest enslavers, calling ninety enslaved people his own. David Outlaw was a powerful white man descended from the state's founding generation. After one undistinguished term representing his district in Washington, he was serving in the state senate when Hagar came to Raleigh looking for her children. If anyone knew where the children were, it was "old David Outlaw," as Hagar referred to him.

Finding them would not be easy. Like Clara Bashop's, Hagar Outlaw's advertisement included important details about where their mother had last seen them—Wake Forest—and the various men responsible for selling or buying them. But the short notice left out other crucial details, such as the complete names of these buyers and sellers and who her children were sold *to*. Outlaw was silent as well about when the children were sold, and details about when or where any of them became free were also missing.

Several local Raleigh newspapers printed advertisements like Hagar Outlaw's, including the *Tri-Weekly Standard*, the *Daily Standard*, and the *Weekly Standard*. None of these papers were Black-owned, and, unlike the *Christian Recorder*, the Raleigh papers published only single ads that were not part of long columns or special sections devoted to formerly enslaved people looking for family members.[1] Single ads from North Carolina freed people could easily be overlooked squeezed in between large print advertisements selling farm supplies and equipment.[2] It's no wonder that, like so many others, Hagar Outlaw placed her advertisement looking for her children in a Black-owned newspaper she'd heard about from a USCT soldier, perhaps, or an African Methodist Episcopal (AME) Church pastor.

Hagar Outlaw paid $1.50 to place the advertisement in the *Recorder*, something that could not have been easy for her. Every word counted; too many cost you extra. Hagar chose her words to appeal to people she knew and to anyone related to, working for, or in contact with members of the extended Outlaw family. With roots dating back to the first families of North Carolina, this latter group was surely rather large, including readers familiar with the state's white slaveholding elite, the properties they owned in the eastern part of the state, and the enslaved people who the white Outlaws had once called their own.

Former slaves often marked their freedom by changing their names, shedding the names given to them by their enslavers and starting life over with names of their choosing. "My slave name was Daniel Cooper," read an ad from a man looking for his mother, father, and seven sisters and brothers, "my name at this time is Daniel West."[3] L. E. Gideon, "owner and originator of Gideon's Refined Negro Minstrels," could not confirm his father's current last name. "He may have went by the name of Rhine or McAfee, having been owned by both slave holders and therefore used both names."[4] His first name was Robert; as a slave he enlisted in the 1st Kansas Colored Infantry, a regiment of escaped slaves from Arkansas and Missouri, like Robert.[5] Robert Gideon became free when he put on a blue U.S. Army uniform; his wife and son, sometime thereafter. Forty years later, his son said in his ad that he was "a gentleman of refinement, culture and wealth. He is one of the leading showmen of the country, carrying thirty people and has been for years. He and his mother would profit considerable if they could locate him." L. E. Gideon had made a good life for himself in the freedom that his father had helped to make possible. Now he wanted to share it with his father, whatever his name or whereabouts. A son's inheritance to his father.

There were good reasons to keep a slave name: applying for a U.S. Army pension, for instance, or retaining a connection to and perhaps the protection or patronage of the planter elite. Keeping a name gave freed people a sense of stability.[6] It could also help a mother find her children.

Hagar Outlaw found three.

Out of the tangled genealogy of slavery, Hagar managed to wrench three of the children the white Outlaws had sold away from her, to live with them as they formed their own families, to "clasp" them to her heart as the "hand of time" stole over her. Hugh Outlaw, one of the men she named in her ad and whose connection to Hagar and her children is unclear, may have helped her to locate them. It helped, too, that Hagar remembered many of the details of each child's sale, as if they were seared in her memory, and that she had made her way to Raleigh, where she enlisted help in writing an ad to be placed in a Philadelphia newspaper. In the years after she became free, Hagar put back together the family she had made in slavery.

Her daughters Julia and Dolly responded first. By 1870, the three had made a home together in Raleigh, Julia and Dolly supporting their mother and Julia's son David. Julia took in wash, and Dolly worked as a "nurse," a term that could have described a number of jobs. And Hagar Outlaw's family continued to grow. Hagar found her son Eli, next, and their two households became one. Hagar Outlaw found the support she needed in her adult children. Making a family together allowed Julia to send David to school. Hagar's granddaughter, Mary—daughter perhaps to Julia or one of Hagar's other children—also attended school. They stayed in Raleigh, did well as she had promised, and avoided the fields where others worked shares for the same families to whom they had been enslaved. Hagar's grandchildren and some of her own children learned to read and write; some owned their homes. They enjoyed happy moments together—all of them made possible by Hagar Outlaw's search for her children. Surely, she hoped to someday find them all.

Of the children's father, Thomas Outlaw, little is known. Hagar made sure that the justice of the peace to whom Eli ("Elijah" is what he wrote, in his own hand) applied for a marriage license on March 27, 1875, recorded his father's name next to Hagar's. The next day Hagar stood beside her daughters at Raleigh's Second Baptist Church to witness Elijah's marriage to Nancy Robinson. Perhaps she thought about her own marriage that day, about Thomas, who may not have survived to the day that his son was married in a Black-owned church by a white pastor from Massachusetts; he did not get to enjoy the comfort of being surrounded by them all without fear of having them taken away again. Freedom Generation experienced moments of joy, of relief at what they had managed to take back for themselves. These moments were surely no less joyful when tempered by the bittersweet memories of what slavery had taken from them forever.

✦

Hagar Outlaw's 1866 advertisement serves as a time stamp, marking the moment when she went to the paper with her family story. That story began decades before.

Hagar and Thomas Outlaw had built a family in slavery, like so many others, aware that it existed at the forbearance of the white Outlaws. Over nearly thirty years, Hagar Outlaw had babies—from around 1824, when Eli was born, to 1852, Cherry's likely birth date—about every three years, from around nineteen years old to forty-seven.[7] There may have been more babies who died at birth or soon thereafter.[8]

With no information about him, we cannot know if Thomas was father to all of Hagar's children. Surely Hagar's son, Thomas Rembry, "taken by Wm Outlaw," was named for his father. By continuing to have children even as the white Outlaws sold them away from her, Hagar Outlaw refused to allow the white Outlaws to deny her and Thomas a family.

Thomas and Hagar were likely married around the time that Eli was born, in a ceremony that was witnessed by family, kin, and friends living on or near the Outlaw plantation in Windsor, North Carolina. Hagar was born in Windsor, so it may have been that members of her family were there that day. Her mother or a sister may have helped Hagar deliver her children. David Outlaw approved of the marriage, but it was not recognized by state law.[9] Neither did the law recognize Hagar and Thomas's claims to their own children. Every one of the children belonged to David Outlaw, a white man, a lawyer well versed in the state laws that gave him the right to dispose of another person's children as he saw fit. Slaveholders made no secret of their interests, condoning marriages that produced children and condemning those that did not. Don't forget, a North Carolina enslaver said at the marriage of two enslaved people, it was their "duty to have a houseful of children" for him.[10]

But enslaved people like Hagar and Thomas had children to pass along their culture, secure their legacy, and affirm their own lives. Having a child in slavery was "an act of defiance, a signal to the slaveowner that no matter how cruel and inhumane his actions," enslaved people would not "be subjugated and destroyed." "'My child him is mine'" was how an enslaved Kentucky mother put it.[11] Clara Bashop said the same about her children, Patience and John, who had belonged to Dick Christian "in name only." Surely Hagar felt the same about hers.

It was not uncommon for enslaved women to have as many children as she did, but Hagar pushed the outer limits of reproductive capacity by giving birth in her late forties. At the same time, enslavers were pushing enslaved people's productive capacities in the cotton frontier of the American South—Georgia, Alabama, Mississippi, and Louisiana. Hagar's son Noah "was taken to Alabama by Joseph Turner

Hillsborough"; Julia "was sold in New Orleans by Dr. Outlaw," the prefix "Dr." referencing David Outlaw's status as a lawyer.

Most never made it back from the labor camps of the lower Mississippi Valley. Julia Outlaw did.

Before the war, sixteen white Outlaws claimed ownership of 244 enslaved people in North Carolina, mostly in Bertie and Duplin Counties.[12] Bertie County is in the northeastern part of the state, where the Chowan River runs into the Albemarle Sound. Duplin is one hundred miles southwest, near the Cape Fear River.[13] The white Outlaws in the two counties were related by blood and strategic marriages that connected them to other prominent families with similar pedigrees. David Outlaw and his wife, Emily, had six children; when each of them came of age they received part of a massive estate made possible not only by generations of slave labor but by the money they made selling children.[14]

In 1860, federal enumerators counted 130 enslaved people in Bertie County belonging to David (91), Edward (21), Jeremiah (9), and Wilson (9) Outlaw. Fifty-three-year-old David Outlaw had tripled his property in slaves over a ten-year period. On the eve of the Civil War, he was among the 2 percent of white North Carolinians who claimed ownership of fifty or more enslaved people. Most white North Carolinians owned none. Planters in Bertie County were not singularly committed to cotton; enslaved people produced a variety of crops, including tobacco and wool for export. Even so, over a ten-year period, the enslaved people in the county were responsible for a fivefold increase in cotton production; in that same time, their numbers grew by only 1.1 percent.[15] This increased cotton production was made possible by higher and higher picking totals from enslaved people.

Pushing enslaved people to pick faster allowed the U.S. South to corner the world's lucrative cotton exports. By the time of the Civil War, Americans produced 88 percent of the cotton fueling England's textile manufacturing boom. This productivity made investors on both sides of the Atlantic rich, but it came at great human cost, as enslaved people were subjected to a cruel disciplinary regime.

The slave population in Duplin County grew, too, but slaves there were scattered among a number of smaller holdings.[16] Outside the elite circles that included people like the Outlaws, white landholders in Duplin County hitched their class aspirations to the backs of enslaved people who, even when acquired in ones or twos, could make it possible to devote another acre of land to the cultivation of a cash crop, the proceeds of which could see a family through a bad harvest or replace farm equipment. The labor of one enslaved person, like Hagar Outlaw or any one of her children, on a farm meant a white woman spent less time in the field and her children could spend more time in school.[17] White men with political aspirations like David Outlaw counted on the votes of the state's small or non-slaveowners. To secure this support, planters hired out enslaved people to their less fortunate white neighbors, as this helped to knit together the interests of slaveholder and non-slaveholder in a system whose benefits flowed disproportionately to the former.

In the middle of epic events such as the settling of America's cotton frontier and the forced migration of thousands of people to work the cotton fields, people like Hagar and Thomas Outlaw and Clara Bashop had children, and, as those children grew, so did their parents' hopes for them. Those hopes were not extinguished when a parent was sold away, as was Clara Bashop, nor when the children were, as was the case for Hagar Outlaw's children. Hagar kept track of each child as they were taken from her, repeating the names of the men who bought them and the details about where the children were headed over and over again so that she would remember them. She may have extracted this information from David Outlaw or gleaned it from the grapevine. Each time she repeated the details to herself, she no doubt attached to each name or location the hope that it would help bring them back to her. Hagar Outlaw made a family in slavery, and when she did, she proved the persistence of hope in the midst of an institution that would betray it. But it wasn't the institution of slavery in the abstract that betrayed her hopes but rather the decisions made over many years by one man.

David Outlaw fancied himself a "gentleman" slaveholder, like Dick Christian. "Whatever evils may be attendant upon the institution of slavery," he wrote to his wife, Emily, from Washington, where he was serving in the House of Representatives in the middle of debates about slavery in the new state of California, "yet its tendency is to beget the high sense of honor, an undying love of liberty, which nothing but death can destroy." Motivated by his sense of the honor that owning people begat, David Outlaw rejected Emily's suggestion that he sell his slaves. "I cannot bring myself to regard them merely as property," he explained. "They are human beings—placed under my control, and for whose welfare I am to some extent responsible."[18]

Reassuring as it was, in the midst of congressional antislavery agitation, for David Outlaw to describe himself as honorable and to insist on the humanity of the ninety enslaved people who worked his Bertie County plantation, his actions spoke louder than his words. As did the actions of his enslaved people who ran away, sometimes repeatedly. When he lost track of three hired-out men, he regretted that he had not "had them severely punished for the fault of which they were guilty last year." Hiring out enslaved people helped him secure the political support of his neighbors, but it was costly. Like Dick Christian, David Outlaw liked to think that these things, like slaves running away or having to be sold away for their own good, happened *to* him and not *because* of him. "The fact is," he wrote in a moment of self-pity at the disappearance of the enslaved men, "I am not fit to own slaves."[19] He determined to sell them, if they could be found.

When it came to selling Hagar's children, maybe Outlaw told himself that he was doing it for their own good. But we should not be deceived by his expressions of self-pity. To claim ownership over another person an enslaver had to convince himself of a number of contradictory things, like when he assured himself and others that an enslaved mother did not suffer the anguish of a lost child like a white woman did even as he sought to shield himself from her anguish. These were things that enslavers repeated to themselves, over and over, to convince themselves of the opposite of what was plainly true. We should read David Outlaw's regret that he had not punished his slaves *enough* for what it is—evidence that he punished them as he saw fit and sold their children when and to whom he wanted. Yet, he liked to play the part of the "good master" in letters to his wife and children. All of this pretending was aimed at covering up the truth about how much enslavers depended on the humanity of people to whom they routinely denied it.

When she went in search of her children, Hagar Outlaw did not appeal, at least in the papers, to David Outlaw for help. If he had her welfare and that of her children in mind, he would not have sold them in the first place.

Hagar's son Elijah was particularly valuable to the Bertie County Outlaws, for he "acted as watchman for old David Outlaw." David Outlaw trusted Elijah when he assigned him to this post, which may have entailed policing the enslaved people that David Outlaw called his, protecting the white family, or both. Elijah's selection for that job may tell us something about David Outlaw's relationship with Hagar, that he knew and trusted her and, by extension, her son. As David Outlaw's watchman, Elijah was privy to intimate details about the white family that he was trusted to handle with discretion.

But then, what are we to make of the fact that David Outlaw authorized Joseph Outlaw to *sell* Elijah? Did Elijah betray David's trust? Or was it something else?

It's striking to read the list of white Outlaws who sold enslaved ones: "Eli Outlaw was sold by Joseph Outlaw. . . . Thomas Rembry Outlaw was taken away by Wm. Outlaw. Julia Outlaw was sold in New Orleans by Dr. Outlaw." Generations of slave-ownership produced a tangle of names and relationships, the consequences of which outlived Freedom Generation. The repetition of names is confusing and the silences about the connections between all of these people are deafening. Whereas Thomas Rembry was likely named for his father and Hagar's husband, could it be that Hagar named her daughter Cherry after old Dr. Outlaw's maternal grandfather, Solomon Cherry? And what about Hagar's daughter Julia, who was sold to New Orleans, where she gave birth to a son named David? In later years, David continued to live with his mother but shed the first name, adopting D.W., for David Williams, which is how his mother, Julia Outlaw, reported his name to census enumerators in 1870. Did he change his name to distance himself from a past about which he had heard from his mother or grandmother, or that he had deduced from their silence? Advertisements like Hagar

Outlaw's indicate that members of Freedom Generation strategically retained and discarded names associated with slavery, but reading the ads feels like trying to decipher a map without the benefit of a legend.

We cannot answer the question *who*, if any, among the Black and white Outlaws were related to one another. Hagar knew the answer, but she may have preferred not to tell anyone. Sometimes it was safer for enslaved family members to keep things from each other, to shield one another from harsh truths that they could do nothing about. "Dissemble" is what one historian calls the strategic omission of information about rape and other forms of intimate violence perpetrated against enslaved people.[20]

Like most families, the white Outlaws had secrets. Some of these were about the mixed-race children in the slave quarters. With landholdings spread out over several counties, the white Outlaws moved their human property from one branch of the extended family to another. Selling children from their mothers was the slaveowner's prerogative; doing so may have helped to keep family secrets.

Scholars once conspired with slave-owning families to keep their secrets. Until recently, for instance, historians took for granted the word of Thomas Jefferson's white descendants who dismissed the claims of the Hemingses to their shared bloodline. And it is still possible for visitors to tour elegant plantation homes that never mention slavery. For too long we embraced what historian Nell Painter called "slavery's family romance, the performance of beauty" that concealed the reality of childhood and sexual trauma that was common in wealthy families who were good at covering it up. Hagar Outlaw lost one child after another to the slave trade. There may have been a white Outlaw who sold a Black child to whom he was related. We have yet to come to account for the psychological toll slavery took on enslaved and enslaver. When we do, we will begin to recognize the "interrelatedness of us all."[21] But first there is much work to be done to atone for these scholarly sins. Some of that work entails tending to tangles of names such as in Hagar Outlaw's missing persons advertisement.

Names don't necessarily indicate a family relationship, but with so few clues to work with, we have to consider the possibility that they do.

Hagar is an Old Testament name. She appears in Genesis as the slave to Sarah, who, convinced she was unable to have children, "gave" Hagar to her husband, Abraham, so that she could have his child. Sarah was a jealous mistress, and when she finally bore a child of her own, she demanded that Abraham cast out Hagar and Ishmael, the son she had had with Abraham, into the desert.[22] Thomas Jefferson was taken by the story of Hagar, on whom he surely projected his desire for Sally Hemings, the enslaved woman with whom Jefferson fathered four children. "Jefferson lived in a world where having a young slave woman" as a concubine was possible and in which the children Hagar bore were "all around him."[23] David, Joseph, William, and "Dr." Outlaw lived in that world, too, surrounded by Hagar's children, some of whom might have been their own. The meaning of her name and the not-so-subtle implications of it were apparent to white men who believed they had a right of access to the bodies of enslaved women and expected to profit from their fertility.

◆

The Civil War changed all that. In February and March 1862, U.S. Army troops came to the coastal regions of North Carolina and stayed there where their camps became destinations for enslaved people making their way to freedom before emancipation was U.S. policy. By spring, federal authorities estimated that about ten thousand people—enslaved men, women, and children who had fled their masters—were building a free community on Roanoke Island.[24] Four columns of the U.S. Army made their way through the state three years later—one worked its way along the coast after securing the forts at the mouth of the Cape Fear River and taking Wilmington, another one moved through the center of the state from the capital, and Sherman's army entered the state in two columns. The Confederate surrender was signed at Durham Station on April 26, 1865. The following day, U.S. general John Schofield, in command of the army in the state, issued an emancipation order.[25]

Enslaved people in the state had already gotten the message. In March, two New England teachers reported from New Bern that the "streets are literally thronged with colored refugees. They come in by hundreds—men, women and children."[26] "[A] huge elephant in our hands" is how the general described North Carolina's freedom-seeking people, a problem he was eager to be rid of.[27] In the same order in which he declared an end to slavery, General Schofield "recommended" that the state's more than 330,000 newly freed people not congregate "about towns or military camps" and, instead, "remain with their former masters and labor faithfully."[28] This may have sounded like freedom to the general but to those who flocked to U.S. Army camps and to the state's cities and towns it was not.

Another of Schofield's orders recognized families made in slavery, granted parents authority over their children, and charged adult children with the support of their parents.[29] People like Hagar Outlaw. I "am growing old," Outlaw said one year after she became free, and need "help."

In place of the paternalism that slavery's defenders had touted as evidence of the South's moral superiority, Northern officials sought to mandate a web of dependent relationships among the formerly enslaved and enslavers that would allow the federal government to wash their hands of the freed people. Surely one way to administer this policy would have been to trace the surnames that still connected freed people like Hagar Outlaw to the men and women who had held on to them as long as their labor was valuable. It was easy to find David Outlaw.

But no effort was made to make former slaveholders support ex-slaves who were too old or infirm to work. Or to pay them restitution or reparation.

Hagar Outlaw came to Raleigh having decided that the city was a good place to start life as a free person. Some former enslavers ignored the fact of freedom, denying it to people they no longer had any legal claim over. Others drove freed people from their homes, sometimes violently. Federal agents and local newspapers reported the murders of freed people at the hands of whites who had once claimed them as their property.[30] This may have been what Hagar had in mind when she sought to reassure her children that Raleigh was "healthy." Safety in numbers appealed to an elderly woman making her way to freedom with no blood kin beside her.

In April 1866, Hagar Outlaw enlisted someone's help in writing an advertisement that described the surviving members of her family, and she called her children to come care for her.

Four weeks earlier, David Outlaw and the other members of the all-white state legislature approved a series of laws that accepted the fact of freedom even as they re-created many of the circumstances of slavery. The tangled genealogy of white and Black Outlaws may have been on his mind when David Outlaw and other legislators drew up "An Act Concerning Negroes and Persons of Color or of Mixed Blood," which defined as Black "negroes and their issue, even where one ancestor in each succeeding generation to the fourth inclusive, is white." With a stroke of the pen, lawmakers acknowledged the race mixing that resulted from the rape of enslaved women and legislated their children and grandchildren into a category of Blackness. And they prohibited interracial marriage. With these measures, white lawmakers sought to legislate a racial separation for others that they had never expected of themselves.

The act did, however, retroactively legalize marriages between enslaved people from "the time of commencement of such cohabitation." This was welcome news for many couples gathered in Raleigh and other towns where they were now invited to go before a justice of the peace and register decades-long marriages, like Hagar and Thomas's. Couples paid 25 cents for the privilege of having their marriages recorded in a book by a white man. Failure to do so could land either or both of them in jail. Once in jail, a North Carolina freed person could be leased out to their former master. What formerly enslaved people gained in this new law was not so much the "right to marry" but a directive to do so.[31] And, in solemnizing marriage, the state of North Carolina found the most efficient way of ridding the state of the care of dependent children, the elderly, and other members of newly recognized free Black families.[32] The laws David Outlaw and other white legislators were busy passing as Hagar Outlaw and hundreds of others made their way to Raleigh ensured that if anyone was going to be responsible for caring for aging freed people, it would be their *Black* family relations.

Taken together, these measures formed North Carolina's Black Code, though they were not labeled as such. It included such things as a vagrancy law and fines for freed people who left the state and tried to return, and it prohibited Black North Carolinians from owning guns.[33] Every word indicated that the men writing it were not ready to give up their prerogatives as slaveowners; they ceded hardly an inch of the power they had for so long wielded over Black women and men. What they had given up was any lingering sense that they were responsible for their formerly enslaved people's "welfare," as David Outlaw had put it—that they owed anything to people whose labor had sustained them in their positions of power.

David Outlaw lived long enough to lose his seat in the state senate and to see Bertie County represented in the House by a Black man, Parker David Robbins.[34] Robbins, a USCT veteran, served as a delegate to the state's constitutional convention, where he fought apprenticeships that granted custody to former enslavers of the children of North Carolina freedwomen and -men. Outlaw was dead when Robbins and eighteen other Black men took their seats in the statehouse in Raleigh, the same seats where former enslavers had tried to hold on to the power over Black people's lives that slavery had guaranteed them.[35]

Hagar Outlaw seized upon the changing legal landscape to reconstitute her family. She might have received help writing and paying for the ad from an agent of the Freedmen's Bureau in Raleigh. In the early months after the surrender, Black men in U.S. Army uniforms were a common sight in Raleigh. In September 1865, five months after the war ended, more than nine thousand U.S. Army troops occupied North Carolina, ensuring that former Confederates laid down their arms and former enslavers obeyed the emancipation order. More than half of these were USCT, themselves mostly former slaves.[36] Over the next few months, the army began reducing the presence of USCT in response to protests by white North Carolinians who complained that the presence of uniformed Black men made freed people "insolent and idle." There were fewer of these men around the following spring when Hagar Outlaw wrote her ad, but there were still enough to raise the ire of whites who resented being forced "to treat freedmen fairly," as a Freedmen's Bureau agent put it.[37]

Black churches in Raleigh did what they could to help freed people streaming into the city. After the war, Black communities throughout the South began their own separate congregations and opened churches to serve them. In Raleigh, the Second Baptist Church, where Elijah married Nancy Robinson, represented the fondest hopes and dreams of Freedom Generation.[38] Built by Black North Carolinians, the church was a place of worship, education, and aspiration. The white pastor, Massachusetts-born U.S. Army veteran Henry Tupper, shared a pulpit with August Shepard, a North Carolina freedman and student at Tupper's ministry school. That school became Shaw University, one of the earliest Historically Black Colleges and Universities to be founded in the postwar South.[39] The Black men who studied for the ministry there went on to start their own congregations and to lead missions around the world.

Finding one's family was a foundational aspiration for Freedom Generation—on it rested the fulfillment of the others. Among the parishioners of Raleigh's Second Baptist, Hagar and her children found people who supported them in fulfilling that aspiration. Hagar Outlaw could not read or write, but among the pastors and parishioners of Second Baptist, she found people who could. To one of them she may have recounted the story that would appear in the papers.

✦

While she waited for word from her children, Hagar Outlaw needed food. For four months—from March to June 1868—she drew rations from the Freedmen's Bureau.[40] Each month, Outlaw brought home meat, bread or cornmeal, and some combination of beans or peas, rice or hominy, coffee or tea, sugar, vinegar, candles, soap, salt, pepper, potatoes, and molasses "when practicable."[41] All were part of standard-issue U.S. Army rations, although freed people—and poor whites—received these items in smaller portions than did soldiers. The food earmarked for freed people was also generally of lower quality. Even so, Hagar was surely grateful to have it. About every four weeks, Outlaw stood in line at bureau offices, answered a few questions about her situation, and carried away the food she would live on until next month. For three of the four months, Outlaw received twenty rations, standard issue for one poor white or "destitute" freed person each month. In April, she received half that much. What she did for food when her rations ran out that month is unclear. And, after June, the bureau cut Hagar's aid entirely.

Hagar Outlaw's experience receiving food aid from the federal government is consistent with what we know about Freedmen's Bureau policies and the agency's concerns about fostering "dependency" among the freed people. A freed person could count on no more than three months of rations, after which a bureau agent visited them to investigate their claim for continued support.[42] Three months was enough time, according to the bureau, for a freed person to find work so that she could feed herself. Hagar Outlaw may have elicited the sympathy of an agent at the Raleigh office when she received an extra month of rations. Or maybe Outlaw made the case that the half ration she received in April could not possibly be the reason the government would let her go hungry in June. Those rations, meager and inadequate, were nonetheless the difference between life and death.

As for shelter, Hagar Outlaw likely made do as best she could. Freedmen's Bureau officials described chaotic scenes immediately after the war as freed people made their way to southern towns with little more than the clothes on their back. In Raleigh, Colonel Eliphalet Whittlesey, the federal officer overseeing bureau operations in the summer of 1865, found "thousands of blacks . . . collected about this and other towns occupying every hovel and shanty . . . many dying for want of proper food and medical supplies." Refugees "were crowding into the towns, and literally swarming about every depot of supplies, to receive their rations."[43] Accounts of overcrowding came in from refugee camps around the state, as did concern about the spread of smallpox and other diseases.[44] Freed people worked to mitigate conditions in the camps and to turn the military-issue tents and other temporary shelters with which they had first greeted freedom into homes they hoped would be permanent. One hundred miles east of Raleigh, under the auspices of the Freedmen's Bureau, for example, freed people at New Bern built a settlement alongside the Trent River on land confiscated from white

North Carolinians who had sided with the Confederacy; there freed people built homes "by themselves of lumber manufactured by hand." White North Carolinians derided these Black settlements and pointed to problems there in order to demand the removal of the Freedmen's Bureau from the state. A reporter for Raleigh's *Weekly Standard*, for instance, found conditions at the Trent River settlement to be "truly deplorable" and "calculated to excite the deepest sympathy."[45]

When they described these places with concern, white officials, even sympathetic ones like Whittlesey, betrayed racist ideas that freed people were deficient in their "domestic obligations"—that they did not understand what family was and had to be taught. This was an oft-repeated complaint, one for which no evidence was ever provided. Indeed, everywhere around was evidence to the contrary, of freed people coming to Raleigh and other places in family units or, like Hagar Outlaw, determined to find them. Harriet Jacobs, former slave from Edenton, North Carolina, was exasperated by freedwomen with whom she worked in refugee camps who insisted on taking in orphans when they could not care for their own children. Jacobs, though, described the problem not as a deficiency in family ties but rather too strong a sense of obligation. "Have patience with them," Jacobs advised northern aid workers.[46] What government officials described as "crowding," "jumbling," and the "collecting" of people into multigenerational, multifamily homes, historian Julie Saville argues was freed people's reversing "the tendency to disperse kinship networks across different properties that had been a key feature of slave life."[47] "Crowding" described the process of reconstructing families made in slavery.

We can only speculate how the reunion between Hagar and Dolly, Julia, and Julia's nine-year-old son, David Williams, came about: Did they meet by chance in Raleigh, crossing a street one day or going to church? Did Dolly or Julia learn of their mother's whereabouts in the newspaper? The census enumerator indicated that Hagar did not read or write; her daughters could read, though, making it possible that they read their mother's advertisement.[48] It is also possible that Hagar knew where Dolly was because she did not name her in the ad; if she did know, Hagar kept that information from the bureau agents who gave her food rations. Having an adult daughter to support her would have disqualified Hagar for aid intended for only the most destitute. In any case, it takes little effort to imagine the joy that Hagar felt seeing her daughters again, making a home together with them. We can imagine the three of them talking excitedly, sharing what information each had about the others, recalling where they last saw each other, wondering who among them was still alive and, if so, where they might be.

And, of course, we can imagine how happy Hagar was to meet her grandson. David Williams was born in May 1861, a little less than a year before Union troops captured New Orleans. If he and his mother were still enslaved in the city, then Julia and her three-year-old son were freed in May 1864, when the Unionist government in the city passed an emancipation order. It would be another full year before Hagar was free and before it was safe for Julia to return to North Carolina to look for her.[49] How proud Hagar must have felt that David attended school.

Unlike her namesake, Hagar Outlaw was not expelled into the desert to die. She survived slavery and the confusing and dangerous postwar years on the thin support offered her by the federal government and among volunteers and officials who had only a vague notion of what she had been through. Through it all, she held on to the memory of her children and the hope that she would find them. Those memories, the details repeated so often over years of separation, served her well in a search that turned up three of the children that had been taken from her. By dint of luck and determination, Hagar lived out the rest of her life under her own "vine and fig tree," in the words of the Old Testament, and in the aspirations of worldly patriarchs like George Washington, surrounded and supported by her children and grandchildren.[50]

Lost Friends.

We make no charge for publishing these letters from subscribers. All others will be charged fifty cents. Pastors will please read the requests published below from their pulpits, and report any case where friends are brought together by means of letters in the SOUTHWESTERN.

MR. EDITOR—I wish to inquire through your paper for my two children that I left near Chester village, Chester county. South Carolina, about 1837. I left them on Jesse William's place, about five miles from Chester village, on a little creek called Pea Ridge. Both my children were girls, named Caroline Williams and Sarah Williams. Their mother died in five years after I left them. Her name was Eliza Williams. She belonged to Jesse Williams. I belonged to James B. Pickett, and I was hired out to Jesse Williams at the time I married Eliza, and I went by the name of Tally Williams; but when I was taken away from Jessee Williams by my master, James Pickett, my name was changed to Tally Pickett. I lived on Turkey Creek two years after I was taken from Jesse Williams, and then I was brought to Louisiana, on Red River, by Col. Williamson. The last account I heard of them they were in Houston, Texas; that is what I heard. I don't know whether it was so or not. Since freedom my name has been changed from Tally Pickett to Tally Miller. I would like to hear from my children very much. Write to me in care of H. W. Ogden, Shreveport, La., 3t TALLY MILLER.

Tally Miller to "Mr. Editor," Lost Friends,
Southwestern Christian Advocate (New Orleans, LA), February 7, 1884

CHAPTER THREE

Both of Tally Miller's Children

Tally Miller was a survivor. He endured the long march from South Carolina to the remote cotton frontier of northern Louisiana, a trip he made largely on foot, chained with others in a coffle. There Miller worked the fields for twenty years until the Civil War came and then, finally, emancipation. Miller survived to experience freedom and then managed to stay alive for at least another twenty years as the region's former enslavers worked to deny him that freedom. The violence came in waves in the 1860s and '70s as southern whites killed Blacks and Blacks fought back. By then, Tally Miller had made two families—one in South Carolina and another in Louisiana. He was father to at least seven children. When his enslaver took him to Louisiana, he endured a separation of more than eight hundred miles from his daughters Caroline and Sarah Williams. By the time he wrote to the *Southwestern Christian Advocate* looking for them, it had been nearly fifty years since he had last seen them.

Tally Miller never left Louisiana. He did not relocate to Kansas alongside hundreds of Exodusters who fled violence in the region and sought refuge in the land of John Brown, the martyred white abolitionist. Miller did not go looking for his daughters, as had Clara Bashop when she tried to pick up Patience's trail. Miller did not go directly to the newspapers, as had Hagar Outlaw, asking his daughters to come to him. He was eighty-nine years old in 1884 when he placed an ad, hoping to hear word of them.[1]

We can excuse Tally Miller for lapses in his memory. In the first line he gave us only one year to work with: 1837, the year he "left" the girls "on Jesse William's place, about five miles from Chester village, on a little creek called Pea Ridge." Miller was not even sure about that; it was "about 1837." And he did not leave them but rather he was taken. Crowded into the following sentences are the names of various white men whose decisions tore apart Tally Miller's family and left his children to grow up without him. Here, Tally notably discarded the verb "left" for "taken away," "taken from," and "brought to."

> I was taken away from Jessee Williams by my master, James Pickett, my name was changed to Tally Pickett. I lived on Turkey Creek two years after I was taken from Jesse Williams, and then I was brought to Louisiana, on Red River, by Col. Williamson.

Some of the details were unclear, but Miller was clear about how it came to be that he did not see the girls again.

That was James Pickett's doing.

James Pickett took from Tally Miller the privilege of a family, the opportunity to watch his daughters grow up, and the comfort of growing old with them at his side. Pickett even took away the last name Tally shared with his daughters and their mother, Eliza. Once, Tally, Eliza, and the girls had all gone by the last name Williams. But Tally had only been on lease to Eliza's master, Jesse Williams. The integrity of the family Tally and Eliza built together relied on the continued forbearance of two white men with an informal business relationship. His arrangement with Jesse Williams terminated, James Pickett had other plans for Tally. "I went by the name of Tally Williams," he recalled, until Pickett changed his name, an assertion of James Pickett's claim to ownership of the man and perhaps also an attempt to break Tally's ties to his wife and children. The children and their mother belonged to Jesse Williams, but Tally was *his*.

Later Tally would change his name to Miller, rejecting the idea that any man could exercise that kind of power over another.

Tally Miller held on to all these details, the names and places that he hoped would someday help him find his daughters. "I wish to inquire through your paper for my two children," he began his letter, in which he repeated the words "my children" two more times, as if by repetition he could defeat decades of doubters. "Both of my children were girls, named Caroline Williams and Sarah Williams." Putting a family back together after slavery could take a lifetime. Formerly enslaved fathers who hoped to find their children faced unique challenges in doing so. Fathers' relationships to their children were attenuated by the law of slavery that tied children's status to their mothers, not their fathers, as was the rule for white Americans. At a time when white men claimed nearly uncontested authority over their children and their wives, enslaved fathers had *no* legal rights as husbands or fathers. Emancipation eliminated these inequalities among men, but slavery's discriminatory laws cast a long shadow over Freedom Generation, complicating fathers' search for their children and the families they had made in slavery.

Fathers working to rebuild families in the middle of white insurgency, like the one that swirled around Tally Miller after the Civil War, confronted daily reminders that the high-stakes project of separating Black families, of the denial of Black fatherhood, did not end with slavery. White people who could no longer claim them as property believed that they could still dominate men like Miller by threats and violence and by denying them the privilege of their children. Yet in hundreds of ads and letters like Miller's, fathers sought to reunite with their children, to build something together with them that could be left behind for *their* children, something beyond the reach of white violence that could protect them from it. What they wanted was, as journalist Ta-Nehisi Coates said to his son, "to put as much distance between you and that blinding fear as possible."[2]

It is likely that Tally Miller never again saw the two girls he left behind. He was, after all, an old man and had survived decades of hard labor, war, and trauma. But to project that doubt backward is to deprive Tally Miller once again of his fatherhood, to miss the pain he felt when he lost his children and the hope that kept their memories alive. That we know how the story likely ended should not lead us to underestimate Tally Miller's hope that he *would* find his children again, a hope he shared with many other Freedom Generation fathers.

◆

Before he sent Tally Miller to Louisiana, James Pickett made clear that he would not be moved by a consideration for Miller's family. The danger of marriages between enslaved people of different masters like Tally's was that slaveholders had little interest in keeping families together when the children could not be monetized. Once he hired Tally out to Williams, Pickett tolerated or maybe even endorsed Tally's marriage to Eliza, an enslaved woman whom Jesse Williams called his own. Or Pickett may not have known, at least at first. Eventually Pickett broke up the family. Miller's reference to leaving them "on a little creek called Pea Ridge" stands out in the letter. That creek cannot be located on a map today. It may have disappeared or been renamed.

Tally Miller tried to keep track of them afterward, hearing that Caroline and Sarah were in Houston and learning of Eliza's death "five years after I left them." He heard they were married. And it may have been Galveston, Tally's son thought, not Houston.[3]

Northwest Louisiana might as well have been a world away from South Carolina. The acquisitive white men who went there were drawn to the frontier, the edge of America's expanding cotton empire. To make a fortune in Virginia, North Carolina, and South Carolina, a man had to play by old rules and limit himself to opportunities tied to dynasty and profits made on worked-over land. In the rich Mississippi Valley, they would write new rules. Many of these white landowners were younger than their counterparts back east. Eager to make their fortune in cotton, they generally brought with them only "prime hands," enslaved women and men between fourteen and twenty-five years old. No families and very few adults over the age of thirty. They made no claims to a kindly slaveowner paternalism; they did not profess a desire to have their "affections" for their slaves reflected back on them. What they wanted were hands to work the cotton fields—until they couldn't.[4] Tally Miller, however, was not a young man.

James Belton Pickett owned various properties in the South Carolina Piedmont, where he made money speculating in property, both human and otherwise. The rules made it possible for Pickett to buy and sell land seized from Indigenous people and to work it with people seized from Africa. Among the concessions extracted by South Carolina's powerful planters in return for their support for the federal constitution was the removal of the Cherokee and other Indigenous people from land they had lived on for generations and the continuation, until 1808, of the legal Atlantic Slave Trade. James Pickett benefited from this grand bargain, filling the fields of his plantations in South Carolina and Georgia with survivors of the Middle Passage. Among them were Tally Miller's ancestors. These "investments" continued to pay dividends, as after the international trade was cut off the price of enslaved people soared. The South's many James Picketts then took their enslaved people with them to the new frontier or sold them to eager buyers who hoped to make their fortune growing sugar and cotton in the rich soil that the Mississippi River deposited along its banks. Tally Miller's family story bridged two forced migrations—from the west coast of Africa to South Carolina and from America's East Coast to its new frontier.

Tally Miller's story begins before 1837, but that year is a good place to begin to understand the world in which he made a family with Eliza. In that year, the U.S. economy lurched, sending markets into a downward spiral. Investors panicked, banks closed, and the livelihoods of many were ruined. At the center of it all were entrepreneurs who speculated in the lucrative trade in cotton and the enslaved people who produced it. Cotton production grew rapidly when Americans discovered that the hardy short-staple variety grew just about anywhere and could be cleaned easily when run through a cotton engine, or "gin" for short. Equipped with this new machine, enslavers turned fields of tobacco and indigo and corn over to cotton and developed new ways of extracting labor from the enslaved people who worked them. The U.S. cornered the international market for cotton.

This spectacular rate of growth made American enslavers and would-be enslavers giddy and rash, buying land and people at premium prices and on credit. As long as cotton continued to sell apace, this growth was sustainable, but when in 1837 the price of cotton plummeted, banks failed and the market crashed. James Pickett had his eyes on the cotton frontier, buying property along the Red River from Bossier to Natchitoches, Louisiana.[5] These investments were risky, as no one knew yet what was possible there, what sort of yields a man could expect, and how long it would take to see them. What was sure was that enslaved people like Tally Miller would work long hours in the cotton fields alongside the Red River, pushed harder than before to pick more and more cotton in hopes that doing so would make up in quantity what American cotton no longer commanded in price.

James Pickett did not live long enough to see his Red River investments pay dividends. He died in 1842, leaving his extensive landholdings, including several Red River plantations, to his wife, Paulina, who steadily grew the family's slaveholding empire. By 1860, Paulina Pickett's property in Louisiana, Arkansas, and Kentucky was worth hundreds of thousands of dollars; she was the largest enslaver in Bossier Parish, Louisiana, with more than two hundred enslaved people at work on three different plantations.[6]

Tally Miller was not the only one who lost his family when James Pickett decided to see if he could grow more cotton in Louisiana than in South Carolina. Between 1830 and 1840, Pickett began sending enslaved people from his South Carolina plantations to Louisiana. Twenty-five women and men ranging in age from their late teens to early forties, "prime hands," were removed from Pickett's Chester County plantation and eleven from Pickett's Fairfield.[7] Years later, when James Pickett's widow, Paulina, died, locals recalled that she was among the region's "pioneers," the generation that turned this as-yet-unsettled frontier into a paradise of exquisite and finely furnished plantation homes surrounded by cotton fields as far as the eye could see.[8] But it was Tally Miller and other enslaved people who had settled the frontier and made Paulina Pickett's generation wealthy.

Tally had met Eliza on Jesse Williams's place, located near James Pickett's in Chester County, South Carolina, sometime after 1830. Hiring out slaves to neighbors knit together the fortunes of men like James Pickett and David Outlaw with aspirational enslavers like Jesse Williams. Paying a neighbor for the labor of an enslaved person was a low-cost solution to Jesse Williams's labor problem. It allowed him to plant crops that he'd harvest alongside the enslaved man he owned and the one he leased from Pickett. With the proceeds, he acquired more slaves of his own. By 1840, Williams owned fifteen people, including Tally and Eliza's daughters, Sarah and Caroline.[9]

Marrying Eliza allowed Tally to carve out a space of affection and intimacy beyond the control of Pickett. Tally spent evenings and Sundays with his wife and children. The close proximity of the two households allowed the couple to get to know one another, to create a small world for themselves. Marriage allowed slaveholders to leverage the emotional bonds between husband and wife to extract obedience, but "abroad" marriages of enslaved couples with separate enslavers attenuated their claims to their slave "property." Writing in 1833, a South Carolina slaveowner complained that "[i]n allowing the men to marry out of the plantation, you give them the uncontrollable right to be frequently absent. For wherever their wives live, there they consider their home."[10] Tally's marriage to Eliza made Jesse Williams's place feel like his home.

If the births of Caroline and Sarah brought joy to their marriage, it was tempered by their parents' fears of all that they could not protect the girls from. "When they told me my new-born babe was a girl," Harriet Jacobs, enslaved in North Carolina, recalled, "my heart was heavier than it had ever been before. Slavery is terrible for men; but it is far more terrible for women."[11] Unable to run away from her sexually abusive enslaver, Jacobs chose instead to hide in an attic for seven years so she could stay close to her children and watch over them. The danger to young girls grew as they reached seven, when they were expected to shoulder the work of an adult and when the eyes of their master might fall on them. Most enslaved children knew their fathers but did not grow up with them.[12] Tally Miller got to know his daughters, and they him. Until they had to say goodbye. Soon thereafter, they lost their mother, too.

Acquired by Williams sometime between the census of 1830 and 1840, Eliza left only a faint trace in the historical record. She does not appear in his Chester County household in 1830, and she was dead by 1840. The names of white men like Williams and James Pickett appeared in the census as heads of households. Hash marks next to their names indicated their dependents, including their wives, children, and enslaved people. In the 1850 and 1860 censuses, only enslaved people remained anonymous hashmarks on the slave schedule.

State officials did not record Eliza's marriage to Tally or the birth of either child. The only proof we have that Eliza lived, married, and made a family is in Tally's ad sent to the papers listing her name alongside his and their children.

It is possible that the girls remained on Jesse Williams's place until at least 1850, when census enumerators counted nine enslaved children in their teens, including two nineteen- and three fifteen-year-old girls and four boys who were fourteen. It is impossible to know who these children's parents were. Though they had neither parent there to care for them, Caroline and Sarah grew up in the company of other children around their age to whom they might turn for emotional support.[13]

It's hard to trace the girls from here. That did not stop their father from trying. By the time he wrote his letter to the paper, their names had likely changed. They were last heard from someplace in Texas, but they might recognize the details in the letter or someone else from the old neighborhood might. Miller picked up word of the girls through the grapevine telegraph after he left South Carolina.

Information Wanted ads like Tally Miller's offer strong evidence of a sophisticated system of surreptitious surveillance by which enslaved people kept track of one another and passed word along to kin, ensuring that loved ones swept up into the Second Middle Passage did not vanish without a trace. The grapevine followed enslaved people wherever they went, transmitting bits and pieces of news about where loved ones went and who was left behind. When freed people began looking for their sons and daughters, this intelligence served as a rough road map of where to begin.

◆

Tally Miller was in his forties when he joined others leaving behind wives and husbands, children, and other kin, and made his journey to the far reaches of America's cotton frontier. From what they heard along the way, enslaved people didn't expect to survive the trip or live long enough to see their loved ones again. Others who had come there before them shared what they knew, warned of what was to come, and risked their lives to pass along information they were not supposed to have. As he walked the miles, Tally Miller may have repeated his daughters' names. He must have wondered, without their mother, who would remember *him* to the girls?

By modern roads, the trip from South Carolina to northwest Louisiana is around 850 miles. There were no roads, modern or otherwise, over most of that terrain when Tally Miller and others made the trip. Chained together at the neck and wrists to the person next to them and then to others in a long double line, slaves in a coffle moved awkwardly, slowly, stumbling at times. Prodded along by a man on a horse, a coffle might manage ten to twenty miles in a day, less if someone was injured or ill, maybe more if the people in the coffle boarded a wagon or a riverboat.[14] West of the Mississippi, river travel was dangerous and unreliable; the Red River became impassable when "rafts" of tree debris formed natural dams, choking off the river's flow and causing it to overflow its banks, flooding the land around it. Until early in the twentieth century, making a trip such as the one that Tally Miller made took weeks.

Solomon Northrup, a free Black man from New York who was kidnapped and enslaved, described the swamps near the Red River plantation of his enslaver as filled with "wild beasts—the bear, the wild-cat, the tiger, and great slimy reptiles, that are crawling through it everywhere."[15] Compared to the tidy farms and towns of upstate New

York, where Northrup had lived, and the tired fields abutting the grand homes of the Piedmont slaveholders familiar to Tally Miller, northwest Louisiana must have felt like traveling back in time.

Tally Miller and Solomon Northrup arrived in Louisiana around the same time, stepping not into the past but into a dystopian future. Slaveholders there pioneered a technique they called the pushing system that held the key to their cotton fortunes: every day they set enslaved people's picking quotas a little higher than the day before. When Miller arrived, Red River field hands picked one hundred pounds of cotton a day, more than twice as much as the same hands had in 1800. By 1850, they were picking two hundred pounds.[16] Thanks to the gin, all that cotton could be cleaned quickly, but there was no machine to make things easier for those who did the picking; for them it was only the master's scale and the driver's whip.

New Yorker Frederick Law Olmsted traveled the South and observed that enslaved people were pushed harder in the Red River region than anywhere else. There he witnessed slaveholder cruelty at its worst, including an incident when an overseer savagely beat a young girl, causing Olmsted to take refuge from the girl's screams by hiding in the bushes. Slavery was a vile institution, he concluded, but the spectacle offended him more than the cruelty. He wrote, "the girl did not seem to suffer the intense pain that I should have supposed she would." At the time, Olmsted had no children; one wonders if he remembered this cruelly treated girl when, years later, he had daughters of his own, Charlotte and Marion.[17] A critic of slavery, Olmsted nonetheless subscribed to mid-century race science that insisted that Black people did not feel pain the same way white people did, the same understanding of Black bodies that drove an overseer to beat a young girl with a rawhide. It's not difficult to understand why Solomon Northrup dreamed that his children had died, that they "had fallen into the arms of that other sleep, from which they never would arouse." Maybe Tally Miller did, too.[18]

The population of enslaved people in the Red River region grew rapidly in the years after Tally arrived, more rapidly than did the number of white people.[19] These forced migrants were taken from their families, and even when they came along with others from the old neighborhood, it took time to build trust, to form relationships.[20] Tally met and married Mahala, a South Carolinian like himself who had also been taken to the frontier by a white person. No records indicate that Tally and Mahala's marriage was ever recognized by the state of Louisiana. The couple had five sons: Ellison was born around 1841, Teague in 1845, Blake in 1849, Milkey in 1853, and Thomas in 1855. When the boys reached seven or eight, they joined their parents in the fields, where they expected to live out their lives working for Paulina Pickett. Tally Miller knew, of course, that like the family he had with Eliza, the one he made with Mahala would exist at the forbearance of the woman who claimed them as her property.

The death or divorce of an enslaver wreaked havoc on the families of enslaved people.

Paulina Pickett remarried shortly after James died. When that marriage ended in divorce, Paulina retained control of the property she and her children had received in her first marriage and built on it with more land and enslaved people. On the eve of the Civil War, Paulina Pickett had achieved the success her late husband had dreamed of.[21] Pickett divided her immense slaveholding empire between her sons John and James, both in their early twenties; she deeded to each enslaved people, cash, and thousands of acres along the Red River.

Pickett made special note of the value of each item of property, dividing it carefully so that there would be no charges of favoritism, no feelings of ill will between the brothers.[22] In consideration of "the Natural love and affection" she felt for her sons, Pickett stated in her gift that she was "desirous to equalize them in property." Paulina gave John ninety enslaved people. To James Jr. she gave her Gold Point Plantation on the Red River and eighty-eight enslaved people, including Tally and Mahala and their five sons. When she registered this transfer of property to James Jr., Paulina Pickett made the only known record of the family of Tally and Mahala Miller.[23]

The property records indicate that Paulina Pickett intended to keep enslaved people's families intact as she divided her property between her two sons. Alongside the list of eighty-eight enslaved people Paulina gave to James Jr., she drew twenty-one brackets marking families large (seven) and small (two), the markings indicating that she was not morally oblivious to the power she had to keep a family together or to wreck it. This was a practice of long standing among slaveholders who grouped enslaved people in family units in the same ledgers where they kept track of the pounds of cotton each person picked. It was the conceit of slave-owning paternalists that they cared for their enslaved people as if they were members of their own family, that they knew about and were involved in their personal lives, their marriages, and the births of their children. But success among slaveholders was measured not in the affection they claimed to have for their slaves or that they fantasized that their slaves had for them but by the number of people they bought and sold, in treating enslaved people not as *people* but as commodities. Success was a column of dollar figures that stood in for the love parents felt for their children. This was Paulina Pickett's expression of her "natural love and affection" for *hers*.

Paulina Pickett estimated that Tally and Mahala Miller and their five sons were worth $4,250 in the slave marketplace. Should James Jr. decide to sell one of Tally's children, which was his "right," he would have to do some math of his own. Was that figure meant to be divided by seven? Or did Paulina Pickett compute a higher value for the older boys because they were "prime hands" as their parents had once been? The profit potential in four-year-old Milkey and Thomas, who was just fifteen months, was limited by the shockingly high rates of infant mortality experienced by enslaved children. It may be that one or more of them would not survive to adulthood, victims, perhaps, of the malaria or yellow fever common to the region or the routine violence of slavery—or perhaps they would become casualties of the war looming on the horizon.

◆

The year that Paulina transferred ownership of her enslaved people to her sons was 1857, when Dred Scott lost his bid for freedom. The Supreme Court rejected Scott's claim that, his master having taken him into a free state, he was no longer a slave. Reaching further, the court ruled that African Americans were fit only for slavery, beings "so far inferior, that they had no rights which the white man was bound to respect." The decision helped drive the nation toward civil war, crystallizing fears among people in states where slavery had been outlawed that slaveowners were planning to reintroduce it there. Slaveowners celebrated the decision as a defense of their absolute right to own slaves, to take them wherever they wanted, no matter what local laws said. At stake were questions about what power the federal government had to regulate slavery as well as whether Tally Miller would ever enjoy the same rights as James Pickett Jr., like the right to marry and raise a family free of the designs of others. The Civil War would settle those questions, freeing Tally, Mahala, and their sons, and Caroline and Sarah Williams, if they had lived that long.

War came to Louisiana early. Union troops seized New Orleans when the war was barely a year old. Tens of thousands of freedom-seeking people streamed into the city. Slavery quickly fell apart there and in the nearby parishes. A new state constitution ended slavery in the state, but this was true only in those parishes that recognized Union authority. And in exchange for their loyalty to the Union, U.S. Army officers gave landowners broad authority to manage the transition to free labor as it benefited them.[24] Success eluded the Union Army in the north, where General Nathaniel P. Banks's ambitious campaign to take the Red River ended in defeat. There as elsewhere, though, the presence of Union troops opened the door to emancipation, just a crack, and when it did, freedom-seeking Louisianans pushed through it. As Banks's men made their way up the Red River, enslaved people fled their enslavers, bringing freedom to the heart of Confederate Louisiana.

Demoralized. From deep inside the perverse moral universe of slavery, "demoralized" is how enslavers described slaves who seized their freedom at these moments. They were "crazy," said one from Rapides Parish: "They become utterly demoralized at once." "The slaves demoralized, refractory, leaving their owners & going to the enemy," complained another from St. Mary Parish. Enslaved people along Louisiana's Red River helped themselves to the livestock and personal belongings of their enslavers, having what one enslaver described as "a perfect jubilee."[25] White witnesses surely recognized the joy in freed people's faces as they celebrated the arrival of Union Army men; in that case, perhaps the demoralization was their own. The Union Army failed to seize the Red River in the spring of 1864, but long after it had retreated to New Orleans, enslaved Louisianans continued to leave their plantations. Perhaps Tally Miller was among them, having ended slavery on his own terms by leaving Gold Point Plantation to follow the U.S. Army or staying behind to ensure the safety of Mahala and his sons.

Northwest Louisiana descended into chaos with the collapse of the Confederacy, and white Louisianans armed themselves against the imperatives of emancipation. "Slavery is at bloody war with us," the Freedmen's Bureau commissioner for Louisiana, Thomas Conway, reported to his superiors after the war as he and bureau agents tried to enforce emancipation. A freedman from Louisiana, Henry Adams, said, "After they told us we were free—even then they would not let us live as man and wife together. And when we would run away to be free from slavery, the white people would not let us come on their places to see our mothers, wives, sisters, or fathers. We was made to leave the place, or made to go back and live as slaves. To my own knowledge there was over two thousand colored people killed trying to get away, after the white people told us we were free, which was in 1865."[26]

Emancipation may have come to Louisiana with Union victory, but enslaved people there were still fighting their way to freedom.

Conditions on the ground shaped the decisions freed people made when they set out to search for their families. Clara Bashop stayed in Mississippi because "she could not get away." She saved her money and learned to read and write before leaving for Virginia to look for her children. Hagar Outlaw made her way to Raleigh, where, supported by a network of Black institutions and occupying United States Colored Troops, she applied for food aid and placed an advertisement in a Black-owned newspaper. Slowly, over a number of months and years, Hagar

Outlaw drew her children to her, rebuilding her family in freedom. Facing a condition of open warfare, Tally Miller would have been wise to wait things out before heading out onto the roads to look for his loved ones. If he was not still living with Mahala and the couple's sons in 1865, going to them immediately would have come with risks. It had been nearly thirty years since he had last seen his daughters, Sarah and Caroline Williams, in South Carolina. As the postwar resistance to emancipation raged on in Louisiana—overwhelming the small contingent of federal agents and the freed people they were charged with protecting—it is little wonder that Tally Miller was unable to get word to them that he was still alive and that he hoped they were, too.

The cotton empire the Picketts oversaw survived the war and the immediate shock of emancipation, but the generation of empire builders died in the war. The same year that Tally Miller took to the papers searching for Caroline and Sarah, Paulina Pickett took out a newspaper ad of her own offering up her "fine Red River Plantation for rent . . . five hundred acres of open land, with new gin house and new cabins. It will be leased on low terms."[27]

Paulina Pickett was unable or unwilling to remain in the business of growing cotton.[28] Perhaps it was the whole business of negotiating labor contracts with people whom she was conditioned to see as property that drove her into retirement. James Jr.'s death in 1880 may have hurried the decision for her.[29]

There is no record that Tally Miller transacted any business with Paulina Pickett once he became a free man. Former enslavers were not oblivious to Freedom Generation's project of reconstructing families they had wrecked. Like other cotton planters, James Jr. and John were interested in preventing freed people like the Millers from leaving the plantations, by deceit and deception if possible, violence if necessary. Tally Miller knew better than to trust them, but his business with the Picketts was not over.

Like others who set out to search for family after slavery, Miller turned to the Black community for help. Help came from white outsiders—such as Freedmen's Bureau agents and missionaries—but their ranks were thin and concentrated in New Orleans. Outside the city, freed people who built the schools and churches and meeting halls and published the newspapers that could sustain communities and support Black families did so in the face of extraordinary white violence. Institutions that were built one day were destroyed the next—Black teachers, proprietors, journalists, ministers murdered or run out of town. Under the circumstances, communication between and among freed people about such things as the whereabouts or condition of loved ones continued to be dangerous.

The history of Reconstruction in Louisiana is framed by shocking massacres—one in New Orleans and another in Colfax. The first occurred in 1866 when white policemen and former Confederates attacked Black soldiers and delegates meeting to revise the state constitution. By the time federal troops arrived, nearly forty people had been murdered, many of them hunted and shot down in the convention hall. Seven years later, white men attacked the courthouse in Colfax because they did not agree with the outcome of an election; Black men inside fought them off while they waited for enforcements. When federal troops did not arrive, the white attackers burned down the building with the Black men trapped inside. The violence in New Orleans marked the beginning of Reconstruction, and Colfax, "the bloodiest single instance of racial carnage," came toward the end.[30] This bookending should not lead us to overlook the fact that for much of the time in between, freed people and free Blacks fought to stave off the return of slavery; to protect themselves on the roads and in their homes; and to defend the schools, churches, and towns that formed the basis for independent Black communities. Just two years after the New Orleans attack, Klansmen in Opelousas—located roughly in the middle of the state—with the help of local white authorities, terrorized the Black community there in the lead-up to the fall elections, killing more than two hundred and ensuring that Black men did not vote and that no one voted Republican.[31]

White Louisianans were determined to keep freed people from exercising the prerogatives of freedom, such as choosing where and with whom they lived and, of course, for whom they worked and under what terms. Black families disrupted the work of white supremacy.

Slaveholders had acknowledged as much as they pulled fathers away from their children and forbade wives and husbands from living together. With slavery now over, whites worried that they had been deprived of the power they had once wielded over Black families, the ability to unmake them at will, to force their will on those who had no family. Reunions like Hagar Outlaw's allowed her and her children to combine their income, purchase property, leave it to *their* children—so that they might live lives free of the struggles their parents had faced. "Wealth," explains journalist Nikole Hannah-Jones, "is accumulated across generations. [And] it is white Americans' centuries-long economic head start that most effectively maintains racial caste today."[32] Once they found each other again, Black families could build the intergenerational wealth that could topple slavery's racial caste system.

For years after slavery ended, Louisiana's free Black and freed people fought to defend Black freedom against a white insurgency.[33] In the remote parishes where there was little federal presence, Black men drilled and formed militias to defend their communities.[34] Federal intervention came in 1867 and, with it, a new state constitution that reaffirmed the fact of freedom and, through a bill of rights, Black equality. Half of the delegates to the constitutional convention were Black men who pushed for Black enfranchisement, integrated free public schools, and a repeal of the Black Codes. The convention did not adopt a policy of land confiscation that would have helped support landless freed people in the state and served as a form of reparations, but other measures aimed to guarantee Black access to property.

Delegate P. B. S. Pinchback, USCT veteran and political activist, secured passage of a measure that recognized the common-law marriages of formerly enslaved Louisianans, such as Tally and Mahala Miller's. "All persons formerly debarred by slavery from legally contracting matrimony," the measure read, "shall be deemed, after the adoption of this Constitution, in all courts of justice, as husband and wife." And, "their offspring [shall be deemed] as their legal heirs though said disability never existed."[35] The measure acknowledged the importance that Freedom Generation placed on reconstructing postwar families.

Louisiana's new constitution declared children born of any marriage—other than those which at the time were prohibited for reasons other than race—as "legitimate children," pushing back strongly against the claims of former enslavers who "apprenticed" children of freedwomen and -men whom local authorities declared illegitimate. Louisiana's new marriage protections removed any doubt that Caroline and Sarah were Tally's. According to postwar marriage laws, the girls were *his*—as were the five children he had with Mahala.

The 1868 law recognizing Tally Miller's common-law marriage to Mahala also expressed the aspirations of men like Pinchback and the ministers who led the state's Black Methodist churches. Removing the taint of illegitimacy from these marriages shielded the Black community from white judgment and supported demands, particularly from the educated Black elite, for racial integration. Among this elite were Revs. A. E. P. Albert and Marshall W. Taylor, Methodist ministers and editors of the *Southwestern Christian Advocate*, where Tally Miller and thousands of other formerly enslaved people posted letters looking for lost loved ones.

Tally Miller may have first heard about the *Advocate* from the pulpit. Unlike in New Orleans, where a free Black community sustained churches, schools, and newspapers and where there was a history of Black proprietorship and landownership, there was no free Black population in northwest Louisiana before the war. Freed people outside of New Orleans built churches and other institutions from scratch, defended them from destruction, and rebuilt them in the aftermath. Shreveport had a small antebellum population and few amenities; it served primarily as a depot for steamboats carrying cotton and enslaved people on the Red River. Confederate civilian and military leaders took up residence in Shreveport during the war and the population swelled with refugees. The arrival of occupying United States Colored Troops in 1865 cleared the way for Black Louisianans to claim space in the city as their own, to begin to build churches and schools and hold political meetings; so effective was this Black institution building that white businessmen-boosters published an 1875 city directory meant to dispel "the delusion" that the city was gripped by a "radical influence and negro domination."[36] Black churches provided crucial support in the transition to freedom: within their walls, couples married, community members attended services, and people connected with others who were looking for their families. Tally Miller found others there who were looking for their children who might come to them in their old age.

Miller was eighty-five years old in 1880 when a census enumerator knocked on the door of the home in Shreveport that he shared with Mahala, now sixty-five, their thirty-one-year-old son, Blake, and another couple. Tally listed his occupation as "farmer," a designation that could have meant any number of things, including working his own land or a share of someone else's or some combination of both. Throughout the region, Black landownership remained uncommon. So many of Tally Miller's neighbors fled the violence and limited economic opportunities in Louisiana for Kansas that that same summer when Miller responded to the queries of a census enumerator, Congress investigated the causes of the mass emigration. Henry Adams, a freedman, traveled to Washington from Shreveport and testified in front of the Senate that freed people "seed that there was no way on earth . . . that we could better our condition there." Adams presented senators with a list of 98,000 men, women, and children, most of them from Louisiana, who were ready to join the exodus.[37] Miller may have considered it, but he did not leave. Having left his family behind once, all those years ago, Tally Miller stayed put even as so many others set out for something better.

The new decade brought new hope that Tally Miller *could* better his condition there. When he told the enumerator that he was a farmer, he and his son Teague were working a two-hundred-acre farm that they hoped to someday call their own. Tally, Teague, and two other men purchased the land from James Pickett Jr. in March 1879. With an X next to their names in place of their signatures, father and son entered into a mortgage with two other men in which they agreed to pay Pickett $15,634.15 in six annual payments.[38] Having picked cotton for white people for most of his life, Tally Miller was now in a position to be his own boss, to answer to no one but himself. There would be no white overseer driving him, his wife, and his sons to pick faster, none in the gin house weighing their bags and recording the weight in a leather-bound book, no beatings if the numbers didn't add up. Tally and Mahala surely celebrated that day, planned what they would do when the land was theirs outright, and thought about what it would mean to pass on that land to their children and their children's children.

Fifteen thousand dollars, though, was a lot of money, even split four ways.

Having worked fields alongside the Red River so many years, the Millers knew what could go wrong: the floodwaters, the armyworms or boll weevils that ruined the crops in the field, for instance, and the yellow fever outbreaks that took the lives of those who worked in those fields. White vigilantes prowled the countryside, assaulting ambitious freed people like Tally Miller. Any one of these could mean a missed mortgage payment, and if it did, Tally and his family would lose the land and the money they had already paid on the mortgage. The terms laid out in the agreement and others the men would sign were grossly lopsided in favor of the white man who had been their enslaver over the Black men whose labor he had by law once owned. But this was Tally Miller's chance at landownership, an opportunity to establish a tradition of family land to pass along to his children and to bind together the family he had made in Louisiana with the one he had made fifty years before in South Carolina.

When Miller took to the papers looking for his daughters, he was hopeful about his chances. Landownership was within reach; surely, he could find Caroline and Sarah, bring them to Louisiana, where they could work alongside him to make it possible.

James Jr. would hardly miss the two hundred acres he agreed to sell, at nearly four times the price he had paid for the land, and it may have been his calculation that doing so would help to secure the men's labor on his own land. There was still plenty of Pickett land to be worked, and Pickett now had to bargain with his workers and compete with other white planters to retain them. Some of these white men were new to the region. Henry Warren Ogden, for instance, who like James Pickett Jr. had fought in the Confederate Army and settled in northwest

Louisiana after the war.[39] Pickett sold land to Ogden, including the Willow Chute Plantation his mother had given him with the same stroke of a pen that she had given him Tally Miller, his family, and twenty other families.[40] When Miller wrote to the papers looking for his daughters, he asked respondents to his query to address themselves to H. W. Ogden. He might have named a Pickett in the return address; that he did not suggests that by 1884, nearly twenty years a free man and with only one remaining payment on his mortgage, he had put the Picketts in his past. He no longer shared a last name with the family, and, in any case, although Paulina and John were still alive, by then James Jr. was dead.

Henry Warren Ogden was a powerful man to enlist in a search such as this. He was elected to the Louisiana House of Representatives in 1880—and then to the U.S. House of Representatives—care of new voting laws that he and other white men wrote to restrict Black access to the ballot. Ogden was part of the white insurgency working to deprive Black Louisianans of the legal equality only recently guaranteed to them.[41] Once the last agents of the Freedmen's Bureau left the state, followed by the few remaining occupying U.S. troops, local governance reverted to former Confederates like John Pickett and Henry Ogden.[42] As Tally Miller worked to establish a tradition of family land to pass along to his children, Henry Ogden and his white allies in the statehouse stood powerfully in his way.

What, then, are we to make of the relationship between Tally Miller and H. W. Ogden? There were clear benefits for Tally in naming Ogden in the letter looking for news of Caroline and Sarah, including giving his plea greater visibility and making it easier for respondents to find him. It's harder to see Ogden's interest in helping Miller. Perhaps he sympathized with the eighty-nine-year-old man, saw something of his own (deceased) father in him. Miller may have worked for Ogden while he also farmed the land he owned together with his son Teague in order to meet the mortgage payments. The simplest explanation is that, because Tally Miller could not read or write, nor could anyone else with whom he lived, he likely enlisted Ogden to write the letter to the *Advocate*.

It is possible to imagine Miller telling his family story to the congressman, sharing the details that he had turned over in his mind so many times: "I wish to inquire through your paper for my two children . . . I would like to hear from my children very much." He may have talked about the land there and how he hoped, once he found his daughters, that they would come to Louisiana to work it alongside their father and half brothers. Ogden wrote the story down and added the last line, "Write to me in care of H. W. Ogden." Included in the envelope addressed to the *Advocate* was $1.50, the cost of printing the letter three times. The letter appeared for the first time on February 7, 1884, and then again for the next two weeks.[43] For three weeks, Tally Miller's story appeared in thousands of copies of the newspaper; his words were read before congregations throughout the South.

Tally Miller told the story, with or without some of the particulars, many times as he sought information about the girls' whereabouts. Each time he told it, he recruited others in the search. After the war, he may have recorded the details with a U.S. government official, Freedmen's Bureau agent, or missionary who, for too short a time, took up residence among the freed people to support them in their transition to freedom. Perhaps at church, when he heard others' stories about searches and reunions, Tally Miller spoke about Eliza and the girls he had left beside Pea Ridge Creek. And, of course, the sons he had with Mahala were familiar with the details about how it came to be that their father was taken away from his two daughters. When they were old enough, they, too, repeated the story and tried to learn about the girls' whereabouts.

In fact, in 1881, Teague Miller had written a letter to the same paper on his father's behalf. Shorter in length and in detail, Teague's letter began with "I wish to inquire for my father's children." It named James Pickett but not Jesse Williams, included no place names or dates, and asserted with some certainty that Sarah and Caroline were married. The Williams surname was left out entirely. Whoever helped Teague with the letter—the S. J. Ziegler to whom responses were to be addressed, maybe—spelled his name "Tuague." But the details square with those that Tally relayed three years later.[44] We know, then, that, like so many others in Freedom Generation, Tally Miller's search for his children was ongoing; it was a legacy they passed on to their children.

As we read Tally's 1884 letter today, the story feels familiar; the details are smooth and worn down at the edges, like something that had been told and retold, each time with the hope that someone hearing it would have something to add and that in the end Tally Miller would get back what James B. Pickett had taken from him.

✦

Tally Miller likely never found Caroline and Sarah. In December 1889, Mahala Miller appeared in the county clerk's office as "widow of Tally Miller, dec'd of Bossier parish." There she affixed an X next to her name on a document selling property to a man named Joseph Boisseau—part of the property that her husband and son had purchased ten years earlier.[45] Tally Miller lived long enough to own a piece of the land he had once worked as an enslaved man. What happened since he bought it dashed the family's hopes that that land would serve as the foundation for the family's next generation.

Construction on a railroad connecting the cotton fields of Arkansas, Tennessee, Louisiana, and Texas to St. Louis, with an important terminus in Shreveport, began in those years. With generous federal support of the sort never extended to Black landowners like Tally Miller, railroad companies built track through a brutal system of convict leasing.[46] To keep the prisons full of Black people who could build the railroads and rebuild the levees that held back the Red River and Mississippi floodwaters, men like Henry Ogden passed state laws that trapped Louisianans of color in poverty and criminalized many aspects of Black life. The extractive economy of mining that came early in the next century aggravated the problem of poverty in the state. When small landowners sold or leased mineral rights, they were often left with land that could no longer support their families.

In 1919, Milkey Miller, another of Tally and Mahala's sons, appeared before a clerk in Bossier Parish to authorize (with an X in place of his signature) a Texas oil company to drill on sixty-four acres of his property, land that had remained in the family since Tally Miller had purchased it.[47] This is the only time, at sixty-six years old, that Milkey Miller could be identified in the public records, when he signed away more in a property agreement than he got back in rent. That none of the Millers ever *signed* these agreements, in their own hands—that they had to trust in the honesty of those who could read them—speaks to the limits of Black freedom in postwar Louisiana.

Tally Miller lived long enough to vote, under federal protection, in elections that brought Black men into the Louisiana statehouse, where they wrote a new constitution that guaranteed his freedom, his wife's, and his children's. If he voted after that, Miller would have been advised to cast ballots for powerful white men—Democrats like H. W. Ogden or John Pickett who were determined to turn the clock back on civil rights—or he kept quiet about it if he voted Republican. He experienced other dramatic markers of freedom, such as the legal recognition of his marriage and acknowledgment that he was father to his children. He bought land, and for nearly ten years he improved that land and prepared to pass it along to his children and grandchildren. That land helped Miller put some distance between his children and the "blinding fear" that continued to threaten them.

✦

As a free man, Tally changed his last name from Pickett to Miller, as did his wife and children, underscoring the point that no one would ever take them from him. Miller fulfilled the duties of citizenship, serving on a jury at least once, deciding on cases involving whites and Blacks charged with crimes—but mostly the latter.[48] Such was the reality of Black life in postwar Louisiana, where emancipation and Reconstruction came late and left early, and where the marks on their property deeds indicated the power of Jim Crow to keep even a successful and determined family like the Millers illiterate. Tally Miller grew old there and, like other fathers and mothers, sought the comfort and company of his children—all of them.

As long as he lived his life in freedom, Tally Miller enjoyed the company of the family he and Mahala had made. Although no one in the family ever reported to the *Southwestern Christian Advocate* that Sarah and Caroline had been found, Miller did not let slavery or postwar racism stop him from trying to find the children a white man had taken from him.

MR. EDITOR—I desire some information about my mother. The last time I saw her I was in Alexandria, Virginia, about the year 1852 or 1853. Her name was Hannah. She belonged to Lawyer Tibbs who sold her when I was quite young to a trader named Bruthing. Lather Tibbs lived at Leesburg, Va., when he sold mother to Bruthing, and afterwards Tibbs moved to Alexandria, Va., and swapped me to Bruthing for another boy. Bruthing put me in jail and I cried, so he told me if I would hush he would bring my mother there next morning, which he did; but I was so young mother hardly knew me, so Bruthing stood four or five boys in a line and asked her which one of them was her boy. She stood a few moments and then said I was the boy. Mother then brought me some cake and candy, and that was the last time I saw her. I now go by the name of Henry Tibbs. I remember the names of two of Tibbs' sons, Abner and Kennedy. Bruthing brought me to New Orleans, La., and sold me to a man named M. Pickett. If mother is found please address me at Deasonville, Yazoo county, Miss., in care of Rev. James Allen. HENRY TIBBS.

Henry Tibbs to "Mr. Editor," Lost Friends, *Southwestern Christian Advocate* (New Orleans, LA), December 11, 1879

CHAPTER FOUR

I Was the Boy

Henry Tibbs wrote to the papers in search of his mother when he was fifty-five years old. Tibbs grew up, without her, in Mississippi, fought with the U.S. Colored Troops during the war, married, and had children of his own, all the while holding on to the details about the last time he saw his mother, when he was a small child. A decade after the war, he wrote a letter to the paper inquiring about her; it described a series of sales or "swaps" that took the young boy away from his mother, sending him to New Orleans, the heart of the domestic slave trade and then on to the Mississippi cotton fields. Scenes of young children being wrenched from their mothers' arms were common in mid-century America; foreign eyewitnesses reported on such incidents in their travel accounts, abolitionists illustrated their tracts with shocking sketches of baby auctions, and, in their published memoirs, formerly enslaved people relayed details about losing their mothers. There was nothing exceptional or unusual about what happened to Henry Tibbs; no laws effectively prohibited the trafficking of young children like him away from their mothers. The laws protected the traffickers, men like those named in Tibbs's letter to the newspaper.

When emancipation finally came, freed people's families were in disarray. Those who had managed to stay together before the war were separated when men and boys enlisted or were impressed into the army, and women and those too old or too young to be militarily useful made their way to refugee camps and abandoned plantations. As soon as they could, freedwomen and -men sought out federal soldiers, local officials, pastors, missionaries, newspaper editors, employers, and neighbors for help finding their children. They went to the papers with everything they remembered and had gathered over the years, including physical descriptions that were eerily reminiscent of fugitive slave ads. Parents filled their ads with details about their children's faces and hands, information gleaned from watching them as they slept and holding their hands when they fell. A father looked for his son, Isham, who was "AN ALBINO—white skinned, but of negro blood, with one black spot on his under lip." A mother wrote for her son William who had a "full mouth with very short white teeth . . . a scar on his forehead, just above his right eye." Someone might recognize a freedwoman's daughter, Martha, by the "little piece chipped out of her right ear." Another mother hoped the same for her seven-year-old daughter, Sarah Francis, who was missing "the index finger of the right hand."[1] Each chipped ear or missing finger marked a moment in a child's life that their parent recalled vividly, painfully; children who were too young to know a name or recognize a place carried with them something—a scar, perhaps—that might remind them of a father or a mother who had once comforted them.

But when a child like Henry Tibbs was separated from his mother at a young age, he was left with little to begin his search—except the memory of that separation and, maybe, her efforts to prevent it. Children had fewer opportunities than adults to fill in the rough outlines of a lost loved one with new information gleaned over the years and transmitted via the grapevine telegraph's many miles. Their memories of lost mothers were frozen in time and could only with some difficulty and limited success be mobilized in the search for family lost to the domestic slave trade.

Henry Tibbs's 1879 letter to the papers inquiring about his mother is full of names, including his mother's, their enslaver's and two of his children's, and even the name of the slave trader who had sold him to someone else.

> I desire some information about my mother. The last time I saw her I was in Alexandria, Virginia, about the year 1852 or 1853. Her name was Hannah. She belonged to Lawyer Tibbs who sold her when I was quite young to a trader named Bruthing. Lather Tibbs lived at Leesburg, Va., when he sold mother to Bruthing, and afterwards Tibbs moved to Alexandria, Va., and swapped me to Bruthing for another boy.

It is unlikely that Henry had seen any of these names in writing, and, as long as he was enslaved, he was forbidden from reading them. He was a child when he learned the names, how they sounded to him and how he said them. And then a white man named Lawyer Tibbs—or was it *Lather* Tibbs?—sold him away from his mother, Hannah. He was "[q]uite young" when sold; "so young" that when he cried the slave trader named Bruthing who had a jail full of children awaiting sale sent for his mother. "I cried, so he told me if I would hush he would bring my mother there next morning. . . . Mother then brought me some cake and candy," is how he recalled it, "and that was the last time I saw her." There was nothing exceptional or unusual about any of this, nothing that set Henry's experience apart from the others, except that Henry had been able to see his mother once more and she had tried to make their parting sweet.

These are the details that Henry hoped would lead him back to her. Except that he got her name wrong as well his own, or at least its original spelling. The date of their parting also doesn't correspond with what we learn from other documentation. The names are close approximations, in some cases homophones, of people Henry Tibbs knew as a child. Tibbs was *Tebbs*; Bruthing likely was *Bruin*; and, as for Hannah? The record is even less clear. Growing up among strangers, Henry held on to the details about the last time he saw his mother because it comforted him to recall her attention to him, her attempt to steal away his tears, as any mother would. And the names held the clues that he would use to find her when the time came.

When it did, Hannah would surely recall the day she brought him cake and candy. Readers would know Lawyer Tibbs—or Tebbs—of

Leesburg and then Alexandria, Virginia. Or maybe the slave trader with a jail full of children. And when they did, they'd get word to Hannah that her son had been sold to an "M. Pickett" in New Orleans, that he was living in Mississippi and going "by the name of Henry Tibbs." Readers would pass this information along to her, and she'd recognize him, just as she had when Bruthing tried to confuse her by placing him in a lineup. "Bruthing stood four or five boys in a line and asked her which one of them was her boy. She stood a few moments and then said I was the boy." Henry's mother had passed the test. They had *both* gotten the better of the trader: first when Henry's tears threatened to upset the other boys and Bruthing sent for his mother. And then, when she saw through Bruthing's trick and picked out her boy. The story as Henry remembered it from the perspective of a child is full of small acts of heroism in the midst of great evil.

Members of Freedom Generation began their search for mothers and fathers with memories like Henry Tibbs's. Letters and advertisements from sons and daughters looking for fathers and mothers fill the archive, many of them published years or decades after their authors became free. Their stories about their parents leap off the page as if the events happened yesterday and were recorded soon thereafter. Children who were sold away from their parents at a young age faced unique challenges in relying on those memories in their searches for mothers and fathers they barely knew and often could not describe. Recent studies show that children can be reliable witnesses to events when questioned soon afterward; over time, though, children's memories become less reliable. Without the support of caretakers, young people forget the particulars about traumatic events even as they continue to suffer the effects. As a result, traumatic memories are disorganized, with some events remembered clearly but not necessarily in order; other vital details are forgotten entirely.[2]

Formerly enslaved children filled their letters with recollections of parents who fought for them and tried to protect them. These vivid memories helped children growing up without their parents, but when the names and dates did not line up, as in Henry Tibbs's case, they could not always help those children find their parents.

We know how trauma affects young people, how they remember it in pieces, and how they can carry it with them. Thirty percent of the nearly four million enslaved Americans were younger than ten when the Civil War began; many carried with them into freedom memories of fathers and mothers from whom they had been separated.[3] Yet the experience of enslaved children is often overlooked, their narratives dismissed as unreliable. What would it mean, instead, to approach Freedom Generation's search for family informed by what we know today about survivors of childhood trauma? How would it change the story we tell about American slavery and its aftermath if we understood the separating of children from their mothers as the rule rather than the exception?

◆

Among the one million people sold from the Upper to the Lower South before 1860, thousands were children sold alone. According to historian Edward Baptist, between 1815 and 1820, 2,646 children under the age of thirteen were sold in New Orleans out of a total of 12,370 sales. Of their number, 1,001 were sold alone. "Their average age was nine. Many were younger—much younger."[4] Children accounted for 20 percent of the sales during the period. If that proportion remained constant throughout the period of the domestic slave trade, then perhaps as many as 50,000 children younger than thirteen were sold in the United States. Many were sold alone, like Henry Tibbs. By one estimate, one in every three enslaved children under age fourteen was separated from one or both of their parents through a long-distance sale.[5] And this does not include local sales. At a time when modern ideas about white children needing and deserving special attention and care were ascendant, America's domestic slave trade was, in the words of historian Erik J. Hofstee, "a continued and structural exercise in child abuse."[6]

Although his exact age remains a mystery, by Henry Tibbs's own recollection he was quite young when he was sold. His description of the events is consistent with what we would expect from someone separated from his mother at a young age. There was a demand for young people in the cotton fields of the Mississippi Valley; and in the Upper South—Virginia, Maryland, Kentucky—enslavers were willing to meet it. Selling Henry from Virginia to Mississippi meant big money for a man like Lawyer Tibbs. In Virginia, a boy under five was valued at $100; by seven years old, that same boy sold for $400 in Louisiana or Mississippi, and $600 by eleven or twelve.[7]

In the middle were slave traders, men like Joseph Bruin, who ran a lucrative slave trade business in Alexandria.[8] Alexandria residents knew Joseph Bruin, could be counted on to relay messages sent to the post office there, and directed visitors to the jail where he kept slaves waiting for transport to New Orleans. As well-known as he was, though, not everyone knew how to spell his name. When in 1850 a census enumerator knocked on the door of his residence next door to the jail to record his name, his wife's, and the couple's five children, he spelled their surname "Brewen," which is how it must have sounded.[9] Henry Tibbs heard "Bruthing."

The name Algernon Sydney Tebbs likely impressed wealthy Virginia planters looking for legal representation, but it does not trip off the tongue. It's no surprise that the Leesburg, Virginia, lawyer's name was often misspelled in public records. In the 1840 Census he was "Alganon Tobbs." Ten years later, he went by "A. S." instead of the ungainly "Algernon Sydney"; the enumerator recorded his surname correctly as "Tebbs." That same year on the slave schedule for Loudon County the name that appears next to the hashmarks indicating that he owned thirteen enslaved people was "A. S. Tibbs," which is how Henry Tibbs remembered the man.

Depending on when Algernon Tebbs, or "Lawyer Tibbs," sold Henry's mother and then Henry to Joseph Bruin (it seems likely to have been earlier than 1852 or '53), he and his wife, Julia, had five children at home, at least three of whom were younger than nine. The two youngest were six-year-old Algernon and five-year-old Clement, likely the children Henry later identified as Abner and Kennedy. Henry may have been close in age to the younger Tebbs boys and so recalled their names, or close approximations of them, all those years later when he wrote a letter hoping to find his mother. Perhaps they had been occasional playmates, or Henry's mother was charged with their care, or little Henry was. But then, like so many other Virginia planters, Algernon Tebbs decided Henry and his mother were more useful to him as cash than as a caretaker or playmate for his children.

Everyone familiar with Joseph Bruin knew that he specialized in New Orleans's "fancy" trade, or prostitution. A. S. Tebbs may have felt the need to come up with a justification for selling a woman into prostitution—maybe it was that "he became involved in debt," as had Dick Christian when he sold Clara Bashop and Patience. He may have told himself that he was an honorable slaveholder like David Outlaw, who sold Hagar Outlaw's children, and assured himself that he did not "regard them merely as property." A slave trader like Joseph Bruin proved useful in such stories, if Algernon Sydney Tebbs found the need to reassure himself. When Bruin bought Henry's mother, Hannah, from Tebbs, he had identified a buyer who did not want her to be accompanied by a small child. That buyer might have purchased her for sex.

Bruin operated a jail in the city's West End neighborhood, on the same property where he lived with his wife and children; by 1860 the Bruins had seven children.[10] Because he was caught up in a number of high-profile cases where abolitionists sought to rescue enslaved people from him, Joseph Bruin was well-known, not only among buyers and sellers of children in the South, but also among a growing antislavery movement in the North.[11] Described as "all smiles and politeness" and with manners "that would eclipse even Lord Chesterfield himself," Bruin charmed them all.[12]

Even Harriet Beecher Stowe found Bruin irresistible, describing him as "courteous" and "gentlemanly," no more to blame for the injustices of slavery than "clergyman and layman, saint and sinner, [who] all agreed on the propriety and necessity of slave-holding."[13] Bruin was the inspiration for Mr. Haley, the character in Stowe's *Uncle Tom's Cabin* who tries to convince Shelby to sell Eliza into the fancy trade. When that fails, Haley, the fictional Joseph Bruin, persuades Shelby to sell Eliza's young son, Harry, assuring Shelby that when it came to white people selling their children, slave mothers "gets used to it."[14] These events are what set in motion Eliza's brave escape with Harry. At the heart of the novel was a mother who refused to be separated from her son; it spoke to white readers who had children and families of their own.

Although in *Uncle Tom's Cabin* Stowe ignored Joseph Bruin's specialization in the sex trade, in *The Key to Uncle Tom's Cabin* published a year later Stowe wrote about Bruin himself. Stowe describes a scene in which two enslaved sisters appeal directly to Joseph Bruin not to sell them: "Mary and Emily went to the house to bid Bruin's family good-bye. Bruin had a little daughter who had been a pet and favourite with the girls. She clung round them, cried, and begged them not to go. Emily told her that if she wished to have them, she must go and ask her father." Which the little girl did. But it wasn't his own daughter that made Bruin relent; it was the enslaved girl Mary, whose tears brought him to the prison to see her. Mary cried and begged Bruin and convinced him to give them more time for friends to come with enough money to purchase the sisters. Which he did, and the girls were purchased and set free. "Bruin," Stowe exclaimed, "was not absolutely a man of stone, and this agonising appeal brought tears to his eyes."[15]

Like those Lost Cause authors many years later who would cover up the history of slavery by claiming that few families had been separated—that, even among those, mothers and daughters and sons and mothers found one another again—Harriet Beecher Stowe insisted that the people who sold children into the slave trade weren't all bad: some of them were Christian and conflicted. To come to this conclusion, Stowe overlooked her own evidence of Bruin's single-minded pursuit of other people's children that he could turn into cash, as when he defended his intention to sell Emily and Mary into the sex trade because "he had had his eye upon the family for twelve years."[16] Bruin may have not been made of stone, but Stowe seems to have been.

Historian Nell Painter has said that slavery "deserves recognition as one of the fundamental influences on American family mores."[17] Stowe—mother of six children, who was moved to write *Uncle Tom's Cabin* while mourning the loss of one of them in infancy—along with her well-known sister, Catharine Beecher, and brother, Henry Ward Beecher, were self-appointed guardians of American family values, even as they ignored the principles in their own lives and embraced white supremacy. Stowe disregarded the fact that Bruin still made his money from the sale of Mary and Emily Edmondson—and all the other children who passed through his jail in the decades he ran it.

✦

That Tebbs "swapped" Henry for another boy suggests that his sale was incidental or related to the sale of his mother; an inconsolable child could disrupt things at Tebbs's place, where there were (in 1850) thirteen enslaved people whose labor could not be spared to look after him. Selling a mother and child was also a common strategy for covering up evidence of sexual assault; a mixed-race child, if that is what Henry was, would have been difficult to hide in a household the size of Tebbs's in Leesburg.[18] A "swap" might solve the problem.

Formerly enslaved people used the term "swapped" in a number of ways. Sometimes it was used in place of sale, as when Charlotte Stuart described how she was "swapped to Evan Thompson" or when Charles Stewart placed an advertisement looking for two sisters, Harriet and Fannie, who "were sold or swapped off to a speculator in slave property." The term also described private exchanges between family or acquaintances, as when, as "a small lad," Allison Washington was "swapped . . . for another boy named Charles." In their ads, freed people used "carried off," "taken," "went to," and many other verbs to describe the sale of adults and children, but "swapped" was only attached to children. The informal exchanges it described captured the dark realities of a traffic in children in which buyers and sellers attached lower values to the young, as if enslaved children were interchangeable or easily replaced. When invoked by survivors like Henry Tibbs, the term might also have implied a rejection of the syntax of the slave trade. It can be read as part of Freedom Generation's sustained refutation of the chattel principle—that people could be reduced to things. Clara Bashop asserted these principles when she insisted that her daughter, Patience, belonged to Dick Christian "(in name only)." In her advertisement searching for her daughter, Lucinda Lowery dispensed with euphemism when she described the two men who sold her daughter as

"Warwick (trader then in human beings)" and "Robert Clarke (human trader in that place)." The words in parentheses come across like real-time translations or stage whispers directed at a knowing audience.[19]

Catharine Mason editorialized in quotation marks about her daughters, who were "'owned'" by one man, and her son, who "'belonged'" to another. Same for Henry and Virginia Thompson, whose daughter "was once 'owned'" by a man in Virginia, and Catherine Rhodes, whose sons "'belonged' to Caleb Dorsey." The quotation marks drew attention to the words.[20]

From Alexandria, Joseph Bruin shipped Henry Tibbs and a few others from his jail to New Orleans by land or sea. The trip was long and dangerous; many did not survive. Children died on the journey; those who made it did so because others with whom they were shackled cared for them as best they could.[21] John Parker was sold away from his mother in Norfolk, Virginia, when he was eight. From Norfolk he walked to Richmond in a coffle chained together with an old man who "made my weight of the chain as light as he could. He talked to me kindly, because I was brokenhearted at leaving my mother." Sold again in Richmond, Parker "began my chain bound journey to Alabama." Years later, Parker recalled his anger: how he threw a rock at a bird and picked up a stick and smashed all the flowers he passed and the bubbles in a stream—because they were free.[22]

John Parker was sure, as children often are, that he had been sold away because he had misbehaved, so he turned his anger inward. In the coffle he became "old in experience and quick at observation"; that education taught him that he "hated the strong." When a younger boy named Jeff joined the coffle and "blubbered and cried" for his mother, Parker kicked him. But then, Parker looked out for Jeff and protected him. As the coffle crossed a river, the adult men lost their footing, and when they struggled to get up, they dragged the children at the end of the coffle under the rushing water. Parker nearly drowned as he pushed Jeff up over his head. "From that day forward," Parker, who later became active on the Underground Railroad, recalled, "I was the champion of the weak. I had found a way to beat at the 'might is right' policy, which had enslaved me."[23]

Like Henry Tibbs's, John Parker's childhood recollection of losing his mother was full of examples of the weak overcoming the strong and the need for enslaved children to be heroes of their own lives. Maybe an adult lightened Henry's chain for him as the coffle made its way from Virginia to Louisiana or he found a champion his own age, but he also learned, at a young age, that he had to be strong.

Joseph Bruin and his associates in New Orleans knew to avoid Louisiana law regulating the traffic in enslaved children. It was illegal to sell a child younger than ten away from their mother or to import one who had been separated for that purpose. These laws did not protect Henry Tibbs, who was separated from his mother in Virginia, where A. S. Tebbs had the right to sell Henry at any age. Once Tebbs sold Henry's mother, disposing of little Henry became easier, for he was no longer a child being sold away from his mother but an orphan. Algernon Tebbs was in good company among his Loudon County neighbors in having made an orphan of Henry Tibbs; one study found that 18 percent of ex-slaves from the county reported having no parents.[24] Virginia's enslavers thus made it possible for traders like Bruin to insist that they never sold children away from their mothers.

In New Orleans as in other American cities and towns, there were many places one could go to buy a child like Henry. English abolitionist Harriet Martineau witnessed the sale of a child in Charleston. When the "little boy of eight or nine years old" climbed up onto the table with the auctioneer, Martineau was struck by "the child's look of helplessness and shame." The awful scene shook her "faith of the spirit of Christianity." "It seemed like an outrage to be among the starers from whom he shrunk," Martineau added, so she left before he was sold.[25] Among the starers who did not shrink was Micajah Pickett, who bought Henry in New Orleans and brought him to one of his Yazoo County, Mississippi, plantations.

✦

Micajah Pickett bought land by the Yazoo River as it was being wrested from the Choctaw Nation. Thousands of Choctaw left Mississippi for

Oklahoma, where the U.S. government promised them "an exchange of lands," something in return for what had been taken from them—as if it were possible to provide a people with something to replace their homelands, the fertile Mississippi Valley that had sustained the Choctaw for millennia. Like the term "swap," "exchange" suggests a transfer of objects of equal value. The official title of the 1830 Indian Removal Act—the forced relocation of Indigenous people from the American South, a policy that made possible the expansion of Anglo-American cotton production and slavery into Louisiana, Mississippi, Tennessee, Alabama, and Georgia, that resulted in the deaths of thousands of Native people in the process of being "removed," and that drew a million forced migrants like Henry Tibbs into the domestic slave trade—is "An act to provide for an exchange of lands with the Indians."[26] Micajah arrived soon after that "exchange" had been effected; his brother Rufus followed him there a few years later. The two "entered it from the Government at a very reasonable price," a descendant of the region's white settlers recalled, many years later, about the process by which men bought the land offered at auction by the General Land Office in Washington, D.C. Micajah and Rufus bought a lot of it; there was still Pickett family property in Yazoo, Mississippi, one hundred years later.

The promise of an exchange between the Mississippi Choctaw and the federal government was never complete, and neither was "removal." In a 1936 WPA interview, a white Yazoo County resident recalled Choctaw camping in the "cane breaks" at the edge of Rufus Pickett's property, where they traded baskets, blow-guns (made of sugarcane), squirrels, and turkeys for food to carry them through the winter and medicine for their children. The Picketts established a "seat of culture" in the Mississippi Delta, where they became known for their generosity, or at least that is how the county's white residents recalled the family that traced their English bloodline back to the Bronze Age. The Picketts, it would seem, had something in common with the Choctaw to whom they dispensed occasional charity—an identity that derived from having lived in a place for thousands of years.

Like James and Paulina Pickett, who hailed from South Carolina—and to whom Micajah was not related—Micajah and his brother Rufus were drawn to the seemingly infinite possibilities of growing cotton in the Mississippi Valley's rich soils. Micajah bought seven thousand acres. He and Rufus chose names for the homes they built there that announced their Scottish-English lineage—Fairfield, Birdfield, Wildwood, Scotland, Floddenfield—as if doing so would establish a claim to the land that title from the U.S. Land Office could not. Over the years, as the two built a kingdom in the Delta, the English names leant the project an air of inevitability, as if cotton would grow there easily despite the floods and a truncated season, and castles surrounded by elegant gardens would emerge naturally from the swamps. When their kingdom building succeeded, the names would ensure that people would credit their success to Micajah and Rufus Pickett's good breeding and not to the brutal disciplinary regime they administered there.

Floddenfield still stood in the 1930s, a place where local whites recalled fondly the mansion for "its spacious rooms, and the royal welcome of the host, who loved to stroll down the long lane" lined with sweetbriar. As they strolled the fragrant lanes, guests of the Picketts recalled hearing "the shuffle feet of the negro fiddlers and banjo players that make the unforgettable pictures of careless joy."[27] It didn't matter that no one had been in that house, or not since they were quite young, and that these memories were likely fiction. Like William Faulkner's character Thomas Sutpen, Micajah Pickett came to the Delta to build an empire, something worthy of the English names he had in mind.[28] There were no spacious mansions or sweetbriar lanes when Henry Tibbs arrived in Yazoo County—only a vast expanse of land to be cleared, drained, ditched, and planted.

To work those acres, Micajah Pickett bought hundreds of enslaved people. In 1860, he owned 181 people, a number that does not begin to capture the cost in human life that accrued as Pickett made a fortune in the Mississippi Delta. The median age of the slaves working his Yazoo cotton fields in 1860 was seventeen. More than half were ten years or younger. Among the one hundred children on his place in 1860, those who survived to their teens could expect to pick cotton until they died, generally by the time they reached twenty-one.[29] The object in the Delta was to grow cotton—a lot of it; more than the competition.

Which meant a brutal work regime and a slave population that was not self-sustaining. Once each year or so, Micajah Pickett boarded a Mississippi steamboat to New Orleans, where he made the rounds paying premiums to purchase more children like Henry to replace those who died picking his cotton or before they were old enough to do so.

Pickett knew how to size up a child standing before him on the auction block: how hearty he was; how likely he was to survive malaria, dysentery, and the other "fevers" common to the region; how many children she would grow up to have—*if* she grew up. He wasn't exactly playing God; perhaps a prophet is a more apt comparison, such as the Old Testament Micajah to whom God spoke and who predicted the death of the king of Israel. Following the lead of prophets like Micajah, a small number of Mississippi Delta enslavers purchased enough slaves annually to sustain a steady growth of the enslaved population there. Between 1850 and 1860, the enslaved population of Yazoo County grew from 10,349 to 16,716; by the latter date, slaves accounted for 74 percent of the total population. Census enumerators found no free Black population to count—*not one person*. A free Black community would have been disruptive to the disciplinary regime sustained by whites, who were outnumbered by enslaved people three to one. Planters in the Delta produced more cotton than anywhere else in the state because they pushed enslaved people to their limits and tolerated no intermediaries to their authority.[30]

Enslaved people in the Delta built networks of communication, worship, and support that existed beyond the detection of enslavers like Micajah Pickett and despite stringent state laws prohibiting most aspects of Black life. That an "orphan" boy like Henry Tibbs survived all of those years, working the fields into his forties, was due to the care he received from the slave community.

Joe Clinton, who also came to the Delta as a young boy, was interviewed by the Federal Writers' Project when he was eighty-six. Clinton recalled the house in the quarters where an old woman cared for the babies and children, a place called the "sick house" where an old man cared for the field hands "until they either get well or die," and the cookhouse where another woman cooked for everyone on the place.

Although his enslaver owned "heaps of people, women and men both and just gangs of children," Clinton referred to everyone as Aunt or Uncle, underscoring the communal ties that bound the enslaved people together, though most were strangers.[31]

Enslaved children and adults came to the Delta from all over the South, bringing with them survival strategies they had employed in Virginia, North Carolina, and Tennessee; some would have to be repurposed. Henry Tibbs's mother may have taught him how to protect himself. He would do well in Mississippi to indulge the pretenses of haughty enslavers like the Picketts. Tibbs was born into a household that included a small number of enslaved people who lived in close proximity to and generally under the watchful eyes of enslavers. He was raised as one of hundreds on Micajah Pickett's extensive holdings, on cotton fields that stretched as far as the eye could see.

Many enslavers in the Mississippi Delta were nonresident, and all of them employed overseers and drivers to enforce discipline. Enslaved people lived and worked cooperatively and communally. Clearing the land, ditching fields, running straight rows, dropping holes, and filling them with cottonseed all required cooperation, as did ginning and packing cotton. Even picking required coordination—and it depended on the communal child-rearing that Joe Clinton described. Enslaved people looked out for and comforted one another, stretched meager rations of food and shelter to accommodate newcomers, and shared what they trapped, hunted, or fished to supplement their rations.

In the quarters and beyond the surveillance of enslavers and drivers, Henry Tibbs learned the ethical code that governed and protected the enslaved community, about not talking to white people, and how to flatter them when they had to. When a white preacher instructed slaves on a Mississippi plantation to report anyone who stole a hog or a chicken, Delia Hill's mother reminded her children that if they did so she would "hang us upside down by our feet, build a fire under us and smoke us."[32] Enslaved children found themselves in an impossible position when enslavers and other white authority figures held children to a standard of behavior that was at odds with what they learned from family and kin. They worked out these conflicts in games, songs, and stories that focused on the weak overcoming the strong; doing so reinforced their sense of self-worth and their adherence to the ethical standards of the slave community.[33] Henry Tibbs's recounting of how his tears convinced a slave trader to bring his mother to him, for instance.

✦

Early in the Civil War, enslaved people began hearing rumors that the Union Army was on its way. A group of enslaved men 150 miles south of Yazoo, near Natchez, plotted to kill their masters. They had heard through the grapevine that "Mr. Lincoln was coming down here" and that "Lincoln would set us free." The men spread the word that the Union troops headed toward Mississippi would "make the South shit behind their asses."[34] Word reached Yazoo County that the white people in Natchez hanged forty slaves. And in nearby Jefferson County, people braced themselves for a July Fourth rebellion. North in Lafayette County, slaves drove away the overseers and seized their enslavers' property.[35] Something like that was rumored to have happened on Micajah Pickett's place; years later locals repeated a story about a white man buried out there, an overseer who "was beaten to death for some cause by the slaves."[36] Whatever happened to Micajah Pickett's overseer during the Civil War, none of the old white residents of Yazoo were sure anymore what the man's name was or what grievance Pickett's enslaved people had had with him—as if it were one "cause."

When the war came to Mississippi, Henry Tibbs was a grown man with children of his own. He may have had them in mind when he engaged in his own act of rebellion, escaping Pickett's plantation and heading for the U.S. Army at Vicksburg. It is also possible that the U.S. Army came *to* Tibbs, for the army detached recruiters to plantations to bring men to Vicksburg. There Tibbs enlisted in the United States Colored Troops, joining an insurgency of some 17,800 Black men from Mississippi engaged in a war against slavery.[37]

Enslaved people heard that the Confederacy's war in the Mississippi Valley was not going well. After a series of losses in 1862 and into

1863, the Confederates surrendered Vicksburg to Ulysses S. Grant in July 1863. What had once been rumor carried via the grapevine telegraph seemed now like premonition.

Lincoln's men did not come to Mississippi to set slaves free, as the Natchez conspirators anticipated, but that hardly mattered to the more than 400,000 enslaved Mississippians, tens of thousands of whom seized freedom for themselves, fled their captivity, and headed to the nearest Union Army outpost.[38] John Eaton, a chaplain traveling with Grant, compared the movement of these freedom-seeking people to "the oncoming of cities. There was no plan in this exodus, no Moses to lead it . . . [A] blind terror stung them, an equally blind hope allured them, and to us they came." Eaton was struck by the physical condition of the refugees "in every stage of disease or decrepitude, often nearly naked . . . the women in travail, the helplessness of childhood and of old age, the horrors of sickness and of frequent death."[39] The enslaved people escaping Mississippi Valley labor camps carried on their bodies evidence of the crushing disciplinary regime that had made possible the U.S.'s cornering the global market for cotton; that had made Micajah Pickett, Algernon Tebbs, Joseph Bruin, Paulina Pickett, David Outlaw, and Dick Christian wealthy; and had relied on an open marketplace for the buying and selling of children.

Henry Tibbs's daughter Nancy was born in 1862, perhaps as her mother, Ann, made her way to freedom. The couple's other daughter, Henrietta, was seven years old. The record is unclear about when Tibbs made his family with Henrietta, Nancy, and Ann. Ann and Henry may have been married in slavery, or Tibbs may have met the girls and their freedom-seeking mother in Vicksburg. Because we cannot find evidence that their marriage was recorded by federal or local officials—and his pension application says little else beyond the girls' names and birth years—it is difficult to know much more about how and when they became a family.[40] In Mississippi as elsewhere, enslaved people's marriages were solemnized by the slave community. As they made their way to freedom, people like Ann and Henry did not universally discard these traditions for legally sanctioned marriages but doing so might help if Ann were to find herself once again behind

Confederate lines. Federal policy moved haltingly to guarantee the freedom of women and children, at first doing so only when they had fled enslavers loyal to the Confederacy and then to wives and children of U.S. Army soldiers.[41]

On November 4, 1863, four months to the day since the Confederate forces defending Vicksburg surrendered the town to Grant, Henry enlisted as a private in Battery D, 2nd Regiment, U.S. Colored Light Artillery (USCLA). The agent recorded his age as thirty-five years old; he stood five feet seven.[42] He gave his name as Henry Tibbs, maybe for the first time out loud. He had always been Henry, but as long as he belonged to Micajah Pickett, he could not be a Tibbs, a surname that connected him to the mother he left behind in Virginia. Suited up in his blue uniform with "U.S." on the sleeve, his mother would have been proud of him. Henry had lived a lifetime since he moved a white man to a moment of mercy with his tears. Now he had a gun—actually, he had a few. That spring, Battery D was detailed to Fort Pillow, Tennessee, where they manned the cannon defending the U.S. troops, Black and white, garrisoned there. As he peered out through the fort's embrasures, it must have crossed Tibbs's mind that he now had the means to fight back against the white violence that had scattered his family and held him in slavery. Maybe he was among those who taunted the Confederates as they came in close to the fort.[43]

When Tibbs left Vicksburg with the 2nd USCLA, the status of the civilian refugees there was unclear. The fate of Ann and the girls, if they were there, would be determined by military officials who insisted that they should not be saddled with the burden of feeding women and children. This attitude reflected the limitations of U.S. Army policy toward contrabands. Although it was often applied indiscriminately to all of those escaping slavery, army officials' use of the term "contraband" underscored their interest in refugees whose labor they recognized as a military asset. It was easy for them to see the strategic interest in enlisting men in the U.S. Army, particularly when they encountered enslaved men impressed into Confederate service building fortifications at a place like Vicksburg. Enslaved men capitalized on these encounters by slipping across the lines to the U.S. Army. So many slaves escaped to Union lines that enslavers openly defied orders and refused to let the Confederate Army impress their slaves.

U.S. Army officials could think of several ways to make use of Henry Tibbs, including digging fortifications and training him in the use of artillery. The agent who enlisted Tibbs registered his occupation as "laborer," a term that described the army's intention to put him to work. Women and children were another issue and a problem for the army, even though, once behind Union lines, they made themselves indispensable as cooks, laundresses, and nurses. By the summer of 1863, the army in the Mississippi Valley was removing women, children, and elderly men from refugee camps and sending them to abandoned and confiscated plantations along the Mississippi River where they picked cotton for the government.[44] For those who had arrived in Vicksburg in family units, this policy was in effect federally sanctioned family separation. Women and children relocated to these camps were easy targets for Confederate raids. At one such raid fifty miles north of Vicksburg, in East Carroll Parish, Louisiana, Confederates attacked and killed refugees encamped at federal plantations, among them unarmed women and children.[45] Freedom, like slavery, was something that Ann, Henrietta, and Nancy would have to learn to survive.

The same was true for Henry. At Fort Pillow, forty miles north of Memphis, Battery D of the 2nd USCLA joined the 6th U.S. Colored Heavy Artillery organized at Natchez and made up of formerly enslaved Mississippians like Henry Tibbs and the other members of the 2nd. The two Black regiments arrived early in the spring of 1864 to reinforce a white Union regiment that was already there. On April 12, Confederate troops surrounded the fort, moving in close to and above the fort's defenses where Union artillery could not reach them; the Americans struggled with defective cannonballs. When the outnumbered Union troops inside laid down their weapons and tried to surrender, the Confederates, led by former Tennessee slave trader Nathan Bedford Forrest, brutally murdered the Black men, often at close range, instead of taking them prisoner. In all, 195 of the 305 Black defenders of the fort were killed.[46]

Among those who survived the Fort Pillow Massacre—either by escaping the fort, feigning death, or evading their captors—was Henry

Tibbs. Many survivors sustained serious injuries from which they never fully recovered. In the days that followed, a congressional investigation exposed the atrocities committed at the fort by armed white men against a smaller and mostly unarmed Black force in the name of white supremacy. Once the two Black regiments laid down their arms to surrender, the Confederates were bound by the laws of war to treat them as prisoners, take them into custody, and grant them basic medical care; instead, they engaged in indiscriminate murder. Thomas Adison, a private in the 6th U.S. Colored Heavy Artillery, had been wounded once already when a Confederate shot him in the face at close range. While he lay on the ground that night, Adison witnessed the Confederates burning people alive and shooting Black children who were waiting on them. Forty years a slave—first in South Carolina and then Mississippi—Adison testified, "I never saw folks shot down so in my life."[47] For the survivors, there was before Fort Pillow and after.

Tibbs lived to serve another two years in the service of the U.S. Army. Sometime that spring, before so many of his comrades were killed at Fort Pillow, Tibbs had been promoted to corporal, giving him the power to give orders and indicating that his superiors recognized in him the qualities of leadership. But the army took away his rank a few months later while he was detailed to Milliken's Bend; his service records give no explanation for the reduction in rank. Thirty years later, when Tibbs applied for a pension, he recorded his rank as corporal even though he mustered out as a private. Tibbs spent about five months of his three-year enlistment in the hospital, recovering from pneumonia.[48]

"Recover" might not be the right word to describe Henry Tibbs's experience: separated from his family as a child, he survived to be put to work in the killing fields of the Mississippi Valley. He grew up to have a family of his own, whom he struggled to keep together even as the army he fought for took them away and put them in harm's way. Then, given the chance to strike back at those who bought and sold children, Tibbs narrowly escaped death at the hands of white men with pistols seeking vengeance. That he remained in the U.S. Army, that he never gave up hope that he could recover the family he had lost with

Hannah, speaks to Henry Tibbs's fortitude and his humanity in the face of sustained, inhumane violence.

People like Henry Tibbs left little evidence behind for us to understand how they lived and continued to hope; he enters into the records at moments of loss: crying for his mother as he was sold away from her, surviving Fort Pillow, and, as we shall see, when he was defrauded of his federal pension. We have to assume that these moments changed Tibbs, that he was different afterward, that he mourned the loss of family, comrades, and his money, but because of the letter he wrote to the papers ten years after the war, we know that the violence and loss did not extinguish his hope that he would find his mother and that he might undo some of what had been done to him.

He also did not give up on Yazoo County. Henry Tibbs mustered out of the 2nd USCLA on December 28, 1865, seven months after the Confederacy surrendered and a few weeks after Mississippi legislators rejected the Thirteenth Amendment that formalized wartime emancipation in the Constitution. The amendment was passed in enough other states, in any case, making Mississippi's rejection of emancipation irrelevant. The first act of state lawmakers two months earlier had been to pass a draconian Black Code that prohibited African Americans from owning or renting land, imposed a stringent system of work discipline on them, and, through a system of "apprenticeship," turned over custody of their children to former enslavers.[49] Separating children from their parents had been an important means of enforcing the regime of slavery, and it remained key to sustaining white supremacy afterward. Like the Virginia law that had made Henry Tibbs into an "orphan," Mississippi's apprenticeship law underwrote a traffic in children. Whites in Yazoo were particularly keen to use the measure, "apprenticing" hundreds of Black children to their former enslavers.[50] In fact, the push to enact measures to protect slavery in the state came from politicians in Yazoo County, where an exclusive group of elites like Micajah Pickett contrived to defy federal authority. Among the architects of the state's Black Code was a contemporary of Pickett's, Judge Robert Hudson, who played an outsized role in drafting the measure that also prohibited Black men from owning guns.

When Henry Tibbs mustered out, he kept his army-issue Springfield rifle and headed back to Yazoo.

◆

Tibbs and other Black vets returned as freed people determined to make a life for themselves and their families; together with a few white allies, free Blacks in Yazoo built the foundations of a democratic society there. But first the county's Black majority had to face down a persistent white insurgency.[51] For a few months after the war, a small contingent of USCT was stationed there to ensure that whites did not continue to hold freed people in bondage. These soldiers were gone before the end of the year, leaving the work of defending Black freedom to veterans like Tibbs who'd done it once before.[52] One white ally, embattled Freedmen's Bureau agent Charles W. Clarke, arbitrated labor contracts between freed people and their former enslavers. Freed people briefly leased property confiscated from Confederates, only to have that land taken from them when the previous owners received pardons from President Andrew Johnson.[53] As their dreams of becoming landowners faded, freed people either signed a contract or risked arrest for vagrancy.

With his confiscated property returned to him, Micajah Pickett submitted to the Freedmen's Bureau a list of 101 names of freed people who had consented to work his Wildwood Plantation in return for food, clothing, shelter, and "kind treatment." Ninety-five of them were listed with the last name "Pickett," suggesting that Micajah believed that his relationship to these people remained unchanged.[54]

There were notable absences on the list provided to the bureau. The agreement made no mention of wages. And Henry Tibbs was not on that list. He may have managed to hold on to some leased property or found better terms working alongside of or for one of the white U.S. Army veterans who had settled in the county, transplanted northerners like Albert T. Morgan and, after he resigned from the Freedmen's Bureau, Charles Clarke.[55] Carpetbaggers, as they were called by local whites who despised them.

U.S. Army veterans served as political organizers, registering Black voters, organizing them into Loyal Leagues, and turning out the vote for Republican Party candidates.[56] With a white ally in the state capital, Republican and U.S. Army general Adelbert Ames—installed both as governor and commander of the state's military occupation—and another one, Ulysses S. Grant, in the White House, Black Mississippians got to work delivering on the democratic promises of the war. In the first interracial elections held in Yazoo, Black men outnumbered white men at the polls by more than two to one. Their numbers grew every year, despite white supremacist violence, until Black voters in Mississippi pushed former Confederates out of office and passed a new state constitution. More than two hundred Black men held elected office during Reconstruction, including Hiram Revels, the nation's first Black senator, who took a seat once occupied by Jefferson Davis, and Blanche Bruce, the second Black senator.[57]

From 1869 to 1875, Yazoo County repeatedly sent Black men to the state legislature to represent their interests.[58] Local leaders built one hundred free (segregated) public schools; before the war there had been none. Black men became property owners in the county, some, like Hilliard Golden, owned quite a lot.[59] No wonder Henry Tibbs cast his lot with the community that had taken him in all those years ago. Yazoo was emerging as a center of Black political power in the state.

These years saw the flowering of Black civic life and an explosion of institution building. Black communities founded their own churches, and congregations pooled their resources to hire Black preachers to minister to them.[60] Perhaps Henry and Ann attended one and helped to support the minister there; maybe this was James Allen, the minister whom Henry enlisted in his letter to the papers. "If mother is found," it read, "please address me at Deasonville, Yazoo county, Miss., in care of Rev. James Allen." Henrietta and Nancy may have learned to read and write at one of those newly built schools, separate from white children, of course, but taught by a Black teacher. Their teacher may have graduated from the state's new Black college, Alcorn University, named after the new state governor, James L. Alcorn, or one of the normal schools founded by missionaries, Rust College in Holly Springs and Tougaloo

College just outside of Jackson.[61] These institutions expressed the aspirations of Freedom Generation to provide for their children what they did not have, including security, an education, and the opportunity to grow up free of the shadow of slavery.

The political power wielded by Black Mississippians yielded federal and local laws that protected Henrietta and Nancy from being sold or "swapped." Ann would not be asked to pick one of them out of a lineup. She, too, could leave the plantation of her former enslaver. The couple moved to Deasonville, twenty miles west of Yazoo City but still in the county, putting some distance between them and Micajah Pickett, the man for whom Henry had toiled for thirty years as a slave.[62] Distance allowed Ann to protect herself and her daughters from sexual assault, although less so if they worked in white homes.

Domestic work offered freedwomen a platform for their politics; during the fall 1868 presidential election, white employers in Yazoo County complained to the papers that freedwomen working in their homes wore Grant campaign buttons on their aprons, an act that seemed aimed to provoke their employers.[63] A generation earlier, white men had come to the Delta to build empires where their authority would be uncontested. Ousted from political power, men like Micajah Pickett were now beholden to the Black men who represented their interests in the state capital and in Washington and were insulted by Black women in their own homes.

✦

Freed people in the Delta wrote to the papers with stories like Henry's of being sold from mothers or fathers quite young. Their letters offer insight into the challenges of searching for people armed only with vivid childhood memories. Henry Tibbs traveled to various posts in Mississippi, Tennessee, and Louisiana with the 2nd USCLA, where he interacted with men with histories like his, with family in Virginia, North Carolina, and elsewhere that they hoped to find. He might have shared some of his story, too. And, while in service, he came across newspapers like Philadelphia's *Christian Recorder* with Information

Wanted ads filling entire columns. Back in Yazoo, ministers read the Lost Friends column of the *Southwestern Christian Advocate* aloud to their congregations, where Tibbs listened for names that meant something to him, some information he could share with others or that could help lead him back to his mother. "I look every week to see if any of them is in reach of the paper," Thomas McAfee said in a letter inquiring about his father in North Carolina; McAfee had been sold away and brought to the Yazoo River as a child. "I do not see the names of any of the McAfee family in the Southwestern."[64]

Surrounded by people with stories like his, who were telling them in public, Henry Tibbs went to the papers with the story of his mother. If Tibbs had learned anything new about her over the years, like the name of the person who bought her or where she might have gone or what her name was now, he would have included it in the letter. Instead, he relayed the story just as he remembered it and carried with him all those years. With the limited information contained in the letter, Tibbs's search likely gained little traction. The person most likely to recognize themselves in it, who knew Henry, was his mother. But, even here, Tibbs betrayed a worry that ran through so many of Freedom Generation's searches for lost loved ones, particularly those involving children—that is, that he "was so young mother hardly knew me."

There were about a million enslaved children when the war began, tens of thousands of whom had been taken from one or both of their parents. Freedom rekindled their dreams of finding mothers and fathers again, even if doing so was dangerous and when they didn't know where to begin looking.

It is not clear how far Henry took his search. If he took to the roads, as had Clara Bashop, Virginia would have been a likely place to try to pick up his mother's trail. Had he been so inclined to help, Algernon Sydney Tebbs was no longer in Virginia, having moved several times since he sold Henry and his mother, Hannah: first to Missouri, then to Texas during the war, and then back to Missouri, where he died. It's fitting that Tebbs spent the war fleeing federal troops to secure his property in enslaved people, while Henry Tibbs ran toward those troops to deprive him of that property.[65]

No Hannah matching the description could be located in the census, although there is no way to know where she went or under what name. Hannah may have had a different name than when Henry last saw her. A woman named Hannah Tibbs Augustus appears in Alexandria, Virginia, on the 1916 death certificate of her son Horace; this Hannah appears in the 1870 Census in Alexandria, the last place Henry saw his mother, in Joseph Bruin's slave jail. Born around 1841, this Hannah Tibbs is more likely a candidate for Henry's sister than his mother. Next door to her lived a Matilda Tibbs, who, at fifty-five years old, was the right age for a woman to have had a son old enough be Henry.[66]

There are problems, too, with the timeline that Henry Tibbs provided in his letter. When he enlisted in 1863, he gave his birth date as 1828, but on his 1891 pension application, the agent recorded Tibbs's birth date as 1824. He may not have known; having grown up without his mother, this is likely. If either of these dates is correct, then Tibbs was most certainly not a boy in 1852 or 1853, the years he recalled that he was sold away from Hannah. It is likely that he was sold earlier, maybe around 1833–34. In which case, the Hannah Tibbs living in Alexandria was born after little Henry was on his way to Mississippi on Joseph Bruin's coffle. There is too little corroborating evidence to know if this Hannah Tibbs and the Matilda Tibbs who lived next door were related to each other or to Henry. Were Henry to have launched his search in Alexandria, he might have pursued this lead, in addition to calling on Algernon Tebbs Jr., a physician, who had made his way back to the city after the war, no doubt to claim his father's property. Algernon Jr. enlisted in the 4th Texas Infantry CSA in Gonzales, Texas, in 1862. Like Henry Tibbs, he spent several months hospitalized in Richmond with dysentery, among other things. Private Tebbs arranged to stay at the Confederate Camp Winder Hospital as "baggage master," a position that he likely arranged through a personal connection.[67] Henry recalled the lawyer had a son named "Abner," but surely that was easier for an eight- or nine-year-old to remember than "Algernon."

Henry and Ann Tibbs could not be located on the 1870 Census; in 1880, they lived in Issaquena County, Mississippi, west of Yazoo.[68] Neither of his daughters, Henrietta and Nancy, lived in the Tibbs household, having died, perhaps, or married and moved on. If Henry left Mississippi to search for Hannah, there is no record of it. There is no indication that Henry found his mother. This doesn't mean, of course, that he gave up. He no doubt continued listening to the names read in church and, perhaps, checking in with Rev. James Allen, to whom he had asked people to address their replies.

Henry and Ann left Yazoo County soon after he wrote to the paper. The heady postwar period of democracy and infrastructure building came abruptly to an end in the summer of 1875 when armed white vigilantes launched a violent campaign against Black voters. Having failed repeatedly to win elections, to effect change through the electoral process, Democrats turned to intimidation, attacking and murdering Black voters. This time, when Governor Ames requested federal support to put down the insurgency, President Grant refused, leaving the matter to state and local authorities. Black men continued to vote, defend the schools and other institutions they had built, and protect themselves and their families, but they could not hold out long amidst the sustained violence. White men in Yazoo organized themselves into a militia company, drove out Albert Morgan and the other white "outcasts," and unleashed a terror campaign on the majority-Black community; Black officeholders became favorite targets for white rage.[69]

Black political power did not collapse all at once, but even when Republicans won elections, the results were not reported that way. Across the South, Democrats developed a playbook called the Mississippi Plan modeled after what had happened there. This plan bore its bitter fruit in a new constitution that disenfranchised and disarmed African Americans, a model that other former Confederate states eagerly followed. If Henry Tibbs had managed to acquire land in Yazoo, his claim to it collapsed with the return of white supremacist rule. There was nothing keeping him there and any number of reasons to leave.[70]

After moving to Issaquena County with Ann, Henry relocated to Shelby, Mississippi, in Bolivar County. There is no evidence that Henry Tibbs ever became a property owner or, if he did, that he retained that property.[71] Ann died in 1884, when she was about forty-four years old; Henry was sixty. Henry married a woman about twenty-five years his junior named Louisa around 1891. In September of that year, as his health began to fail, Henry applied for a U.S. Army pension as Corporal Henry Tibbs. He stood for a physical examination that confirmed that he suffered from arthritic shoulders and knees and failing eyes and ears. "I can find nothing in this case," the physician concluded, "but what can be attributed to old age." Had he thought about it, the doctor might have wondered if Tibbs's hearing loss began thirty years earlier when he served as an artillerist in the U.S. Army. And if the doctor was a bit more generous, he might have awarded Tibbs the full pension. Henry told the doctor that his lungs had never fully recovered from the pneumonia he had suffered while serving in the army and that he often had to rest while working "a hard days work"; this also did not impress the doctor. At sixty-eight years, Henry Tibbs was awarded a pension of $12 a month from the U.S. government, enough money to support himself and Louisa.

It was also enough money to attract the attention of an opportunist.

For about a year, Ben E. D. Donnell, whom investigators described as "a slick colored man," stole Tibbs's pension money. Donnell collected Tibbs's checks from the post office, cashed them, and "settled" Tibbs's debts around town—including the money he owed Donnell for his services. He then gave the old man the little that remained. Tibbs wasn't sure how much Donnell had taken from him, but when investigators deposed Tibbs in 1893, he had received a total of only $33. In a small community like Shelby, Donnell found several easy marks, Black veterans like Henry Tibbs who could not read or write and trusted a Black man like Donnell who could. "He came there with nothing, has done nothing and now seems to be in comfortable circumstances," the investigator said of Ben Donnell. "I have no doubt but that he is swindling others as he seems to be doing this man Tibbs."[72]

The papers were full of stories of swindling pension agents making bogus claims on behalf of Black veterans and widows. Maybe Tibbs and the others thought Donnell was different or, more likely, they went to him because no white proprietors in Shelby would cash a Black man's check.[73] "My att[orne]y Ben Donnell" is what Tibbs called him, even though it is likely that what he meant was that he had granted Donnell power of attorney to handle his pension paperwork. Tibbs had some experience with lawyers, the authority they commanded, the respect afforded people who hired one. If Lawyer Tebbs, the man who stole him from his mother all those years ago, crossed his mind when he was fighting to have his stolen pension returned to him, Henry was surely convinced that lawyers were only good for protecting white men's property.

Henry Tibbs died on August 28, 1906, three weeks after he received what would be his last pension check. He was eighty-two years old. No record could be found indicating where he was buried.

Do You Know Them.

I would like to find my relative. I was born near Louisa Court House, Virginia and was sold in Richmond, Va., to a negro trader by the name of Smith. It has been thirty-six years ago I think. I belonged to the Burruss family in Virginia. My old mistress was Mrs Lucy Burruss, she had a son by the name of Dr. John L. Burruss. The Doctor's sisters were Caroline and Mary Eliza. The widow Burruss moved from near Louisa Court-house to Hanover Co., and took my brother Jim and my sister Louisa, and myself (Susan). By marriage my name is Susan Anderson. My mother was named Rachel, and my father Martin; both belonged to the Burruss. I think I had three brothers, Jim, Carter and Dave. Two uncles, Charles and Henry. He was a shoe-maker by trade and lived in the town of Louisa, Va. My sister Louisa had two daughters, their names were Isabelle and Charlotte.

They lived in Hanover County with me and the widow Burruss. Some of my cousins are Joe, Mark, Hunter, Margarett and Millie. I knew people when I lived near Louisa, Va.; Dr. McGee Lisby; and Dr. Goodman. If any one can give any information of these persons, please address at once

SANDY OR SUSAN ANDERSON,

Mineola, Wood Co., Texas.

"Do You Know Them?,"
Richmond Planet (Richmond, VA), July 14, 1894

CHAPTER FIVE

The Andersons of Mineola, Texas

Mineola, Texas, seemed an unlikely place to find hope. Hundreds of miles from cities like New Orleans and Galveston to which newly freed people relocated after emancipation, the tiny East Texas town was even farther away from Kansas, which drew Black Texan Exodusters hoping to find a promised land ten years after the end of slavery. Whites in East Texas first called the town Sodom, an Old Testament name that marked the place as sinful, inhospitable, or doomed to destruction, although it's not clear why.[1] Once the railroads arrived and Sodom became Mineola, people did not ask. The town remained little more than an isolated outpost surrounded by a thick forest of hardwood and pine trees. Both the Texas and Pacific and International–Great Northern Railroads reached Mineola in 1873. The I-GN got there first, but, having decided to go no farther, slumped back down toward Tyler—as if it found the place as inhospitable as had the angels who appeared in Sodom to rescue the righteous.[2] Decades later Mineola remained little more than a depot with a few shops whose merchants could afford to pay railroad company premiums for the plots of land nearby. Most of the town's white residents lived and worked farther off, where the land was cheaper, and they could get a lot of it to raise livestock and grow cotton. Black Texans hoping to buy land there were turned away by the state's Black Code that prohibited the railroads from selling to them, even if they could afford it.[3]

When the Andersons arrived there in the 1870s from one county over, the biggest business was the prison camp, where about eighty prisoners cut wood into railroad ties. Most of the inmates were freed people like them.[4] Inside the camp, there was little that distinguished their lives from when they had been enslaved except that in slavery they had made families and had at times been able to live with them. Mostly what happened in the prison camp was dying. Black prisoners were expected to cut a cord of wood a day; when they did not, white guards whipped them with branches cut from persimmon trees, put them in stocks, or shot them. Eighteen prisoners died in Mineola over a four-month period in 1879 in what one town resident described as a "wholescale slaughter of convicts." Everyone in Mineola knew what went on in the camp, heard about the prisoners who died there at the hands of the guards; people knew to steer clear of the prison guards.[5]

It's hard to imagine what drew freed people like the Andersons to Mineola. East Texas was not a place they could have expected to nurture their hope of starting a new life in freedom or of finding the families they had lost in slavery. Susan and her husband, Henry Anderson, had been sold away from their families in Virginia and Maryland when they were children. So, too, was Henry's brother John. Others in their kin group lost their families during the Civil War or immediately afterward; they were orphans, widows, and adopted children. None of them had been in Texas very long or had roots there or anything keeping them there but each other. If what they hoped to find by settling in Mineola was some land on which they could earn enough money to make their way back east to loved ones they had last seen years ago, then those hopes were not realized. If, on the other hand, they could get word from their families, reconnect with them, learn of their fate, and share news of their own, then the most unlikely town of Mineola, Texas, turned out to be the Andersons' promised land.

Enslaved children taken from their mothers in Virginia and Maryland—and Georgia, North Carolina, Tennessee, and Mississippi—exchanged hands a few times before they were sold into East Texas cotton fields. Nothing they experienced along the way or when they got there should have given them any hope of finding the people they had left behind until they lived in a town with trains that brought people and things from places just as far away. When they arrived in Mineola, they started writing to the papers.

The Lost Friends column of the widely circulated New Orleans *Southwestern Christian Advocate* was filled with letters from freed people in Texas searching for their families. Mrs. Ann Carter and her husband, Edward, posted their letters from Mineola on February 23, 1888; they were looking for their families in Tennessee and Mississippi, respectively. "I wish to inquire for my people," Ann wrote. "Mother died in Tennessee, ten miles north of Memphis." Edward started his letter with the exact same words: "I wish to inquire for my people. I left them in Mississippi." Perhaps they sat next to one another when they wrote, or one of them wrote both letters; surely they sent them in the same envelope to save the postage. Then, three months later, when Ann announced in the paper that she had found a brother and sister living two hundred miles south in Oakland, Texas, word spread that such a thing was possible, even in—or maybe it was *particularly* in—Mineola. "I am glad to say," Ann wrote in May, "that through the SOUTHWESTERN I have been able to find . . . Mary Jane Granger and Arch. Williams."[6] It's not hard to imagine Ann Carter's joy in learning that her sister and brother were alive and that she might see them again. The news rekindled hope among her friends and neighbors that they, too, might find the families that they had lost in slavery. Ann Carter may have been the first freed person in Mineola to find the family she had lost in slavery, but she was not the last.

Sandy Anderson grew up hearing about how Ann Carter found her family by writing to the papers. His mother, Lucy Mead, told him a story that started like Ann's, when she was sold as a child; so did his father, John Anderson, and his uncle and aunt. He was told similar stories by others in Mineola, some of whom he was related to by blood, some by kin and sentiment. When he came of age, Sandy helped them to reconstruct their families; as he did, he worked to reconstitute his own. At least eight people from the small town of Mineola went to the papers in search of the family they lost in slavery. In a testament to the persistence of hope and the dedication of a son to the work of rebuilding families, half of these searches ended in reunion. Half.

Sandy Anderson was not a pastor or teacher, nor did he hold local office, work for the Freedmen's Bureau—prominent people to whom others turned for help locating lost family. He was a product of the blending of families that occurred all over the postwar South as people searched for blood kin and made families with those who had none. Mineola's Black community was made up of many such families, made in slavery and afterward, of husbands and wives lately recognized as such, children born to mothers they hardly remembered or never knew, and people who began their lives in freedom hoping to find blood kin while holding on to those who had brought them up and carried them through. Hope spread along overlapping lines of kinship and shaped the search for family that took place there.

✦

Born in Texas after the Civil War, Sandy Anderson learned from his mother how children used to be sold away from their parents. When Lucy Mead was nine years old, her enslaver took her from her family in Hampton, Virginia, and sold her, the first of several times the girl changed hands. She recalled all of them: Lewis Davis sold her to "Goodbah. He took me to Norfolk, Va., and put me in jail at night. He then took me to Richmond, Va., and sold me to Silas McHunder, who sold me to Roberson in Mobile, Ala. He sold me to Judge Perkins in Louisiana." Lewis Davis and his wife, Rosa, had seven children of their own when they sold Lucy. Lucy and the Davises' daughter Sarah both turned ten years old in 1860, but while Sarah celebrated her birthday surrounded by her parents and siblings—now there were eight—Lucy was making her way to Alabama or maybe Louisiana by then, chained together with strangers in a coffle.[7]

In Louisiana she crossed paths with other trafficked children owned by a man named Perkins—people like Henry and John Anderson, who were not much older than she was when they were taken from their mother on Maryland's Eastern Shore. Lucy met Harry Mead in

Louisiana, maybe on Perkins's place, too. When the Civil War began, Perkins was eager to get his valuable property out of the way of the U.S. Army and took them to Texas, where they would be secure. By then, Lucy had married Harry. Their marriage ended abruptly when Harry was "killed in Texas by a mob."

Reconstruction in Texas was not marked by one or two massacres of freed people, such as those in Tennessee and Louisiana when Black men gained political rights, grabbing headlines in Washington, D.C., and moving federal lawmakers to demand they be protected. A slow-moving massacre began in Texas at the very moment that slavery ended as whites bent on preserving slavery murdered newly freed people who dared to leave their former enslavers. White men shot into a crowd of freed people who gathered in Wood County to elect representatives to the state constitutional convention in 1867. In Harrison, two counties over, local police joined other white men in violently breaking up a meeting of freed people.[8] Freedwomen were often targets of violence in East Texas. Two white men beat Lucy Grimes to death, but, because no Harrison County judge would allow Black witnesses to testify, Grimes's murderers went free.[9] One study counted more than a thousand murders in the state in the first three postwar years. By the time Black Texans gained the right to marry and to vote in the new state constitution in 1868, many had died by the hands of their former enslavers.[10] Harry Mead, Lucy's husband, was among them.

Lucy Mead began her life in freedom as a young widow. She had seen and survived a lot by then, including the Second Middle Passage and Civil War; she had worked fields belonging to Perkins in Louisiana and East Texas and witnessed the murder of her husband at the hands of a white mob. Sometime in 1870 or 1871 she gave birth to her son Sandy, whose father, John Anderson, she had also met in Louisiana and who had been taken as Perkins's property to Texas. Mead appears not to have married or lived with John Anderson; instead, she found a home with his brother Henry and Henry's wife, Susan.[11] Lucy Mead's life had been marked by trauma and the repeated loss of the people she loved; in Mineola among neighbors and kin she found reason to hope. She told her story to her son Sandy when he was old enough to understand and he told it in the papers.

Susan and Henry Anderson's kin group changed in size and composition to meet their needs and circumstances, the sort of adaptability and improvisation common among Freedom Generation. Susan had arrived in Texas, also as someone's enslaved property, around the same time as Henry and John Anderson and Lucy Mead. She married Henry in 1870, when she was twenty or twenty-five years old and Henry was thirty. Their household included a man named James Thomas; the young widow, Lucy Mead; and two young children, George and John Mays, ages three and one, who had lost one or both of their parents—perhaps to the same violence that had taken the life of Harry Mead. Sometime before 1880, Susan and Henry left Smith County for Wood County and brought with them their adopted son George and Lucy Mead and her nine-year-old son, Sandy; the fate of George's brother John is unknown.[12] Without kin, a child like George would not have survived long in a hard place like East Texas; by state law, he was liable to be apprenticed until the age of twenty-one to a "master or mistress" who was authorized to use "moderate corporeal chastisement as may be necessary and proper" and to have him arrested if he ran away.[13] The language of slavery was not incidental; once arrested, George could find himself cutting railroad ties for the Texas and Pacific.

The odds were long, too, for women like Lucy Mead raising children on their own. Landowners negotiated sharecropping agreements or tenancies with nuclear families only, pushing unattached women to the margins of society.[14] In an aspiring railroad town like Mineola, Mead might eventually find alternatives to field labor, but it would be some time before she was able to support herself and her son Sandy. Marriage would have provided Lucy and Sandy support and protection, the nucleus with which to begin a new kin group.

Postwar Black family life moved to a traditional patriarchal norm in response both to preference and external pressure. Hostile whites used laws granting freed people marriage "equality," like the one passed in Texas in 1868 that legalized slave marriages, to punish African Americans who did not marry or remained outside of those norms.[15] As part of the Anderson household, Lucy found relief and protection, and so did Sandy, but things had been hard for her.

Over thirty years of marriage, Henry and Susan Anderson raised and helped to raise a number of children, including George and John Mays, their nephew Sandy, and a girl named Mary White. Each time they made room for a child who was not their blood relation but who nonetheless became their responsibility. Orphaned by America's traffic in children, the Andersons made a family in freedom of children and adults displaced by slavery and the Civil War and marginalized by the postwar labor regime. One of these children, John's son Sandy, learned to read and write and determined to help them find their families. Over an eight-year period, Sandy wrote a series of thirteen letters and advertisements in Black newspapers documenting his family's stories and seeking information that would connect his extended kin network in Texas to their loved ones in the East, beginning with his aunt Susan.

✦

Susan Anderson was ten years old when she was sold away from her mother, father, sisters, and brothers. Nearly forty years later, she began searching for them from the far west of the Second Middle Passage. Anderson sent word from Texas back to Virginia, where she had last seen them. "I would like to find my people," she wrote. "I was called Susan Burrus in Virginia; I belonged to the widow Burrus. My mother was named Rachel. She belonged to Dr. John L. Burrus."[16] Susan Anderson was born around 1850, more than twenty years after Henry Tibbs and Clara Bashop.[17] During that time, Susan's mother and father, Martin, raised six children who grew up among an extended family, including uncles, aunts, and cousins.

By the mid-nineteenth century, the white Burruss family of Virginia included at least two distinct branches clustered in Louisa County, neighboring Goochland County, and Caroline County. In 1850, fifty-year-old Lucindy or Lucy Burruss, widow of John (date of death unknown), lived in Louisa County with her thirty-year-old son, also named John; a census enumerator credited to his household twenty-five enslaved people, including three girls under age ten: one five-year-old girl, a one-year-old, and another child who was just six months old.

Susan and her sisters, Mary Jane and Louisa, might have been among them.[18] Among the enumerator's inscrutable hashmarks it is impossible to find Susan or her mother, Rachel—or her three brothers, two sisters, uncles, and cousins. "My mother was named Rachel, and my father Martin," Susan would recall. "I think I had three brothers, Jim, Carter and Dave. Two uncles, Charles and Henry. He was a shoe-maker by trade. . . . My sister Louisa had two daughters, their names were Isabelle and Charlotte. . . . Some of my cousins are Joe, Mark, Hunter, Margarett and Millie." We can't piece together families or see all the relationships between people as Susan experienced them as a child. The invisibility of these families did not reflect inattention on the part of enumerators but rather the designs of the system of chattel slavery in which the bonds shared between enslaved people were routinely broken.

In the settling of accounts among the heirs of the late John Burruss, Susan's mother, Rachel, came to belong to Dr. John Burruss. Her father, Martin, may have belonged to Dr. John Burruss or to another of the white Virginia Burrusses. The syntax of Susan's sentence, "both belonged to the Burruss," isn't much to go on. The widow Lucy Burruss took Susan, her brother Jim, and sister Louisa to Hanover County; when she did, the Burrusses separated at least two families at once, taking Susan, Jim, and Louisa from their parents and Louisa away from her two daughters Isabelle and Charlotte. The white Burrusses surely thought nothing of sending three of Rachel's children to the next county and leaving Louisa's children in the care of another of their enslaved people. They may have assured Rachel that the separation was temporary, that she could still on occasion see her children.

Then Martin and Rachel lost Susan for good when Lucy Burruss or her son took ten-year-old Susan to Richmond and sold her "to a negro trader by the name of Smith." From Richmond, Susan changed hands a few more times before she ended up in Texas. When emancipation came to Texas in 1865, Susan was around twenty years old. She married Henry Anderson five years later. The couple settled in Mineola among other freed people who had been sold away from families in Virginia, Maryland, North Carolina, South Carolina, and Georgia, all of them with different stories to tell. They stayed there, even as many Black

Texans migrated north when they gave up hope that their lives would be better in Texas. Susan, Henry, and their neighbors told their stories to their children and kin and shared them with each other, and that is how they learned that people in Mineola were finding the families they had lost in slavery.

Susan heard about how Ann Carter found a sister and brother living in Texas. Like Susan, Ann had been sold when she was a child, but their experiences differed in important ways. Ann came through the Second Middle Passage with siblings, and she received updated information about various members of her family. Susan was sold alone, and, like Henry Tibbs, she had heard nothing of her mother, Rachel; her father, Martin; or the others since. With the information she had, Susan turned to the papers for help, posting two ads four months apart, in two different newspapers.

On March 3, 1894, Susan placed a short ad in the *Freeman*, a Black newspaper published in Indianapolis, asking readers to send word of her family's whereabouts. "Address, if you please, Susan Anderson, Mineola, Tex."[19] Susan then wrote a longer letter on July 14 to the *Richmond Planet*. This one contained more details, including information about where she was born, how Lucy Burruss took her from her parents, and how the Burrusses sold her. "I would like to find my relative(s)," she began her second ad. "I was born near Louisa Court House, Virginia and was sold in Richmond, Va., to a negro trader by the name of Smith." The two events, her birth and sale, served as brackets for the life she struggled to recall, the one she lived before being sold into America's traffic in children. Susan provided no details about how she came to Texas from Richmond, nothing about how and to whom she exchanged hands in between. These details would allow us to tell a more complete story of her life in slavery. The July ad included a crucial time stamp that allows us to estimate how old she was when she lost her family. About her sale in Richmond, she recalled, "It has been thirty-six years ago I think."

Sandy signed on to Susan Anderson's second ad, the first of several efforts to reconstruct his extended family. Sandy likely prompted his aunt to include additional details that she was not sure of, such as when she added "I think" to signal to readers that she may have been sold in 1860 or thereabouts. The new ad left open the possibility that Susan had more brothers. In the March ad there were three; but in July, Susan wasn't sure that was all. Susan was sold alone; she had no one with whom to rehearse and recall these details since. Thirty years later she sat down with her nephew and put down all the names. The white Burrusses had sold ten-year-old Susan to a man in Richmond who then sold her to someone else who took her to Texas—away from everyone she loved. Now she reached out to a Black newspaper in Richmond in hopes that someone would help her find them.

She did not wait long. Within a few weeks, Susan received information about her family from readers of the *Planet* in Virginia and Louisiana. Charles Braxton wrote from Louisiana to say that he knew a few of the people Susan named in her ad, including her uncle Henry, a shoemaker, who "lives about two hundred yards from" Braxton's father's house in Virginia.[20] A skilled tradesman like Henry Burruss was in high demand; Henry likely repaired shoes for Black and white residents and others who were passing through. It is not surprising that a reader of a Virginia newspaper knew Henry.[21] In early August, Susan received a second letter, and by the end of September she had found her brother and relatives in Virginia.[22] It is not hard to imagine what it meant for Susan to find her family after all those years. For the middle-aged woman to hear from loved ones whom she feared she had lost forever. How it must have felt to learn from one brother of the whereabouts of the others and of her sisters, cousins, uncles, and nieces. In just a few short months Susan got back some of what the Burrusses had taken from her decades ago. Her story is a testament to her determination—first as a young child and then as a woman—to hold on to the details when she had no one to share them with, no one who recognized any of the places or names. Susan organized these memories into a rough timeline of her life and went to the papers twice with a story that must have been painful for her to recount but that she nonetheless felt some urgency in telling.

Finding her family the way she did speaks to the crucial role played by Black newspapers in connecting people enslavers and traders had separated and scattered. Two ads placed in two different newspapers—one in the South, another in the Midwest—allowed Susan to reach freed people who remained in or made their way back east after emancipation and those who lived in small Black communities in Indiana but who were still connected by blood and affection—and railroads—to the South. The Black community in Mineola was supported by both a Baptist church and a Methodist Episcopal church; freed people there had access to Black newspapers published in New Orleans, Indianapolis, and Richmond. Susan heard *Advocate* advertisements like those her neighbors the Carters' read in church, but she chose to write to the *Freeman* and the *Planet* instead. Both papers were founded a decade after the *Advocate* and were edited by Black men who were not affiliated with any church. Both were decidedly political and dedicated to Black advocacy.

George L. Knox, publisher of the Indianapolis *Freeman*, was prominent in local Republican politics. Knox called his paper "The Leading Afro-American Journal of the World"; the *Freeman* reported a circulation of more than sixteen thousand made possible by the agents they recruited in "every city, town, and hamlet in the U.S."[23] Editor of the *Planet* John Mitchell Jr. supported the Republican Party and ran a courageous anti-lynching campaign. When Susan wrote to the *Planet*, the paper reported more than six thousand subscribers, and many more heard the paper read in churches and barbershops, like Mr. E. S. Jones's "first class barber shop north of Pratt's house" that Sandy Anderson reported on in a news report he filed from Mineola.[24] The *Freeman* and the *Planet* paid agents to report on local news and to circulate the papers in their communities; Sandy Anderson worked for both. He wrote columns that reported on cotton exports aimed at a national audience and that included items of local interest such as deaths and funerals and the professional jealousies of Mineola's Baptist and Methodist pastors.

Appearing alongside the news published in these widely circulated newspapers were Sandy's updates on people searching for families lost in slavery. "Mrs. Susan Anderson has found her long lost brother and relatives in Virgin[i]a," read his September 29, 1894, announcement in the *Freeman*. Railroads collapsed the distance between a barbershop in Texas and a shoemaker's bench in Virginia; Black editors and their agents turned railroads and the newspapers they carried into powerful allies in the search for family.

For Sandy Anderson, the work of finding family was both professional and personal.

◆

Inspired by Susan Anderson's success, Sandy helped his father next. Later that year, when John Anderson wrote to the *Richmond Planet* with his family's story, Sandy co-signed the letter. As was the case with his aunt, he likely had a hand in writing it. Regardless of the relationship between Sandy's mother and father, John Anderson remained part of Susan and Henry's extended kin group. He hoped he would find his family and share in the joy that others in the small town felt when they found theirs. Sandy grew up hearing the stories about Maryland's Eastern Shore, where his father and uncle were born and lived with their mother, siblings, uncles, aunts, and cousins, some of them free, others enslaved. He learned how Eastern Shore enslavers continued to wring profits from slavery, not primarily by extracting labor any longer but by selling other people's children.

John told Sandy about the day that one enslaver—a white man also named John Anderson—sold the boys from their family. This John Anderson, identified in the records as John D. Anderson, sent them from their home, where freedom was at times as close as a neighbor or an uncle or aunt, to Louisiana; from there they were taken to Texas, where freedom must have seemed nearly an impossibility. Now, nearly forty years later, a child of their own who had known only freedom sought to take back what had been taken from them. Sandy did it for these two men, now old, who had nonetheless survived, and for himself.

In two letters published almost exactly one year apart, Sandy Anderson searched for news of John and Henry's mother, aunts, and uncles, and appealed for help finding the men's sisters, brothers, and cousins. John Anderson's letter appeared in the *Richmond Planet* on December 8, 1894; Henry's was published on December 7, 1895, in the Indianapolis

Freeman.[25] The next day, December 8, 1895, Sandy Anderson married Lizzie Williams.[26] In the years that followed, the couple had two children, both boys. George was born in 1896. Sandy was born two years later.[27] It could not have escaped the notice of those who attended Sandy and Lizzie's wedding that, even as Sandy began a family, he continued the work of rebuilding one.

The two letters differed in some of the particulars, indicating either a difference in the brothers' memories or that Henry's letter included information they had just received. "I would like to find my relatives. I was born in Sommerset County Md.," John began his letter to the *Planet*; he added "Prencesam, Md." to the location, referring to Princess Anne, the county seat of Somerset County, where their enslaver John D. Anderson lived with his wife, Leah ("Layer" is how Henry said it and Sandy wrote it), and their children.[28]

Sandy wrote down the names of the people and places as his father, and later his uncle, recalled them. Peggy was their mother's name. Neither John nor Henry ever mentioned a father, although John identified a man named Adam Lankford as Peggy's husband; Henry referred to him as his stepfather.[29] Also unclear is how many children Peggy had, although we know that she had two daughters, Sarah Ann and Malinda. John named six brothers: "vis: Horace, Charles, George, Alexander, Henry and Sandy." When Henry wrote to the *Freeman* the next year, he left both George and John off his list: "I had a brother named Geo. who drowned at Montgomery, Ala., on the Alabama River." It may be that John had also died since he placed his own ad in the paper. Or his brother lost track of him. John Anderson left virtually no trace in the historical record, other than the advertisement. When Sandy Anderson picked up the search again the following year, he did not mention his father in any of the series of ads he placed for his uncle Henry.

The slave schedule provides few answers. Fourteen enslaved people worked John D. Anderson's Maryland property in 1850, including two adult men, two adult women, and ten male children aged one to seventeen years old.[30]

Henry was ten years old in 1850, about the same age as John D. Anderson's son Samuel. Samuel lived in the same household with his mother, father, and siblings.[31] Henry did not. In his advertisement written all those years later, Henry recalled the names of four enslavers who "owned" various members of his family. Because Maryland slaveholders owned a small number of slaves, enslaved Marylanders were born into families made up of people claimed as the property of various enslavers and others who were free.[32] Families that were beholden to the whims of more than one enslaver were particularly vulnerable to separation. Samuel was about fourteen when his father died. He lost his father that day, but he still had his mother and siblings.

Henry and his brother John lost everyone.

John D. Anderson died in 1854. "[M]y master died in Baltimore, Md., before I left," Henry recalled in a second ad, "but was brought home on King Branch five miles from Princess Anne County." John D. Anderson's widow, Leah, and heirs sold Henry and John away from their mother, brothers, and sisters.[33] At fourteen or fifteen years old, Henry was sold into America's marketplace for children. John's age is unknown, but he may have been older and better able to recollect the details about the multiple times the boys changed hands. "I was sold by John Anderson to John Sanders, a Negro trader;" read John Anderson's advertisement, "he sold me to Smith, a Negro trader; Smith sold me [to] Robertson, a Negro trader and Robertson sold me to Judge Perkinson of Louisiana."[34] This man Perkinson—or it may have been Perkins, as both Henry and Lucy Mead identified him—then brought Henry and John and Lucy Mead to Texas, where he thought they'd be "safe" from wartime emancipation and where they would not attempt to free themselves as the Union Army came near. They'd forget about their families, be beholden only to him.

But they did not forget. Over the years, John and Henry shared stories about their mother, Peggy, siblings, uncles, and aunts with each other. They recalled details about the white Andersons and their neighbors who "owned" various members of their extended family. Morris Adams, for instance, who owned their uncles, aunt, and cousins and who helped John D. Anderson's widow, Leah, settle her late husband's affairs. "The widow Dryden was our neighbor," Henry said in a second ad that included the names of white neighbors and their enslaved people.[35] These additional details were surely useful to readers of Black newspapers in the Midwest and on the East Coast and all the other places where members of Freedom Generation accessed the *Freeman* and the *Planet*. Within two weeks of placing his second ad, Henry, too, had received a letter from someone with information. By April, four months after he began searching for his family, Henry found them.[36] Like his neighbor Ann Carter and his wife, Susan, Henry Anderson experienced the joy of finding his loved ones again, of learning the fate of his mother, Peggy, his sisters Malinda and Sarah Ann, and his surviving brothers. Nothing could erase the lost years—thirty-seven, by his count—or the regret he felt at learning about those who had died. Henry Anderson never forgot them, and with Sandy Anderson's help, he found them. And they found him.

Children who were taken from their loved ones and sold into the Second Middle Passage faced considerable odds in finding them again. They often had trouble recollecting names they had heard only once and when they were very young. Henry and John improved their odds, perhaps, because they could help each other recall the details of their separation. Among the freed people of Mineola, four of eight people who searched for their family found them for a success rate of 50 percent. There may have been more.

The successes in this small East Texas town are striking, particularly since white Texans had dragged enslaved people like them far away so that they would not go looking for their families.

✦

Slavery expanded rapidly in Texas in the decade and a half before the Civil War as Americans from other parts of the South pushed the cotton frontier beyond the Mississippi River Valley. They demanded federal protection for their "enslaved property" in a region where, when it was part of Mexico, slavery had been outlawed. Protection came in 1845 when Texas became a state with a constitution guaranteeing the rights of slaveholders. Even this did not conciliate those who settled there only to have their enslaved people escape to Mexico where they could not be extradited. "There was no reason to run up North. All we had to do was to walk South" recalled Felix Haywood, formerly enslaved in San Antonio. "We'd be free soon as we crossed the Rio Grande."[37] From East Texas, enslaved people could also walk to Indian Country, territory that would become Oklahoma.[38]

The expansion of cotton's slave labor camps in Texas showed that, far from reaching some sort of "natural limits" there, slavery was dynamic and adaptable to the conditions of America's southwestern frontier. Unable to expand, historian Charles Ramsdell wrote early in the twentieth century, "slavery would have declined to extinction"; the Civil War would have been unnecessary, and a national bloodletting that might have been avoided had abolitionist agitators simply waited. "Even those who wished it destroyed had only to wait a little while," the argument went, "perhaps a generation, probably less." *Patience.* Enslavers demanded patience from their enslaved people, with whom they found themselves negotiating. Early the next century, white authors agreed. Scholars of slavery and the U.S. Civil War insisted that Texas was an inhospitable place for slavery, and the institution never really took root there. People's children trafficked into Texas's cotton fields, people like Susan Burruss and Henry Anderson, needed only "to wait a little while," for surely *their* children would live to see freedom.[39]

This "natural limits" argument helped sustain the Lost Cause mythology. Ramsdell and others who wrote those histories ignored the complaints of unhinged enslavers whose slaves ran away to Mexico or escaped Texas to Indian Territory, where they allied with Texans' enemies and posed a continuing threat to the security of their slave property. These men attracted powerful allies in Washington and elsewhere who were bent on expanding slavery *beyond* Texas, proposing the annexation of Cuba, Nicaragua, and even Mexico to ensure slavery's survival in perpetuity, to build an armed buffer zone around the Mississippi Valley to keep international forces of abolition out.[40]

There is no reason to believe that white Texans weren't really committed to slaveholding, that the slavery that took hold there was "milder" than elsewhere. When Susan and Henry wrote to the papers about being taken from their families as children, they had already raised their own children free of the shadow of slavery: a daughter, Mary, and son, George, whom no white man would ever take from them and sell to another one.[41] Their stories revealed the casual cruelty of suggesting that they might have simply waited, that the price paid for their freedom had been too high.

There were 182,566 enslaved people in Texas in 1860, 70 percent of whom had arrived in the last ten years.[42] The slavery they endured there was not "milder" than in the Mississippi Valley. Traveling through the state in 1857, Frederick Law Olmsted was shocked by the material deprivation in which all Texans lived, white and Black: homes with no floors and partial roofs, no medical care, a dull and innutritious diet. On a cold December day in East Texas, Olmsted saw "a young black girl, of twelve or fourteen years, sitting on a pile of logs before a house we passed, in a driving sleet, having for her only garment a short chemise." Inexplicably, Olmsted mused that it was "impossible to say whether such *shiftlessness* was the fault of the master or of the girl." He witnessed the same brutality directed at enslaved people on the smaller, isolated Texas holdings as he had seen on the large estates of the Mississippi Valley. Olmsted interpreted East Texans' rough cruelty toward their slaves, the way they cursed their slaves at every turn, as evidence of their conflicted consciences; he guessed that they knew slavery to be wrong but were nonetheless determined "to face conscience down" in the name of "selfish profit." As a result, the slavery he observed there was not the settled sort he saw elsewhere in the South but a "state of war."[43] What gave the New Yorker the sense that Texas enslavers were ambivalent about slavery he never said, but what he saw in the cotton fields of East Texas left him searching for an explanation.

Nothing in Henry's brief childhood on the Eastern Shore or Susan's in Virginia prepared them for the vastness they would encounter in Texas; the diverse people who lived there and languages they spoke added to a sense that they had left one country and arrived in another.

Texans' imperial fantasies did not consist of building white-pillared mansions with Scots-English names. Instead, white Texans were restless—Olmsted described them as "nomadic"—working land for a short time and then moving on, dragging their enslaved people with them as they did. The empires they sought were always in front of them; behind them lay exhausted fields and the wrecked remains of enslaved families.[44] Susan and Henry Anderson arrived in this state of war, children without their families, attached to restless white people determined to master their own consciences and to extract obedience from their slaves. Without their parents, it was difficult for Henry and Susan to recall the names and the dates that they might use to find them again. The isolation must have felt complete, the separation final. Susan's mother, Rachel, and her father, Martin, surely tried to keep track of her and the other children—perhaps the same was true for Henry's mother, Peggy. Texas stretched the lines of the grapevine telegraph to their limits.

White Texans passed a series of laws to secure their "slave property," each one providing evidence that the last one had failed. Among these were steadily escalating measures to deal with the problem of fugitives, including a law that deputized any non-Black Texan to act as a bounty hunter and offered cash rewards for seizing suspected fugitives. Another law created a statewide network of slave patrols composed of men who had vast powers to detain and interrogate suspected fugitives and their allies. At each revision of the state constitution, lawmakers sought new ways to make it illegal to be a free Black person in the state. These laws had their desired effect. There were fewer than four hundred free Blacks living in Texas in 1850; over the next decade, that number declined even as the state's population grew. But white Texans were unable to eradicate Black freedom entirely. Enslaved children and adults trafficked into the state found allies and opportunities to transmit and receive information along the grapevine.

Texans' state of war with slavery flared in the hot summer of 1860, brought on by whites' nagging uncertainty that they had or could secure the loyalties of their slaves as the grapevine connected free and enslaved Blacks in the region and outside of it. Henry was twenty years old and Susan was ten or fifteen when vigilance committees began rounding up and executing enslaved people suspected of starting fires that leveled towns, burned gin houses to the ground, and destroyed millions of dollars in property. As white fears grew, the mysterious fires spread. Texans eyed one another with suspicion in the tense weeks before the presidential election. Who could be trusted? Which white men—or Mexicans or Cherokee—were stirring up rebellion among the slaves? Or was it Lincoln and the Republicans who were behind these events? Messages buzzed along the telegraph's many wires, ensuring that rumors overheard in Texas reached people in Louisiana and Mississippi. Nervous enslavers expressed their fears openly and often in front of enslaved people, particularly children whose silence they took for granted, and enslaved people passed the word along. Susan may have heard from her enslaver that white Texans were executing slaves nearby in Upshur, Rusk, Cherokee, and Anderson Counties, or perhaps other enslaved people reported that something was making white men "shit behind their asses."[45]

Once the Civil War was underway, enslaved people in Texas heard that the U.S. Army was coming to free them. Eleven-year-old Lu Lee "heard powerful talk of the war that was heading that way"; her Navarro County enslaver extracted a promise from Lee that she would not run away.[46] If Henry, Susan, John, or Lucy considered it, their chance never came. Enslaved Texans who might have escaped to Union lines during the war waited in vain for the federal army to get close enough. In the fall of 1863, General Nathaniel Banks sent four Union gunboats to the mouth of the Sabine River, at Sabine Pass, where Confederate defenders easily defeated them.[47] Had they succeeded there, the five thousand Union soldiers on board the gunboats and army transports—and others that would have followed—might have made their way up the river into the East Texas counties with the heaviest concentrations of slaves. This would have opened the opportunity for Susan and Henry and thousands of enslaved people to beat their own paths to freedom. Perhaps, like Henry Tibbs, Henry Anderson might have enlisted. Susan might have fled, too.

But fewer than fifty enslaved Texans enlisted in the USCT, and over the next two years, General Banks failed repeatedly to establish a Union foothold in Texas.[48] Without one, the institution of slavery remained largely untouched, and it was business as usual in the East Texas slave labor camps: steamboats transported cotton down the Rio

Grande into Mexico and blockade runners carried it out from the port of Galveston.[49]

After Union troops took Vicksburg, the roads filled with white men driving their slaves away from the federal armies of liberation. Thousands of enslaved evacuees were forced to march in the opposite direction of their aspirations.[50] Each one brought news of a war going badly for people like John Anderson and the widow Burruss. "We just marched behind the wagons like soldiers," Smith Austin recalled how his enslaver drove him, his mother, and his thirteen siblings into Texas. The children were afraid to run away in this "strange country," Austin recalled, even though they knew they were leaving behind the "Freedom War."[51] They also left family members behind; when the Freedom War finally overtook them, many went looking for them.

The liberating army arrived in Texas in the summer of 1865, weeks after Confederate armies elsewhere had surrendered. "Soldiers all of a sudden were everywhere. Coming in bunches—crossing and walking and riding," Felix Haywood recalled.[52] U.S. Army general Gordon Granger landed in Galveston on June 19 and issued an emancipation order there, later celebrated as Juneteenth. He faced the unenviable task of informing white women and men who had fled to hold on to their slaves that they had not fled far enough. "The people of Texas are informed that . . . all slaves are free," the order read.[53] There were more than 240,000 enslaved people in Texas that day—perhaps many more.[54] The late precipitous growth of slavery in the state does not support the claim that the institution would have died there on its own, "naturally," that what was required was patience. When U.S. Army troops brought slavery to an end in the state, their hands were steeled by the resistance of tens of thousands of enslaved people who had escaped their enslavers throughout the South and offered their services as spies, guides, cooks, washerwomen, and soldiers. "We all felt like heroes and nobody had made us that way but ourselves," Haywood explained. "We were free! Just like that we were free!"[55]

A regiment of white U.S. soldiers from Illinois crossed over into East Texas and occupied the town of Marshall in Harrison County; by the end of June, two regiments of United States Colored Troops had set up quarters in Tyler in Smith County and got to work enforcing emancipation.[56] These same troops soon proved inadequate to protect freed people from white supremacist violence, but in those early days, their presence made Black Texans feel like heroes.

Sometime that summer, Susan, Henry and John Anderson, and Lucy Mead learned that their enslavers could no longer command them to stay, that if they chose to remain, they'd be paid wages for their work. They may have learned this from a Black soldier or via a white man tasked with making the announcement; they were advised to "remain quietly at their present homes and work for wages." Experience told military men to be prepared for this advice to be disregarded, and, Felix Haywood recalled, "right off colored folks started on the move. They seemed to want to get closer to freedom so they'd know what it was—like a place or a city."[57] As people had been doing throughout the South over four years of war, enslaved Texans turned up en masse in U.S. Army camps in order to get closer to freedom.

For many this was not close enough; once they hit the roads, they kept on going, retracing their steps, hoping to pick up word of loved ones and kin they had left behind. Doing so came with considerable risks, as white Texans violently resisted emancipation and overwhelmed the 52,000 troops that had been sent to enforce it. After two white soldiers were murdered in Houston and two Black soldiers, members of the 80th USCT, were ambushed and shot to death by the sheriff in Jefferson, General Philip Sheridan admitted to his superiors that he was unable to secure the safety of his own men, much less the freed people they'd been sent to protect.[58] Instead of reinforcements, Sheridan received orders to pull his men out. Troops stationed in the interior of Texas were sent south to reinforce the border with Mexico and west to fight Indians.[59] Black Texans who had waited four long years for the U.S. Army to get close enough to strike for freedom now faced painful choices about how to move on while also protecting themselves and their families. Leaving was dangerous, but so was staying.

✦

By the time the Andersons moved to Mineola, many Black Texans had their sights on Kansas. Word reached Black Texans about land available to them there, of aid societies ready to help them set up homesteads, free transportation even. At a state convention in Houston in July 1879, activist and political organizer Richard Allen appealed to his fellow Texans to go to Kansas: "Ask no more from the white people, but go."[60] Reports came in from across the state of Exodusters gathering at train stations; perhaps as many as twelve thousand Black Texans left for Kansas.[61] There as elsewhere in the South, freed people realized "that their oppression was inextricably bound up with Southern or perhaps American life."[62]

In his work for the papers, Sandy Anderson was aware of fierce debate about whether freed people should abandon the South to the white supremacists and Democrats or, as Frederick Douglass and others insisted, stay and ensure that the Republican Party, still the best guarantor of Black people's rights, did not collapse there.[63] The trains that pulled in and out of Mineola each day to points north carried people who were not convinced by Douglass or anyone else to stay on in Texas. At the Mineola train depot, the Andersons caught glimpses of these passengers, maybe even heard from them about what they hoped to find in Kansas, what drove them to leave Texas. Black passengers peering out the windows of the trains as they left the station saw Black men cutting railroad ties at the prison camp, where, as the delegates to the Houston convention reported, prisoners were "subjected to barbarities disgraceful to civilization and humanity."[64] But the Andersons stayed. Maybe Sandy convinced them to stay. Or it was something else.

Susan and Henry Anderson and their kin settled in Mineola in the 1870s among other freed people who had been sold away from families, all of them with different stories to tell. Susan, Henry, Lucy, and their neighbors told their stories to their children and shared them with each other, and that is how they learned that people in Mineola were finding the families they had lost in slavery, starting with Ann Carter. Hope spread through Mineola, inspired by stories like Ann's, Susan's, and Henry's and nurtured along by those willing to help them look.

Black institutions provided key support in their search. Institution building began in Mineola as elsewhere, with freed people founding a church and sending their children to school when it was safe to do so and so long as they could spare their labor. St. Paul Baptist Church was founded in 1871 in the home of Bettie and Pinkney Brooks, a couple about the same age as Henry and Susan. Newcomers like the Andersons surely found the Brookses' home welcoming, with the couple's young children there to entertain them when they came to worship.[65] In a few years, the growing congregation began meeting in their own church building, with the minister baptizing parishioners in a nearby creek.[66] Mineola's Black community organized a Methodist Episcopal church in these early days, too.[67]

By the time the Andersons arrived, Freedmen's Bureau schools were shuttered or destroyed and the teachers driven away in the paroxysm of white violence. Once white Texans removed, replaced, or murdered Black officeholders, support for the construction and support of public schools evaporated. The first (segregated) public schools in Wood County did not open until 1884. Even so, around 24 percent of Black Texans were literate by 1870, a testament to self-teaching and the instruction that literate freed people delivered in their homes and churches.[68] Pinkney and Bettie Brooks could not read or write, but their son Robert learned, as did Lucy's son Sandy. Working for the papers, Sandy helped his aunt, uncle, and father find their families. Finding his mother, Lucy's, family proved harder.

✦

Lucy Mead's advertisement appeared in the papers a few months before Henry Anderson's but with less success. Unlike with the others, Sandy placed no follow-up announcements, nothing indicating that his mother found her mother, father, three sisters, or two brothers. It is unclear if she ever heard from any of them. "When I left my native home," Lucy said, "I was about nine and half years old. A man bought me named Goodbah. He took me to Norfolk, Va. and put me in jail at night."[69] Her story began like many others, with the still vivid memory of when she last saw her loved ones, the names of the white men who took her from them, a jail where they kept children before they sold them. As in the other letters Sandy helped to write, Lucy included additional names in hers that she hoped might lead someone to help her. But this is not where Lucy Mead's story ended. As late as 1902, Sandy was still trying to find his mother's people.[70] Sandy Anderson grew up surrounded by the stories of his ancestors, people he had never met in places he had not seen. He told their stories in the papers and continued to hope that one day he would find them.

◆

Like the railroad lines that ran through it, Mineola never lived up to the dreams of its boosters. Despite its name, the Texas and Pacific Railway only reached Abilene in the dead center of the state before it went bankrupt. The company tried in vain to encourage (white) immigration to the towns springing up along its lines, like Mineola, listing in big letters on promotional maps all the reasons passengers should "TAKE YOUR FAMILY WITH YOU OVER THE GREAT THROUGH LINE." But the line did not take passengers through Texas; it never would. The other railroad line that stopped in Mineola, the International–Great Northern, had better luck, but it was never international and passengers continuing on to Chicago, St. Louis, and Cincinnati could not do so on its lines.[71] Mineola remains today a small town with high rates of poverty.[72]

The Andersons continued to live among their kin in the Black community in Mineola into the new century. In 1900, Susan and Henry shared a household with a nineteen-year-old woman named Mary J. White, whom the enumerator identified as their daughter. Sandy, his children, George and Sandy, and Lucy Mead lived nearby. Sandy's marriage to Lizzie was cut short when she died, leaving him with two young boys to raise. Perhaps he recounted to them the stories in the papers about how the Andersons of Mineola became a family and about the ones they had left behind.

Susan and Henry did not retrace their steps along the Second Middle Passage to reunite with the families in Virginia and Maryland that Sandy helped them find. Maybe it was enough to know what had become of them. Ann Carter stayed in Mineola after finding her brother and sister two hundred miles away in Oakland, Texas. In 1900, Ann, now widowed, lived and worked as a cook in the household of a white man; perhaps her husband, Edward, had lived long enough to hear from his family in Mississippi. Henry Anderson died sometime after 1900, but not before he, too, had received word from his family in Maryland. Susan Anderson appeared one last time in the 1910 census; it is unclear what became of the rest of the family she and Henry had made in freedom.[73] The others, including Sandy, George, Lucy, and Mary, had either moved on or passed on. That same year, state legislators voted to end private prison contracting, closing camps like the one in Mineola where men, perhaps some the Andersons knew, had cut the ties that built the railroads that brought news in and out.[74] The measure came too late to protect the Andersons and their neighbors from harsh daily reminders of the limits of their freedom. No further trace could be found of Sandy Anderson or his children. We do have though the extraordinary series of letters he wrote to the papers helping people find the families they had lost in slavery.

Do You Know These?

I would like to know the whereabouts of my brother, (Lias Tibbs), who belonged to Mrs. Moore Carter. He left Warrenton, Tarquier County, 58 years ago, and was sold. His father's name was Adam Tibbs; mother's name, Lucy Tibbs. Had a brother by the name of George Tibbs, who has another by the name of Beverly Tibbs, who is the youngest one. Anyone knowing anythng of his whereabouts will kindly notify his brother.

GEORGE TIBBS,
19 Cross Street,
Montclair, N. J.

George Tibbs, "Do You Know These?,"
Richmond Planet (Richmond, VA), January 1, 1916

INFORMATION WANTED

Information is wanted about Lias Tibbs, who was sold before the war at Fauquier county, Virginia. It is thought that he is in Greenville, Ga., or Columbia, Ga., or thereabouts. In the country out from Greenville, Ga., are some Tibbs, John and William, whom I think are my brother's children. Any information about my brother Lias will be gladly received by Beverly Tibbs, 29 Carroll St., Worcester, Mass.

Beverly Tibbs, "Information Wanted,"
Chicago Defender (Chicago, IL), May 26, 1917

CHAPTER SIX

Looking for Lias

Brothers George and Beverly Tibbs (not related to Henry Tibbs) came north before the Great Migration. They left Virginia around 1888 and headed to Montclair, New Jersey, twenty miles outside of New York City. They made a home there among a community of freed people, some from their old neighborhood in Virginia; most of them worked as servants in the homes of the town's white elite. After a few years, Beverly became restless for more and headed north again, to Worcester, Massachusetts, where he found work as a porter at Union Station.[1] The position allowed Beverly to move steadily into the Black middle class; by the time he died he owned the home where he lived with his wife, Alice. The trains he traveled as a porter connected Worcester to Boston in the east; westbound travelers could ride all the way to Chicago via a connection in Albany. From Albany, one could instead head south to Jersey City and board a ferry to New York City or disembark at various New Jersey towns—bedroom communities like Morristown, where Clara Bashop lived and looked for Patience, and Montclair, where George Tibbs lived with his wife, Julia. The job made it possible for Beverly to stay in touch with George as he traveled back and forth seeing to the comfort of the white passengers in the Pullman cars.

As a porter, Beverly witnessed the trains filling with Black passengers fleeing the South in the 1910s, as Europe descended into war.

Beverly hoped to find a familiar face among the migrants; when he didn't, Beverly and George tried a more direct approach, placing two advertisements in the papers, in 1916 and 1917, looking for their brother Lias. Beverly addressed the papers from his home in Worcester. George wrote from Montclair, where the streets were illuminated by gaslight and electricity lit the graceful hillside homes, and where Black men worked as carpenters and pharmacists. "Even though it was dark," another southern Black migrant to the "beautiful little town" recalled the first time she saw Montclair through the window of her family's car, "it looked very special to us, with its gaslights blinking like stars."[2]

It had been more than fifty years since Lias was sold away from them. Since then, George and Beverly had witnessed the epic and violent birth of freedom; together, they navigated "the long emancipation," witnessed the slow death of slavery, and sought a way to mend their family while they built new ones.[3] Civil War had broken out soon after Lias was taken, scattering Black families like the Tibbses further as people fled slavery and sought refuge in Union Army camps. Separations continued when army officials surveyed the labor potential of refugees, enlisting some men and impressing others. Women, children, and the elderly were placed where their labor was needed. Relocation to a refugee camp or an abandoned plantation was temporary and changed abruptly according to the location of the two armies. Parents pressed federal officials in these camps for help finding children they remembered vividly and whom they continued to imagine growing up. When the war was over, mothers like Clara Bashop retraced their steps along the Second Middle Passage to pick up traces of their missing children. Sold-away fathers returned or, like Tally Miller, stayed put and hoped to draw sons and daughters to them. Through repeated dislocations, daughters and sons kept their ears to the grapevine for word of family from whom they had been sold, even when no new information about them was forthcoming and as their parents grew old. Some families were rebuilt over a few years, but many people continued to search, to hope, for decades. Even as they lived out their lives, built new families, loved and lost.

Freedom Generation's determination to find sisters and brothers was enduring. Fifty years separate Hagar Outlaw's search for her children and George and Beverly's search for their brother Lias. Well into the twentieth century letters continued to appear in the papers from freed people describing lost sisters and brothers. As years passed, younger members of Freedom Generation came to accept the fact of their missing parents' passing, perhaps, but as long as they lived, they continued to hope that their siblings did, too.

George and Beverly wrote to the papers during World War I as the first wave of southern migrants arrived in the Great Migration. Fleeing deteriorating conditions in the former Confederacy, African Americans boarded trains heading north hoping to fill the jobs left open when European immigrants no longer arrived to take them. In an era of civil rights reversal, freed people's ability to move was, author and early twentieth-century civil rights leader Howard Thurman said, "the most psychologically dramatic of all manifestations of freedom."[4] Freed people exercised that freedom, moving first to the South's urban centers and then to the North. From the 1910s to the 1950s, nine million African Americans left the South in search of new opportunities.[5]

Before the mass of migrants came north there were individual journeys made by people determined to make their homes outside of the South, people like Clara Bashop and Beverly and George Tibbs. These pioneers built support networks that attracted a slow and steady stream of migrants from among their families and friends. Early migrants provided shelter and support to those who followed and helped to expand the geographic imagination of their generation. When George and Beverly wrote to the papers in search of Lias, they sought to rebuild on this new ground the family that had been taken from them in slavery.

✦

Lias Tibbs was around ten years old when Lucy Carter, or Mrs. Moore Carter, sold him from his family in Fauquier County, Virginia. His brother George was a bit older. Beverly was younger—so young that it is hard to imagine he remembered Lias at all. Carter had six children of her own under age thirteen at home. She and her husband, Moore, had more children over the next ten years, for a total of at least ten.[6]

Orphan making was not the exclusive prerogative of white men; women may have been more likely than men to see the financial opportunity in selling or buying a child.[7] As their household filled with their own children, the number of enslaved people working for the Carters shrank, leaving more work for the six enslaved people who remained.

Not all Northern Virginia slaveholders were downsizing. For instance, Samuel Tebbs, one of the Carters' Fauquier County neighbors, claimed twenty-eight slaves in 1860, four more than he had ten years previously; George, Beverly, and Lias's father, Adam, may have been among these people. As we have seen, Virginians spelled that surname in a number of ways, including "Tubbs" or even "Tibbs." The boys' mother, Lucy, belonged to the Carters; that explains why Lucy Carter could sell Lias. If Adam's enslaver was Samuel Tebbs, then, he and his wife, Lucy, retained a variant spelling of that last name in freedom.[8]

As the critique of slavery grew louder and antislavery agitators became bolder, Virginians continued to augment their slave population and to profit from selling other people's children. They rehearsed stories about debt and business deals gone bad, half-truths that they used to convince their enslaved people and themselves that they had no choice in the matter. But within a few months after the start of the Civil War, the artifices enslavers had erected to inoculate themselves from self-doubt and to shield slavery from external criticism crumbled as enslaved people walked away.

But cracks in slavery's edifice had already appeared by then. In 1859, thirty miles north in Harpers Ferry, Dangerfield Newby, a freeman from Warrenton, Fauquier County, joined John Brown and other Black and white men in a bold attempt to start a slave rebellion. Having failed to free his wife and children through legal means, Dangerfield Newby hoped to do so as part of the rebellion.[9] But the rebels, including Newby, were caught and executed. Afterward, white Virginians stepped up the surveillance and policing of Black Virginians, and it was then that Lias Tibbs was sold.

George and Beverly grew up in a climate of heightened white fear about what enslaved Virginians were thinking and what they were capable of. Lucy and Adam Tibbs surely entreated their sons to keep their heads down lest they be sold or prosecuted—or worse—by local authorities looking to make examples of them. But the boys were also aware that men were arming themselves in a battle against slavery.

Enslaved Virginians began slipping across the lines in the early months of the Civil War as the first U.S. Army troops appeared in the state. When a massive army arrived as part of General McClellan's Peninsula Campaign the following summer, many freed themselves and sought amnesty in the army camps. Thirty thousand men, women, and children had quit their enslavers in Virginia by 1863.[10] Freedom came for many "not by proclamation but through perambulation."[11]

Positioned between Richmond and the Shenandoah Valley, war raged in Fauquier County and in the adjacent counties of Loudon, Prince William, Fairfax, and Culpeper. Each time federal troops appeared—as they did repeatedly—enslaved people fled toward them seeking safety. In November 1864, General Philip Sheridan sent an army into Fauquier that seized livestock, freed enslaved people, and set barns and fields on fire. "We could mark the progress of the Yankees, in every direction dense columns of smoke arising one after another, from every farm through which they passed," Ida Powell Dulany, a Fauquier County enslaver, noted in her diary. "At night we could look out and see the whole country illuminated by immense fires."[12] George Tibbs slipped away amidst the confusion and followed the columns of smoke eastward toward Washington. As war swept through Northern Virginia, the Tibbs family was separated again.

Lucy and her youngest son, Beverly, left Fauquier, too. Once the Carters got wind that George had enlisted, they might have wanted to make Lucy pay for her son's disloyalty. She wasn't safe; neither was Beverly. They made their way to Union-occupied Alexandria. Adam's whereabouts during the war are unknown.

It's hard to overstate how dangerous it was for Lucy to walk those fifty miles to Alexandria with Beverly, who was three or four years old at the time. She would have proceeded slowly, cautiously, as it wasn't clear whom she could trust. Lucy wanted to avoid crossing paths with soldiers from either army who might take them back to the Carters. And then there were guerrillas who fought by their own rules and terrorized soldiers and civilians, adding to the war's chaos. Men like Confederate John Singleton Mosby, whose armed band operated everywhere Lucy walked, often with Beverly in her arms. Had Lucy and Beverly been intercepted by guerrillas, they would likely have been executed.[13]

Once in Alexandria, Lucy and Beverly were safe from immediate threat, but at times the city provided cold comfort. The swelling refugee population found shelter where they could, either in the rough army barracks or among the free Black population. At the L'Ouverture Hospital, Beverly and Lucy each received a pair of shoes donated by a Quaker relief organization. A volunteer added their names to a long list of "indigent freedmen" living in the freedmen's village adjacent to the hospital.[14] Harriet Jacobs, working as a teacher and Quaker relief agent, reported with compassion about the poor conditions faced by refugees there, about how they arrived destitute, how many of them died of exposure and smallpox soon after. She was moved by the faith that freedom-seeking people like the Tibbses invested in the Union soldiers they first set eyes on, and she was shocked when their faith was repaid with cruelty. "In return for their kindness and ever-ready service," she wrote, "they often receive insults, and sometimes beatings, and so they have learned to distrust those who wear the uniform of the U.S."[15]

But Jacobs refused to let the army's casual cruelty toward refugees define the epic human drama of emancipation as it unfolded before her. "I see the dawning of a better future for us," she wrote in January 1865. "I feel that this Republic will live, and in her new life learn justice and a broader humanity to the race she has hitherto despised."[16] That future, Jacobs believed, began with Black enlistment. Like the hospital's namesake, Haitian revolutionary Toussaint L'Ouverture, the people Harriet Jacobs encountered in Alexandria were fighting their way to freedom. Harriet Jacobs, too, had fought her way to freedom.

Being in a city swelling with refugees put Lucy in direct contact with people with information that she might use to find her son Lias and to keep track of George.

George enlisted in Washington on November 26, 1864, as the substitute for a white man named Mckendree Moulden. Although U.S.

Army regulations officially prohibited it, Black men preferred to go into the army as paid substitutes for white men. The army paid them nothing to enlist on their own, and, until late in the war, they were paid less than white soldiers.[17] The clerk who enrolled George in Company F of the 6th USCT, a regiment organized in Philadelphia, spelled his name "Tabes," a mistake that would complicate life for George later.[18]

George was with the 6th when the regiment boarded transport ships on the way to North Carolina, where the men helped to capture the Confederacy's Fort Fisher on the Cape Fear River. The victory cut the Confederate Army off from a crucial supply of food and drove up desertions among Robert E. Lee's soldiers defending Richmond, but fighting on the swampy banks of the Cape Fear River took a toll on the Union men as well.[19] George and the others cut their way through "jungle-like thickets" and then, standing in waist-deep water, dug a line of defensive trenches to prevent Confederate reinforcements.[20] Thirty years after the war, when George applied for a pension, he complained of chronic back pain and trouble with his kidneys "from working in trenches partly filled with water at Fort Fisher N.C. . . . and from cold and exposure while marching in rain and wading streams . . . and lying on wet ground and lying in the mud."[21] The injuries prevented him from working for long periods of time.

From Fort Fisher, the 6th USCT joined William Tecumseh Sherman's army in Raleigh in time to witness the Confederate Army's surrender. The war was over, but Private George Tibbs's enlistment was not. He spent the remainder of his time in the army serving as part of the occupation in Wilmington, North Carolina. Dissent spread through the 6th's ranks. Men complained to the papers that they were paid half as much as white soldiers, their pay was chronically late, and their families suffered in their absence; their commanding officers were racist. "I am a soldier in the 6th USCT," one of George's comrades wrote to Philadelphia's *Christian Recorder*, but "our officers tell us now, that we are not soldiers; that if we were, we would get the same pay as the white men; that the government just called us out to dig and drudge."[22] George may have entered the army with a political education, as enslaved people throughout the South held clandestine meetings to discuss politics. But serving with free and enslaved men hailing from Pennsylvania, Maryland, and Delaware surely enriched George's thinking and expanded the universe of possibilities he imagined for himself and his family.[23] The 6th's chaplain, Jeremiah Asher, for instance, appealed directly to President Lincoln on behalf of Black men who sought appointments as chaplains, when the army was not prepared to do so.[24] There were many lessons to be learned from men like Asher, including the potential for Black political organization and not allowing oneself to be defined by white racism. Later, when George Tibbs served as vice president of Montclair's Colored Republican Club, he put his political experience to good use organizing African Americans to vote for candidates who had their interests in mind.[25]

George mustered out of the 6th USCT in September 1865 and made his way to Philadelphia with the men he'd served with for the better part of a year. Perhaps it was those personal connections that convinced George to stay in Philadelphia instead of returning immediately to his family. The prospects looked good in a city with a large and vibrant Black population. Young USCT veterans lobbied for voting rights and equal access to the ubiquitous streetcars that plied the city. With so many Black soldiers arriving at Camp William Penn from all over the South, George may have hoped to find Lias. By 1865, the *Christian Recorder* ran a regular column of Information Wanted advertisements from people like George hoping to find lost family members. The paper circulated widely in the city and throughout the South where USCT regiments had served, and editor Rev. Elisha Weaver invited freed people to take their search for family to the paper by sending in Information Wanted advertisements. If George learned anything about Lias in Philadelphia, he left no record of it. In April 1866, George made his way back to Virginia. He stopped in Alexandria, where he was treated for his injuries, and sometime that fall he collected his mother and brother and headed back to Fauquier County.[26] There they caught up with Adam Tibbs.

Separated during the war, the Tibbs family moved forward together into those first few heady post-emancipation years. They lived under one roof, maybe for the first time, or for the first time as freed people.[27]

Of Lias, they had many questions. Had he survived the war? Whom had the Carters sold him to? Where had they taken him? In 1870, Moore and Lucy Carter lived in Warren County, just west of Fauquier, where George might have inquired for information about Lias.[28] It must have pained freed people to appeal to their former enslavers for help finding loved ones they had taken from them. "Please let me know where they are or when you only could let me know something of one of them," Frank Marten wrote to the man who had once enslaved his wife and six sons. "I am getting old . . . but I would [forget] age and poverty in the joy to hear something from my boy, which I hope you will be able and kind enough to give."[29] Adam and Lucy Tibbs were sixty and fifty-five, respectively, but surely they still hoped to experience the joy of hearing from Lias again.

George returned to Virginia a free man and a U.S. Army veteran. He had fought alongside men determined to end slavery and lived for months in the company of idealists who now saw the postwar South as a laboratory for democratic experimentation. Some followed him back home, where they worked to support and build up the institutions that free Black Virginians had sustained for decades. White women from Boston and Philadelphia opened schools for freed people in Fauquier and Loudon, the two counties adjacent to where George lived and worked.[30] Freed people built Black churches whose sanctuaries doubled as political meetinghouses, where men, women, and children participated in drafting petitions, vetting candidates for local office, and laying out community priorities.[31]

Black men's votes in local and state elections secured the Republican Party's foothold in the state and sent eighty-five Black men to elected office during Reconstruction. George and Adam may have voted as early as 1867, with the occupying army overseeing elections. Under Virginia's new constitution, formerly enslaved people's marriages were legalized—among them Adam and Lucy's—and freed people's other basic rights were secured.[32] Military victory had made possible a striking course correction in Virginia. The state where for decades enslavers had recklessly separated wives from husbands, children from parents, and siblings like George, Beverly, and Lias from each other now recognized the integrity of Black families, a belated acknowledgment of the bonds of affection that had held enslaved families together even as people were sold away.

And then Reconstruction in Virginia came abruptly to a halt. Federal troops pulled out of the state in 1870, and Virginia was readmitted to the Union. Black Virginians were not immediately stripped of their rights, but they found themselves with fewer and fewer political allies.[33] When Republicans lost their majority in the state in 1873, white Virginians launched a campaign to drive out Black officeholders and to disfranchise Black voters, including resorting to violence, as was the case in Danville in 1883, when white men killed four Black men and then blamed the attacks on the city's Black population. "The white people of Virginia," the Richmond *Dispatch* declared, warning of further violence after the Danville murders, "do not intend to hold their rights at the will of the negroes."[34] Seeking protection and self-sufficiency, African Americans in Virginia relocated to freedmen's villages or left the countryside and headed for towns. Some decided to rebuild their communities elsewhere and joined a trickle of migrants headed north. There they provided crucial intelligence and support for the many who followed.

George Tibbs returned to Virginia hopeful about what the future held. He lived in various locations around the state working for white landowners. He met Ellen Noyes, and the two were married in 1871. Ellen worked for Ida Dulany at the stately Oakley Plantation in Fauquier County. Dulany had remained a devotee of the institution of slavery to the bitter end, refusing to allow a USCT soldier to retrieve his wife and children from Oakley late in 1864, even as slavery was falling apart around her.[35] Ellen may have quit once she was married.[36] She was ten years older than George when they met and had a two-year old son named Walter. George and Ellen had two children together, a girl named Ida and a boy they named Elias, after George's brother.

Ellen and George shared a sense of rootedness to the place where they were born and where they married and had their children. They stayed, even as the possibilities for landownership shrank and white violence against African Americans escalated. The couple took comfort that their children would not be taken away from them. George hoped to raise his children on stories about how their grandmother slipped away from the Carters during the war carrying her child in her arms, their uncle Beverly. These stories would help make Ida and Elias brave and strong. But they could not save their children from the racism that ensured that Black people in the postwar South remained poor, even those who had fought bravely for their country, and that deprived them of their health and the medical care they needed when ill.

Elias—the child who might one day have told people to call him Lias—died at thirteen months. The coroner determined that he had died of bronchitis.[37] A doctor would have been able to do little to help Elias, who struggled to breathe between coughing spells. Ida died, too. There is no record of what took her life. Ellen died sometime after 1880.[38] George and Ellen had been married fifteen years. There is no record of Lucy Tibbs from these years. Nothing is known of Adam either. He would have been sixty-seven the summer his grandchildren died.

George built a family in freedom, and then, like the one he had as an enslaved child, it was taken from him. Losing his family sent him looking for someplace new to put down roots, where, as historian Carole Emberton has put it, they "might grow deeper and strong, and where old ties might be stretched and even broken."[39] Maybe if things had been better in Virginia—if he had been able to find work he could do with his weak back, if he had been able to save enough to buy a plot of land where he could be his own boss, or if his wife and children had lived—George Tibbs might have stayed. Maybe if Lias had returned and the three brothers had seen a way forward together. "I feel that this Republic will live," Harriet Jacobs had predicted during the war as she cared for Black soldiers and their families in Virginia, "and in her new life learn justice and a broader humanity to the race she has hitherto despised." If Private George Tibbs, 6th USCT, shared Jacobs's optimism, then he hoped that new life would begin in New Jersey.

◆

George and Beverly arrived in Montclair, New Jersey, in 1888, joining a small Black community high up on cliffs overlooking the Passaic River.

Looking for a way out of tenancy, freed people from Virginia worked in the homes of the town's elite white residents and on farms that fed the growing population of New York City. Southern Black migrants hoped to eventually bring their families along with them. Over time, some worked their way into the middle class.

State lawmakers, however, had done their best to make New Jersey an inhospitable place for freed people looking to put some distance between themselves and slavery's long shadow. The state earned the distinction of being the only one to pass and then *rescind* their vote for the Fourteenth Amendment, the federal law protecting the rights of Black Americans.[40] On the other hand, an 1881 state law integrated public schools. The law was unevenly enforced, but for many years Black and white children attended the same schools in the northern part of the state, as in Essex County where George Tibbs settled, married, and remained.[41] Black children born there faced many of the same hardships as did those born in the postwar South. But they learned to read and write alongside white children and grew up wanting the same things.

Booker T. Washington visited Montclair and delivered a speech applauding Black achievement there. Washington estimated that the town's 3,500 Black residents owned property valued at $500,000. They supported one Methodist Episcopal, one African Methodist Episcopal, and two Baptist churches; a YMCA and a YWCA; a chapter of the Boy Scouts and of Campfire Girls; and a Black newspaper, the *Eastern Observer*. He ticked off an astonishing list of Black-owned businesses and Black professionals, including "two barber shops, one billiard parlor, three beauty parlors, one contractor and builder, one carpenter, two medical doctors, two druggists, one domestic service and cooking school, nine dressmaking establishments, four employment agencies, two expressmen, one furniture and piano mover, one hair-dressing establishment, one house-cleaning bureau." Black residents of Montclair worked in a variety of skilled and semiskilled trades.[42] By 1914, Black residents of Montclair had found the new life for the Republic that Harriet Jacobs had imagined, Freedom Generation living out their aspirations.

George and Beverly Tibbs did not "cast down [their] buckets" where they are, as Booker T. Washington advised freed people thinking of leaving the South. Instead of counting on "friendly relations with the southern white man, who is their next-door neighbor," they found a home in New Jersey, where within a few decades the children of Black migrants from Virginia and elsewhere could be found working in every trade Washington might have imagined.[43]

George met Julia soon after he arrived in Montclair. "I must have been a fine looking girl for he fell in love with me at first sight," Julia recalled years later when a pension inspector asked her about their marriage. Julia was born in Campbell County, Virginia, and like George, she came north after her first husband died. She worked for a white woman in New York City briefly before leaving for Montclair, where she lived among people who had settled there from the old neighborhood.

George and Julia married in April 1888, weeks after a spring storm blanketed the region with ice and heavy snow, shutting businesses in New York and New Jersey and paralyzing train travel.[44] The local Montclair newspaper described residents pulling together to help one another during the storm. People appeared along the train tracks to help stranded passengers climb out of cars, including "a colored man, who rigged a ladder to rescue the passengers." And, when Rosier Hooe, "a colored boy living above Mountain Avenue," fell in a drift on his way home from school, a white passerby pulled him out and took him home.[45]

It may have been the extraordinary circumstances of the storm that produced these moments of interracial harmony. White residents of the small New Jersey town welcomed Black southerners who arrived to help solve "the servant question." An early Montclair historian described the first migrants: "most were born in servitude. . . . As a class they are quiet, industrious and well behaved. They retain many of their old time customs." The arrival of a servant class who understood their place, he assured readers, was a positive feature of a town known for "its elevated, moral and religious life."[46] If it comforted white residents to imagine that people like Julia, George, and Beverly were there temporarily—like people stranded in a storm—or that they had limited aspirations, or that they would not seek to bring along others, they were wrong about that.

The Blizzard of 1888 may not have been Julia's first taste of a spring nor'easter, but the sleet that stung George's face and his back that ached in the frigid cold might have made him wonder if he'd made a mistake in coming. No wonder he fell so fast for Julia. Her voice sounded like home to him, and he saw something in her that made him think he could once again find happiness. They married at Union Baptist Church, or First Baptist, as people called it because it was Montclair's first Black church. "Mr. George Tibbs and Mrs. Julia Stevens of this town were united in matrimony," read the announcement in the *Montclair Times*, alongside notices of the European travel itineraries of the adult children of the town's elite white residents.[47] With her first husband, Julia had had one child who was stillborn; she and George had none of their own. They grew old together in a town with streets filled with children, walking to and from school, where spring storms stung your face and where Freedom Generation came together around what they had lost and whom they hoped to find.

Julia and George lived just outside the Fourth Ward, a Black neighborhood at the southern tip of the town. When they first arrived, Beverly and George worked for Phebe Crane, widow of James, the heir of wealthy cotton magnate and enslaver Israel Crane.[48] The brothers lived in Crane's barn, built decades before by Crane family slaves. After they married, Julia and George lived in various locations before they settled into their home on Cross Street, a short walk from First Baptist.[49]

George and Julia Tibbs welcomed into their home Virginia freed people making their way north. The Tibbses purchased the house on Cross Street with the money they earned working a number of jobs in the homes and on the property of white town residents and by renting part of the house to tenants.[50] Julia washed other people's clothes alongside her female tenants who supported themselves and paid the rent doing the same.[51] Each day, Julia carried clean and pressed laundry across town to the spacious homes along the foothills of the Watchung Mountains, where she knocked on the back door to conduct her business not with the white lady who lived there but with the Black servants. At the back door or in the kitchen, Jane exchanged news with the servants, finding out what she could about people back home and learning who was looking for a place to live while they got settled in.

News traveled fast in Montclair on Thursdays, when all the servants had the day off and gathered in each other's homes—the Thursday grapevine, they called it. "It was a powerful communication system," Carrie Allen McCray recalled, "our own private intelligence service." When the Allens, McCray's parents, had moved from Virginia into a big house on Bloomfield Avenue, the Thursday grapevine reported that white residents were petitioning to get them out.[52] The Allens were a formidable couple and not easily intimidated: they stayed put.

So did Julia and George Tibbs. George worked and attended night school, where at fifty years old he learned to read and write. "I learned to write my name about two years ago," George reported in his pension application. "I can't write very well and for that reason sometimes in order to save time still sign my mark but generally have written my name in signing papers since I learned how."[53] Until he could do so on his own, Julia read the newspapers to George in addition to relaying the intelligence she had gathered with the dirty laundry. In this way, they stayed on top of news in Montclair and back home in Virginia. If anyone in Montclair knew about Lias, they'd hear about it.

George and Beverly got involved in Republican politics. Democratic victories at the state level in the 1880s, even as Republicans managed to stay in power in Washington, D.C., further diluted enforcement of civil rights throughout the country, but particularly in the postwar South. This was the case in Virginia, where in 1884 a Democratic-controlled legislature passed a series of measures effecting a more complete disfranchisement of Black voters. In New Jersey, as Republicans struggled to break the stranglehold that Democrats had held in the state since the war, white party leaders accepted that they needed to appeal to Black voters.[54] At the state's Republican convention in Asbury Park in August 1888, attendees named two Black men to represent their districts but dismissed as "out of order" a proposal to put a Black man on the state's delegation to the national convention.[55] Beverly Tibbs was there for the debate, representing Montclair, where he and George worked to turn out votes for Republicans.[56]

When, years later, New Jersey elected Republican John Griggs as governor, George and Beverly Tibbs could take satisfaction in the fact they'd helped to build a political apparatus in Montclair to make it happen. Southern Black migrants like the Tibbses tipped the scales in favor of Republican candidates. By 1920, in battleground states like New Jersey, W. E. B. Du Bois observed that "the Negro voter easily holds the balance of power."[57]

It helped that the Tibbses knew so many people, family and kin relations connecting them to Montclair's Black community and back to their families in Virginia. Marriages among Virginia-born members of Freedom Generation strengthened this web of belonging: George's marriage to Julia and Beverly's to Alice Young, for example. Beverly was married twice, both times in Montclair. After his first wife, Mary, died, Beverly returned to Montclair and married Alice.[58] Beverly had been living in Worcester, Massachusetts, for more than ten years, and during that time he visited Montclair often as a porter on the trains. Alice and Julia knew one another before they became sisters-in-law, and Alice had known George since she was a child. "I knew Uncle George from [the] time I knew anyone. That was in Loudon County, Virginia," Alice explained to the pension inspector investigating Julia's application for a widow's pension. "I was always told that Uncle George was in [the] army during the war."[59] Because of her previous marriage, the inspector was skeptical of Julia's claim to a pension as George Tibbs's widow, but he had no difficulty in finding people willing to be deposed to speak on her behalf, blood relations or kin from Virginia. Leslie Irvine, Julia's half sister, was one of several who had known George in Virginia.[60]

The community sustained Julia and George over their thirty-six years of marriage; they grew old together there, helping to lay the foundation for Black institutional life and welcoming new migrants from the South. They stretched the ties that bound them to Virginia and their families there, living and dead, but they did not break. The brothers kept up with one another, and they gathered information about Lias. George asked about Lias when he spoke to those arriving from the South, with greater frequency now than when he'd first arrived. And on board the trains where he worked, Beverly Tibbs learned what he could.

George placed his advertisement in the *Richmond Planet* on January 1, 1916. That October, he would turn seventy years old. It had been nearly sixty years since he last saw Lias, although it seemed longer to him. "He left Warrenton, [Fauquier] County, 65 years ago, and was sold," George wrote in his ad appearing alongside others under the headline "Do You Know These?" in the *Planet*. George poured everything he knew about Lias into five short lines, starting with "I would like to know the whereabouts of my brother, (Lias Tibbs). . . . His father's name was Adam Tibbs; mother's name, Lucy Tibbs. Had a brother by the name of George Tibbs, who has another by the name of Beverly Tibbs, who is the youngest one."

Black men worked as carpenters, pharmacists, and, like Carrie Allen McCray's father, doctors in Montclair, where gaslights illuminated the night sky.[61] George had access to a number of newspapers, including the local white-owned paper, the *Montclair Times*, and the new *Eastern Observer*, edited by a Black man; in New York, he could have reached the *World*, *Times*, *Herald*, or *Sun*. Perhaps George placed his ad in the *Planet* because of the paper's circulation or its politics. Nothing in the ad indicated that George had learned anything new about Lias.

✦

Beverly Tibbs wrote to the *Chicago Defender* sixteen months later, including more information about Lias. "Information is wanted about Lias Tibbs, who was sold before the war at Fauquier county, Virginia," it read. Beverly did not include George's name, nor did he name their parents or former enslaver. Instead, he repeated something he'd heard about Lias—that he was alive and living in Georgia. "It is thought that he is in Greenville, Ga., or Columbia, Ga., or thereabouts. In the country out from Greenville, Ga.," Beverly said, "are some Tibbs, John and William, whom I think are my brother's children." Had Beverly met someone, perhaps on a train, who knew these Tibbses? Or, did this new information come as a result of George's earlier ad, with someone writing to George in New Jersey that they suspected a relationship to the Tibbses living in Georgia? Beverly was convinced that he'd found

Lias, or he'd found his brother's sons. If the latter, they would be able to tell him what had become of their father.

Beverly's decision to go to the *Defender* for help finding his missing brother underscores the links between his and George's earlier migration to the one that brought tens of thousands more. The newspaper's publisher, Robert Abbott, enthusiastically supported Black migration as a means of punishing white southerners for racial discrimination and violence. The paper regularly featured letters from earlier migrants who spoke in glowing terms of their lives in the North. As had other Black papers, such as the Indianapolis *Freeman* and the *Richmond Planet*, the *Defender* relied on information gathered by the Black men who worked near the tracks or on the trains.[62] Beverly may have chosen the *Defender* because he distributed it on the trains where he met people in the midst of a southern exodus.

It seems unlikely that the information that Beverly had about Lias's family in Georgia turned out to be useful. The two locations—Greenville and Columbia County, if that is what Beverly was referring to—are on opposites sides of the state. Greenville is in Meriwether County, in the west, about one hundred miles east of the border with Alabama, while Columbia County is in the east, on the border between Georgia and South Carolina. Between the two are hundreds of miles with a number of railroad lines converging in Macon and Atlanta.

New South race relations were made on these trains. Throughout the 1880s and '90s, Black passengers sued railroad companies for denying them the first-class accommodations for which they had paid. By 1900, southern states had passed railroad segregation laws, requiring companies to provide separate coaches for white and Black passengers. The measures were billed as a compromise that allowed Black passengers to ride without suffering the violence of whites who tried to force them from the trains, but the "Colored" waiting rooms were cramped, dark, and dirty and Black travelers were prohibited from entering through the doors marked "Ladies" or "Gentlemen," because the assumption was African Americans could be neither. The only African Americans allowed to pass through white spaces at the new terminals were servants and porters.[63] If Beverly traveled to Georgia to look for Lias, his porter's red cap may have granted him some minor privileges not afforded Black passengers, but making a trip like that would have been dangerous and inadvisable. He could have lost his job, or worse. That no record can be found of these Tibbses—John, William, or Lias—does not necessarily mean that George and Beverly were unable to find their brother. But there are other indications that their search for Lias did not succeed.

◆

An Elias Tibbs, born in Fauquier County, enlisted in Company H, 1st USCT, in June 1863.[64] He was twenty-three years old when he enlisted on Mason's Island, "a wooded, swampy 75-acre" strip of land in the Potomac River, a couple of miles from the White House.[65] The capital city had filled with freed people after slavery ended there in 1862, and both free Blacks and freedmen filled the ranks of the 1st USCT. In August 1863, the 1st was sent to North Carolina to guard refugees, then in September they were reassigned to the Virginia Peninsula to reinforce the federal army and navy bases in Portsmouth and Norfolk. In November they were joined by the 4th USCT, recruited in Maryland, and the 6th, who were stationed at Yorktown.[66] For a few weeks, the 1st USCT and the 6th USCT were camped within fifty miles of one another. If this was "Lias," then he lied about his age when he enlisted, for he could not have been much older than sixteen.

But when fifty-three years later George placed an advertisement in the papers looking for Lias, he said nothing about his brother becoming a soldier. Also, Private Elias Tibbs died in Portsmouth, Virginia, in September 1863. It is unclear what the young recruit died of because his enlistment record says only "disease." Maybe Elias Tibbs died as a result of the fatigue duty that USCT were disproportionately ordered to do. He enlisted for three years, but he died after only three months. George didn't join the 6th USCT until the following year.

If this was Lias, then Lucy and Adam Tibbs never learned of their son's enlistment or his death, nor did Beverly or George, who kept looking.

✦

America's domestic slave trade ripped apart families like the Tibbses, then the Civil War scattered people further, disrupting the logic of an already impossible search. The work of rebuilding proceeded for decades. It began for some at the very place where parents, children, aunts, uncles, brothers, sisters, and kin had once lived together, in the old slave neighborhood or nearby, where proper and place names were familiar to those who might have heard something. Others began searching from new places where they worked to replicate and rebuild the affective ties that had sustained them in bondage. The great distance and time that separated them never extinguished the hope that brothers and sisters would find each other again.

Many younger members of Freedom Generation lived long lives. When Federal Writers' Project interviewers caught up to them in the South in the 1930s, they were old and frail; their bodies showed all of the signs of poverty and ill health. But their minds remained sharp, and they vividly recalled what they had eaten, worn, and sung when they were children. They recalled the names of the sisters, brothers, and cousins from whom they had inherited the clothes, recollected the last day they had seen them. But government interviewers had been sent to their doors to preserve the folklore of the "old South," not to document the long emancipation of people who had been torn from their families when they were young. Not freed people's family stories. These memories were carried into the twentieth century in letters and missing person advertisements published in Black newspapers.

Perhaps it was talk of war that inspired George to write in 1916. A year later, young Black men were enlisting eagerly to fight in Europe, certain that they would return to full citizenship and the right to an intact family. Once again, these expectations failed to materialize. The U.S. entered World War I in April 1917; in July, St. Louis erupted into violence in the first of a series of race riots. Black soldiers were hanged in Houston the following summer for fighting back against racial provocations. And hundreds of Black men, women, and children were murdered throughout the South and in northern cities like Chicago in

1919. "This is the country to which we Soldiers of Democracy return," W. E. B. Du Bois wrote in *The Crisis*, channeling the anguish and determination of Black veterans and their families. "[B]y God of heaven, we are cowards and jackasses if now that the war is over, we do not marshal every ounce of our brain and brawn to fight a sterner, longer, more unbending battle against the forces of hell in our own land."[67]

These sentiments might have resonated with George Tibbs, a "Soldier of Democracy" who returned to Virginia having helped to save his country, only to have that country turn its back on him. Like a good soldier, he kept fighting, resuming that longer battle from new ground.

George Tibbs died on March 15, 1924. His military experience was important to him, and after he died, it became part of his family's history. George's $50-a-month pension had provided crucial support as he and Julia grew old and his weak back worsened, as did the $30-a-month widow's pension that Julia received for the four years between George's death and her own. To get it, Julia fought an "unbending battle" against Pension Bureau agents who were disinclined to support her because she had been married previously, and because USCT widows were subjected to more invasive scrutiny than their white counterparts.[68]

There were a lot of things that Julia couldn't recall or never knew—her own age, for example (she was sixty-four in 1925, at her pension deposition), or her late husband's (George was around seventy-eight when he died)—but she knew that George had served in the 6th and that the two fell in love at first sight. She called in a broad range of people to be deposed on her behalf, and, in so doing, she created a further record of the Tibbs family. One after another, friends and family gave statements testifying to their marriage and to George's military service; many had known the Tibbs family before the Civil War. Others knew Julia and George and Beverly only after they had arrived in New Jersey. Julia and George had no children, no one who would carry on the family name or continue to tell the story of his family.[69] George created a record of his family in the advertisement he placed looking for Lias, and Julia filled in the critical missing details that she had heard from George repeatedly over thirty-six years of marriage.

The boys were young when they lost Lias, so they surely had few memories to draw from when they looked for him. How many times did their mother, Lucy Tibbs, tell George and Beverly about Lias, about the day that he was sold away from them? The ache Lucy felt for Lias lived on in George and Beverly, in their continued hope they would find him. Like so many thousands of others looking for brothers and sisters long after their parents had died, George and Beverly reached out to a brother they had hardly known yet could still imagine by their side.

CHAPTER SEVEN

Emeline and Julia

AFTER MANY YEARS.

AFFECTING MEETING OF TWO SISTERS.

Special Telegram to The Inter Ocean.

BATTLE CREEK, Mich., Nov. 19.—Forty years ago Julia and Emeline, two sisters, were slaves upon the plantation of a master by the name of Hall, in Kentucky. Emeline left her sister one night, and with a party of fugitives crossed the Ohio River at Cincinnati, and by means of the underground railroad made her escape to Michigan and thence to Battle Creek, where she has since resided, the wife of Joseph Skipwarth, now dead. In all these years she has never heard of her sister until recently, when by accident she learned that she was now Mrs. Julia Lyon, living on a farm near Troy, Ohio, in good circumstance. Yesterday Mrs. Lyon arrived in this city, and the meeting of the two sisters after forty years separation was very affecting. Mrs. Skipmarth is one of our most respected colored ladies, and the two happy sisters have received a number of calls to-day from our leading citizens. The reminiscenses of slavery days and their escape by the underground railway, out of the changes which have since taken place, are of the most interesting nature.

"After Many Years," *Daily Inter Ocean* (Chicago, IL), November 20, 1885

Emeline escaped her Kentucky enslavers and made her way to freedom in Michigan when she was sixteen years old. She left her sister, Julia, behind, expecting never to see her again. Forty years later, a story appeared in newspapers in Battle Creek, Michigan, and then in Chicago announcing that the two women had found one another. "After Many Years. Affecting Meeting of Two Sisters," read the November 20, 1885, headline of Chicago's *Daily Inter Ocean.* The paper did not publish advertisements placed by freed people looking for their family members, nor did its coverage include stories that directly addressed Black readers. By the time the story ran, white Americans had grown impatient with talk of equal rights even in towns like Battle Creek with a reputation for racial tolerance. But a moving account of two sisters' reunion made for compelling reading, and it allowed the paper to tap into a regional nostalgia for stories about the Underground Railroad. The *Inter Ocean* described Emeline's escape from a Kentucky plantation, her marriage and widowhood, and her discovery of her sister, Julia, "by accident." In a scene that harked back to the town's antislavery radicalism, elite residents turned out to pay their respects to Emeline and Julia. After all, their own ancestors had spirited Emeline to freedom; it was fitting that the descendants of the town's Underground Railroad conductors attend a reunion of two old women whom slavery had torn apart. The *Inter Ocean* invited readers to share in a sweet moment of celebration and self-congratulation.

From towns throughout the Midwest white readers told Underground Railroad stories that claimed for themselves and their communities an inheritance of virtue. What they did had helped to end slavery. Sharing heroic stories of white Underground Railroad operatives relieved white audiences of the moral responsibility of sustaining the civil rights gains made by an earlier generation and from addressing the racism that limited Freedom Generation's economic opportunities. From recognizing that slavery's still separated families prevented those who managed to emerge from poverty from passing along their property and creating intergenerational wealth. Emeline's story offered readers "reminiscenses of slavery days" long gone, a way for them to measure "the changes which have since taken place." Emeline, the widowed former slave and longtime town resident, was the perfect subject to carry that message. She came to Battle Creek as a teenage girl, and now "Mrs. Skipmarth [Skipworth] is one of our most respected colored ladies." We learn little else about Emeline and nothing about Julia's journey to freedom.

The account featured two happy endings, one when Emeline arrived via the Underground Railroad and the other when her long-lost sister, Julia, found her. Battle Creek's "leading citizens" sought to take credit for both. Although originating in the North, the motivation behind the *Inter Ocean*'s coverage drew from the same emotional well as did the

Lost Cause—white Americans' desire to see slavery as ancient history, a problem solved. The real story of Emeline's and Julia's lives challenges this narrative.

The Last Seen Collection is full of stories of sold-away brothers and sisters who looked for one another for decades after emancipation, into the twentieth century even, and well after white Americans began burying the truth about slavery under mountains of nostalgia. Despite the extraordinary challenges of looking for people who moved about, changed their names, or never settled on one spelling of them, Freedom Generation's sisters and brothers searched for one another. Looking for *sisters*—and mothers, daughters, and wives—whose names changed with each marriage presented unique challenges. Women often included several names in their ads, leaving trails for their loved ones to find them. "My last matrimonial name is Ethrington, maiden name was Octavia West, and by first marriage, my name was Newby," Octavia Ethrington wrote from New York City. From Chicago, Fannie Roly placed an ad looking for two sisters and a brother, "Katie Butler and Caroline and Walton Carter. These were the maiden names of my sisters. Caroline was sold to a man in South Carolina named Pickens. We belonged to Alfred Duern who sold us to Issac Winston."[1]

There are no ads from Emeline or Julia in the collection, either because they didn't place them or because we have not yet found them. Women were hard to find, and they continue to be. The *Inter Ocean* account—and the local coverage on which it was based—is all we have to follow the sisters' trail even though it is full of silences and was intended for a white audience. But if we trace Emeline and Julia's search backward from the white press's coverage of their reunion, then we can learn something about how two sisters separated in slavery found one another in freedom, and, by extension, how others hoped they might, too.

EMELINE HALL

Newspapers in Battle Creek first reported on Emeline and Julia a year earlier, in 1884, when the sisters found one another and began planning Julia's visit.[2] The *Battle Creek Daily Moon* ran a short announcement about the women's reunion on Wednesday, November 18, 1885, then a longer story based on an interview with the sisters appeared four days later in Battle Creek's *Sunday Morning Call.*[3] When a reporter showed up at Emeline's house asking her to tell him about her escape from slavery, she may have hesitated. She had been careful not to share her story with strangers, perhaps even other freedom seekers who came through Battle Creek before the war and whom she had helped to feed and shelter. Surely she'd confided in her husband, Joseph Skipworth, as he was also self-emancipated, and Emeline told her daughters Aurena, Rebecca, Frances, Jennie, and Carrie about how she had found the courage to do what she had done and how she hoped they'd be courageous.[4] Now she told it before her sister and a white man with a pencil, and then it appeared in the newspapers. The account flattened out some of the details of her escape, but there was no mistaking the pride Emeline took in telling her story.

It may have been one of the white women for whom Emeline washed clothes who tipped off the newspaper about Julia coming to town. Emeline would have had to complete the wash early that week so that she had time to spend with her sister. That woman surely told Emeline to expect someone from the paper, so she gave her small house on Pittee Street a thorough scrubbing and pulled down the clothes drying on the line before he arrived. Maybe, as in the Federal Writers' Project interviews some fifty years later, Emeline offered the reporter a seat, apologized for not having more to offer him. Living in that town for forty years, washing white women's clothes, and keeping her head down, Emeline had a reputation for respectability. "Most of our citizens are acquainted with Mrs. Skipworth and her family," the brief November 18 announcement reported, "as among the best of our colored population."[5] The good people of Battle Creek had taken her in, and she'd repaid them by her accommodation to the limited prospects she and Joseph had found there. For forty years, she'd carried heavy baskets of their dirty laundry to her home on Pittee Street and returned them full of clean and pressed clothes and linens. But when she presented herself to the reporter, Emeline did not speak of the strain of the work, the little she was paid for it, or the toll it had taken on her body. At fifty-five, Emeline must have wondered how long she had before her back gave out. Until now, she'd kept quiet, too, about her past and about how she had lost Julia and hoped to find her.

"[I] lived only eleven miles from Covington, on the Ohio river," Emeline recalled the details clearly, including the exact distances she had traveled in what was no doubt a carefully planned and deliberately executed escape. Covington, located in the slave state of Kentucky, is just across the Ohio River from Cincinnati, which was in the free state of Ohio. She had never been more than seven miles away from her home, not to Covington or anywhere else. Emeline "walked four miles to Taylor's hill, where she laid down by the road side, out of sight of any travelers, and slept until morning. Before daylight she waded across mill creek, and started on the road to Covington. Arriving there she walked boldly onto the ferry boat. . . . When the captain came around she told him that she was Jesse Pettee's [Petty's] slave, and he passed her by."[6] The reporter who wrote the November 22 story spelled the last name "Pettee," maybe because it sounded like the street where Emeline lived.

Having claimed that she was on an errand for her master, Emeline made the short trip to Cincinnati, hiding in plain sight. "Landing in Cincinnati," read the account in the *Sunday Morning Call*, lingering on her youth and good fortune, "Emeline, tired and hungry wandered along in the city, knowing not where to stop for shelter or assistance." Until she knocked on the door of a woman who directed her to an agent of the Underground Railroad. "He took her in charge," and after a time Emeline, along with three others, was "started on the underground railway through Ohio and Indiana for Michigan."[7] The Battle Creek reporter was convinced that Emeline had been lucky, when she had likely planned every step of her journey, including the part when she talked her way onto a boat by telling a convincing story about how she was there by permission of her enslaver.

Emeline's solitary escape was unusual. Of the thousands of enslaved people who fled Kentucky every year, few were women, and only rarely were they alone. Because most freedom seekers were in their late teens and twenties, women were likely to have children and less likely to risk trying to escape with them.[8] If Emeline ever discussed her plans with her sister, Julia might not have wanted to attempt it with her four-year-old son, Henry, in tow.[9]

Henry Bibb, William Wells Brown, Lewis Clarke, and Lewis Hayden escaped slavery in Kentucky around the same time as Emeline and published accounts telling of their daring escapes.[10] These narratives were intended to support the cause of abolition and to sustain these men and their families in freedom.

Emeline did not write about her escape; she did not go to the papers in search of Julia. She kept her head down and blended in, quietly protecting the freedom she had seized for herself and no doubt hoping to see Julia again.

Without a published narrative, we are left to imagine Emeline's journey north, how she avoided those who would try to betray her. Battle Creek resident Perry Sanford recalled how it took him and the group of enslaved people from Kenton County six hours to get to Covington, as they traveled across fields to avoid the roads. Then, after a week of waiting in Cincinnati safe houses, they began making their way across Ohio. Traveling only by night, armed with a club and pocketknives, they crossed into Michigan one month later. Sanford described the midwestern prairies they crossed as teeming with slave catchers and related his narrow escape from a party of forty of them who raided a Quaker community southwest of Battle Creek. It was several more weeks before Sanford made it to Battle Creek, but they were not safe there. "We were in a constant state of alarm," he recalled, "and when the fugitive slave law was passed, every colored person left Battle Creek for Canada except for Wm. Casey and myself."[11] Having survived that perilous journey, Emeline kept her ear to the grapevine for any news that her master, John R. Stephens, was sending someone for her—or if his daughter Catherine was.

However Emeline may have planned to escape, it most certainly did not happen as reported: "One pleasant day in May, Emeline, then past her sixteenth birthday, resolved that she would never live in slavery and decided then and there to leave the plantation and make her way to freedom in the north."[12] What did it mean that she resolved never to live in slavery? Emeline understood her condition well, knew the power wielded over her by John Stephens and, by proxy, his married daughter Catherine and her husband, Jesse Petty, whom she was sent to live with. She was well aware of how vulnerable she was to sexual abuse, by John, Jesse, or really anyone—particularly once separated from Julia. No mention was ever made of her parents, but it may be meaningful that the reporter described Julia as her half sister.[13] Census records indicate that Julia, who was older than Emeline, was light-skinned, which could have been merely a matter of perception or could indicate that her father was a white man, perhaps her enslaver.[14] What lay ahead for sixteen-year-old Emeline may have been the sexual abuse her mother had experienced.

Julia and Emeline kept the details about their early lives to themselves. We cannot recover what it meant to them that they were half sisters, or even if this was a term that they used to talk about one another. When members of Freedom Generation placed Information Wanted ads looking for half siblings, sometimes the terms "half sister" or "half brother" implied a hierarchy, as when Abram White wrote looking for his sister and others who were "only half brothers."[15] But using "half" also helped brothers and sisters who were trying to be accurate. That these fractions appeared so regularly in advertisements is a reminder of the multiple dislocations that were common in the Second Middle Passage. Take for instance Sarah Ann Lewis, who was eleven when she was sold from Maryland to Tennessee and then to Missouri and finally to Texas. She placed one ad looking for a sister, three half sisters, and two brothers, in that order.[16] Julia and Emeline likely shared a mother but had different fathers. When white men raped enslaved women, they asserted the same prerogatives as they did when they sold women's children, to make and unmake enslaved people's families as they saw fit. We don't know for sure what made them "half sisters," but when she turned sixteen, Emeline devised a plan to protect herself from whatever she feared was coming next.

Emeline may have decided to leave around the time Jesse Petty died. In the settling of accounts after an enslaver's death, enslaved people's families were often broken up and sold away. That did not happen after Petty's death, for his will stipulated that his slaves would be freed. "It is my true intention to Emancipate my slaves" and "to bequeath until all of them at my death there [*sic*] immediate freedom." To be sure there was no mistaking his intentions, Petty listed all eight of them by name; they included "Henney, Henson, Fortunatus, Alfred, Alexander, Eliza, Seleney [*sic*], and Tory [or Toby?]." To Henney, Petty also gave land and a cow.[17] As to those enslaved people belonging to Catherine, including Emeline, Petty's will was silent—likely because Catherine retained her rights to them as part of her dowry.[18] If this was the case, then, while the other enslaved people in the household were given their "immediate freedom," Emeline was not. The news must have been crushing. It's not hard to imagine how sixteen-year-old Emeline might have taken it, how she might have "resolved" to right the wrong done to her by taking freedom for herself.[19]

The Last Seen Collection includes seventy advertisements describing enslaved people's flights to freedom, all of them resulting in separations from family members. Before emancipation, the pages of white papers everywhere, even in states where slavery had been outlawed, carried ads aimed at recapturing people; these were very different public announcements. The enslavers who placed "Runaway Slave" advertisements spared no expense to offer rewards for the return of their "property." Enslavers often knew where these people went. When a man named Burwell escaped, his enslaver suspected he was "lurking about the plantation of Gen. Robt. Haywood . . . as I purchased him of his brother." "I suspect she is about Newbern, among her relations," an enslaver wrote about a woman named Carry who absconded with her baby. From Tennessee, an enslaver wrote, "I expect that he started to Richmond, Va., where he was raised," when fourteen- or fifteen-year-old Littleton escaped to be with his mother. When young people ran away, enslavers expected that they were trying to get to a parent, sibling, or another kin relation, because they often were.[20] When Emeline ran away, her enslaver, Catherine Petty, may have "suspected" that she was headed to Julia, a couple of miles away; if she did, she was wrong. Emeline did not run to her sister—she did not "lay out" nearby or "lurk around," as young people often did—because none of those things were freedom.

Only three Information Wanted advertisements taken out by self-emancipated people have been identified in newspapers before the Civil War; all of them sought family members who were already free or presumed to be.[21] Each ad documents the assistance of a community of Black and white abolitionists in the U.S. and Canada; these people were crucial allies for freedom seekers who were still in danger of re-enslavement. William Robinson placed an advertisement in William Lloyd Garrison's paper, *The Liberator*, looking for his brother who had escaped to Philadelphia. John Murry placed one from Canada West (Ontario) looking for his father, who had escaped to Canada twenty years earlier. Ellen Nettleton also wrote from Canada looking for her husband and children from whom she had been separated while they were all escaping "at one of the Stations west of Hamilton."[22] Of the tens of thousands of enslaved people who escaped, it is impossible to know how many made it to freedom, but that so few of them went to the papers to search for their loved ones underscores how dangerous it was for them to take their search for family public as long as slavery was legal anywhere.[23]

✦

When Emeline arrived in Battle Creek in 1845, the settlement was not quite a decade old; whites numbered perhaps a thousand.[24] The federal government's attempts to "remove" the Potawatomi and Ottawa people who lived in the Kalamazoo River watershed had largely failed, and white people and Indigenous people continued to live in close and at times tense proximity to one another.[25] The first white entrepreneurs built flour mills and woolen factories powered by water running through a man-made canal connecting the Kalamazoo River to a little stream called Battle Creek. The earliest freedom seekers traveled back and forth across the Canadian border, returning to the U.S. to pick up word about still enslaved family members; they settled in clusters close to the border and served as "beacons for slaves contemplating flight."[26] The small refugee community in Calhoun County, home to Battle Creek, was made up of people determined to get their family and friends out of the South.[27] White Quaker Erastus Hussey parked a wagon outside of his store that he used to smuggle freedom-seeking people to the next stop on the Underground Railroad.

Emeline married Joseph in Battle Creek soon after she met him, trading the simple surname Hall for Skipworth, which seems never to have been spelled the same way twice. They had two girls in about as many years. As she watched her daughters grow, Emeline may have thought about the sister she had left behind. Her daughters were born in a free state and in a town settled by people who were hostile to slavery. But any comfort she took in those facts was tempered by the persistent claims made by enslavers who regularly rode into the state seizing freedom seekers and dragging them back into slavery.

Joseph survived such a raid southwest of Battle Creek, where he, Perry Sanford, and a group of Black residents were ambushed and seized by Kentucky enslavers. They narrowly escaped with the help of white Quakers and reached Battle Creek. In 1847, the year Emeline's daughter Aurena was born, white residents of a town around seventeen miles east of Battle Creek prevented bounty hunters from seizing a family of freedom seekers. Later that same year, a Detroit crowd broke into a jail and released a man who was being held while his Missouri enslaver awaited court authorization to claim him as his property.[28]

A year after Emeline's daughter Rebecca was born, white men in Washington, D.C., passed the Fugitive Slave Law, emboldening enslavers to continue raiding Black communities like those in southern Michigan and making it a federal crime for anyone to stand in their way. It must have crossed their parents' minds that the girls weren't safe there: if Petty came for Emeline, she could have claimed the girls as her property, too. "[W]hen the fugitive slave law was passed," Perry Sanford recalled, "every colored person left Battle Creek for Canada."[29] Among them were Emeline, Joseph, and their two young daughters; the couple stayed in Canada long enough for Emeline to give birth to a boy she named after her husband. They returned to Battle Creek soon after, this time for good. Joseph surely hoped to own property, land that would support his family. At thirty-seven, he may have also been done running.

Petty did not come for Emeline. Neither did whoever once claimed Joseph as their property. Aurena and Rebecca grew up in the small Black community of Battle Creek. In 1860, the Black residents of Calhoun County numbered 376, more than three times as many as the previous decade but still only a tiny fraction of the population.[30] They were big enough, though, to sustain two Black churches, Second Baptist on Michigan Avenue and Mt. Zion African Methodist Episcopal (AME) Church on Champion Street, just about a half mile and a mile, respectively, from the Skipworths' Pittee Street home. Mt. Zion AME was founded by families of freedom seekers.[31] Fellowship with this community brought them in contact with others who'd left people behind as they made their way to freedom.

The girls attended school, perhaps in the home of one of their Black neighbors; the town's public schools were more than five miles away from their home north of the creek, too far for them to walk.[32] Joseph and Emeline opened the doors of their home to various Black Kentuckians from whom Emeline might have heard news of Julia and her children. Through Mt. Zion, Emeline came across the *Christian Recorder*, which by the 1870s and '80s carried their regular column of advertisements from people hoping to find loved ones. She listened as the pastor read the ads aloud. Perhaps after all those years, Emeline still did not want to put her name in the paper.

Among Battle Creek's new residents in 1860 was a woman famous in northern antislavery circles, Sojourner Truth. Born enslaved, Isabella Baumfree was freed decades earlier via New York State law; she changed her name to Truth, traveled the North on behalf of the American Anti-Slavery Society, and attended women's rights conventions. With the help of antislavery allies, Truth came to Michigan and settled in Battle Creek. She lived there with her two adult daughters and grandson, Sam, who also attended school. Truth transfixed audiences, relaying her own experiences of slavery and entreating listeners to act to end it. Her fame grew during the Civil War, when Harriet Beecher Stowe published an essay about her in the *Atlantic*. She met President Lincoln, although an eyewitness reported that the president did not treat her with the respect her reputation should have elicited. After the war, tourists who came to visit Truth at her Battle Creek home were impressed by her still powerful voice and clear mind, but her health declined. Despite the help of her well-connected friends, she and her family lived in poverty and died that way in the town that had been settled by the friends of freedom. No one knew for sure how old Truth was. Local papers claimed she lived to be 108; she was likely around eighty-six.[33]

Emeline was fifty-four in 1883 when Sojourner Truth died. Visitors streamed into town to pay their respects, and the pews of the elite Congregationalist Church were filled for the funeral service. "Hardly a person in the history of the country," declared the local paper about the significance of the moment, "is more universally well known and her death will be greatly regretted by them."[34] Local accounts of the funeral painted a picture of the white racial conciliation that had transpired there since its Underground Railroad days, when white and Black activists had driven slave catchers out of town and then watched as their own neighbors burned down the offices of their antislavery newspaper. Inside the church, whites gathered to mourn Truth. Outside, "a concourse of people, composed of all classes and creeds" waited to file past the open casket that was placed in the vestibule. The death of Battle Creek's most celebrated former slave did not elicit public reflection on the community of ex-slaves who worked in mills and foundries and in the homes of "some of the more prominent citizens" and who jockeyed for positions as pallbearers at the funeral.[35]

Emeline may have been among the crowd who waited to file past Truth's casket. If she was, she would have been struck by the contrast between that funeral and the one for her husband. Joseph had died two years earlier and like Truth was buried at Oak Hill Cemetery. There is no record of who attended. Joseph was likely in his late sixties or early seventies, although the county death record says he was eighty-two.[36] After he escaped from slavery in Tennessee, Joseph had stayed in Michigan; there he helped to transport other freedom seekers to safety. Joseph had worked as a gardener. He'd managed to acquire a little property in Battle Creek but didn't earn enough to buy the home he and Emeline lived in on Pittee Street. Joseph and Emeline raised their children in a city that, after emancipation, moved rapidly to embrace legal equality. West of Battle Creek, in Cass County, Black men became landowners and acted as a powerful voting bloc in local elections. Lawmakers integrated public schools, extended the franchise to Black men, and legalized interracial marriage. Just a few years after Joseph died, the state guaranteed Black Michiganders equal access to restaurants, theaters, and other establishments. Emeline and Joseph navigated their lives together in relative safety, free from the racial pogroms members of Freedom Generation faced elsewhere.[37]

Access to the ballot did not translate into representation. William Webb Ferguson was the first Black man elected to the Michigan statehouse in 1893, and it wasn't until 1955 that voters in the state elected a Black congressman.[38] There never was a reckoning with the territory's early tolerance for slaveholding, laws restricting Black migration, and the discrimination that kept formerly enslaved people locked in the most menial jobs. When Joseph died, his widow struggled to pay the rent on the house on Pittee Street with the money she made as a laundress.[39] Emeline could not afford to buy a headstone for his grave; her daughter Carrie's grave also remains unmarked. Emeline was among the town's "most respected colored ladies," but respectability had not made it possible for the Skipworths to acquire wealth that might have become intergenerational. In Battle Creek they had found a safe haven and a community of sympathetic whites for whom they worked and who accepted them because they were not aspirational.

Sojourner Truth's daughters also worked in white women's homes, perhaps some of the same ones who hired Emeline. Maybe Emeline crossed paths with them when she delivered baskets of clean laundry. At age fifty-six, as she sat next to her sister Julia, her hands folded in her lap, cracked and dry from handling sodden towels and sheets in another cold Michigan winter, Emeline broke her silence and told the white reporter about what it had meant to lose a sister.

Emeline's life was punctuated by losses. She had lost Julia and her mother. Then there was the child born in Canada, named Joseph for his father, who died sometime before he turned thirteen. Joseph and Emeline's daughter Carrie was fifteen years old in 1880 when she died of typhoid fever. White people came to Battle Creek's famous sanitarium to get their health back, while Black children died from drinking contaminated water.

But Emeline also experienced joy. Frances was born the first year of the Civil War, and Jennie arrived three years later. Her girls attended school, and Aurena, Rebecca, and Frances—people called her Franc, for short—survived to adulthood. All three married men in Battle Creek, settled there, near their mother, and started families of their own.[40] After Joseph died, their presence was a comfort she did not take for granted. Emeline had arrived alone in Battle Creek, but she never was alone after that. The community of migrants around her grew, and together they built and sustained churches and schools and explained to their children how they came to be in a place so far from where they were brought up and what it took for them to get there. Frances was having dinner with her mother—perhaps Aurena or Rebecca was there, too, maybe Rebecca's daughters Luttie and Carrie—when Emeline rushed out of the house and into the arms of her sister, Julia.

JULIA VICKERS

Battle Creek's *Sunday Morning Call* broke the story on December 14, 1884, that Emeline had received a letter from her sister. "About thirty-five years ago a young slave woman made her escape from Kentucky across the river to Cincinnati," the *Call* recounted, "where she found friends of freedom, agents of the underground railroad, who passed her from station to station until she reached Battle Creek." The paper mentioned her only once by her last name: "The lady referred to is Mrs. Skiperth, one of our esteemed colored ladies, residing at No. 3 Pittee street." Julia was unnamed. "She left behind her an only sister of whom there has been no tidings in all these years, until a few days ago a letter was received from her." The two planned to meet at Christmas. As would the *Inter Ocean* the following year, the *Call* found the story compelling, in particular for how it allowed readers to appreciate "the great changes in this country within a few years" and the part that the "friends of freedom" had played in those changes, which likely meant emancipation.[41] There was little detail about Emeline, her escape from slavery, and her life afterward, other than that she was a wife, now a widow, and mother, and that she was "esteemed," something that the paper said twice.

Surely Julia's letter included details about Emeline that only her sister could know; perhaps it named their mother. Julia filled it with clues. She listed her various surnames, perhaps also referring to her sister as Emeline Hall. How did one find a sister who in her lifetime was assigned various names by enslavers, called herself a name of her own choosing—perhaps something that connected her to her ancestors—and then by convention changed her name each time she married? More particularly, how did one find a sister who was so adept at *not* being found? John Stephens and his daughter Catherine Petty may have tried, but it was Julia who found Emeline.

In 1850, a few years after Emeline escaped, when John Stephens wrote his will freeing his enslaved people at his death, he reported to the census enumerator that Emeline was a "fugitive from the state." She was in good company: Kentucky census records showed there were ninety-five more just like her that year.[42] Stephens died seven years later, freeing Julia and her children. "The other sister, now Mrs. Julia Lyon, of Troy, Ohio," the reporter from Battle Creek explained, "lived with her master until his death, which occurred 28 years ago the 26th of last April, when she and her four children and her uncle were given their freedom, by his will."[43] Julia was thirty-five; the names and ages of all but one of these children have been lost. The oldest, Henry Vickers, was sixteen, the same age as Emeline when she made her escape.

Julia married Isaiah Lyons, a free man and Ohio native, two years after she left Kentucky with her freedom papers.[44] She had had four children with her first husband, Samuel Vickers, before he left them. Julia and Isaiah's son Walter was her first child born free; he was followed by Arthur in 1862 and Eliza in 1865. All these Ohio-born children attended school where they learned to read and write. Julia's older children, Henry and Harriet, who was born after Stephens wrote his will, came with her from Kentucky, and together they built a family in Troy, Ohio. After Isaiah died, Julia's older children helped support her and the younger one.[45] Julia worked as a laundress, like her sister. Harriet worked as a domestic.

Alongside other men from Troy, Henry had served with the 5th United States Colored Troops at the siege of Petersburg in the fall of 1864. Then, like Private George Tibbs, Henry was deployed to North Carolina, where he helped defeat the Confederate Army at Fort Fisher. He got sick there, too, and was hospitalized; he suffered from a cough and intestinal problems long after his enlistment. "We charged through water waist deep and got very wet," a Troy neighbor and fellow veteran of the 5th explained to the pension agent to whom Henry applied for an increase to his pension, "and remained in wet clothes all night and then and there is where Henry Vickers took a bad cold."[46] (His request was denied.) Henry never married; the $8 a month he received from the government helped provide for his mother and her younger children—Henry's half brothers and sister.

Like her sister, Julia and her family became part of a community of freedom seekers and free Blacks; the Black community in Troy, though, was more than two times the size of the one in Battle Creek.[47] Julia drew support from that community, where Isaiah's brother lived and others who knew her from when she had first arrived there from Kentucky. More refugees from slavery arrived during the war, bringing with them stories similar to those that Julia shared with her children, about how she managed to hold on to Harriet and Henry and about how she'd lost others, including her sister, Emeline.

People in Troy, as in communities everywhere, wrote to the papers looking for the families they had lost in slavery. Elizabeth Smith wrote to the *Christian Recorder* looking for her sister and others she had last seen in Mississippi; she had been able to track some to Alabama and included their married names in the ad. Anna Cox wrote to the *Southwest Christian Advocate* in September 1884 to say that she had received a letter from her sisters in Georgia, where they had all been enslaved. Her sisters wrote to tell her that they'd heard that their brother, Thomas Henry Burrah, was a Methodist preacher in Alabama. Anna hoped someone reading the paper could help her to find him. George Green received a letter from his son Sam in Illinois. He had found and brought two of his other children to Troy from Tennessee and hoped to bring Sam along, too.[48] Similarly, Julia Lyons was looking for her sister, Emeline, hoping to share in Anna Cox's and George Green's great good fortune by receiving a letter of her own.

And she did.

The story of the sisters' reunion is remarkable. Even with the help of digitized records, it is difficult to find records for either of them today. Emeline's married name appears in records with at least six different spellings: "Skipworth" and "Skippworth" (census); "Skiperth" (city directories); and in the newspapers as "Skiperth," "Skipwerth," "Skipwarth," and "Skipmarth." If Emeline placed an advertisement looking for Julia, we have not yet found it, nor have we found one from Julia. Enslaver John Stephens had called Julia "Judy." She took the name Vickers in 1840, when a "colored preacher" married her to Samuel Vickers, a free man. Her "true name," she said years later to the pension agent, was Julia Vickers.[49] Or at least it was until she married Isaiah and became Julia Lyons. Sometimes the papers left off the *s*. Yet, despite marriages and remarriages and moves for both sisters, Julia found Emeline.

It was likely Julia's son Walter who tipped off his mother that there was a woman in Battle Creek who might be Emeline. "A year ago she [Julia] was visiting a son in Detroit and there, by mere chance," the paper in Battle Creek said, "learned that her sister was living in Battle Creek. They had not heard a word from one another in forty years." Walter, now in his twenties, toured the Midwest performing as a vaudeville comedian.[50] Raised on his mother's stories about a sister who had freed herself, Walter could have picked up Emeline's trail while on the road. Julia wrote to Emeline in Battle Creek, and by Christmas 1884, nearly forty years after they had last seen one another, Julia and Emeline prepared to meet again. Julia may have been inspired by those in the Black community of Troy who wrote letters looking for family. And when it came time for her to make the two-hundred-mile trip to Battle Creek, Julia may have turned to them for help raising money to pay her train fare and for a seat on the omnibus that took her to her sister's door on Pittee Street. It takes little effort to imagine Emeline's joy in receiving Julia's letter, and the reply Emeline wrote Julia. How that joy must have been shared by their children who had helped make their reunion possible.

Yet, all these details are missing in the white newspaper coverage of Emeline and Julia.

REUNION NEWS

It was November 1885, a year after they began exchanging letters, that the sisters reunited. Perhaps the delay was due to the fact that Julia had been reported to be living in Detroit—not two hundred miles away, in Troy, Ohio. A long trip like that took time and money, things that Julia Lyons, a sixty-seven-year-old widowed washerwoman, would have little of. This was not a meeting of two "well to do" old widows, as the paper reported it, but Julia and Emeline's reunion that fall day in Battle Creek, after all of those years, was "joyous." The *Sunday Morning Call* captured some of what the two women felt. "Mrs. Lyon rode up to her sister's house, on Pittee Street, Tuesday afternoon, in the bus. Mrs. Skipwerth and family were at dinner. When she espied her sister, although she has been sick for several weeks, she sprang to the door and outran the remainder of the family to the bus, where the sisters embraced one another for the first time in forty-one years."[51]

Surely over the year, as they exchanged letters, the two had imagined what it would be like to see each other again. Emeline must have been transported back to the time when she and Julia were young, when they had been enslaved in Kentucky. And here they were, two sisters separated in slavery together again, after forty years.

The two women obliged the *Sunday Morning Call* reporter with the details about Emeline's escape from slavery and how Julia "remained on the old plantation" after her master died before she "removed to Ohio." They revealed no other personal details. Nothing was said about how they had searched for one another. The reporter wrote that each assumed the other was dead, until by chance they learned differently. But that wasn't true. Some of the other reporting wasn't true either, or they told him what they thought he wanted to hear.

In fact, this newspaper story wasn't about slavery's survivors. It was about the town of Battle Creek, Michigan, the antislavery legacy that was built there, and what one historian has called a "yearning to bask in the moral glow of the old abolitionist generation."[52] White newspapers throughout the country published reunion stories that made slavery seem like a problem that was solved long ago. Underground Railroad nostalgia stories were the Midwest's unique contribution to the Lost Cause project, and from Illinois, Indiana, Ohio, and Michigan came stories of white ancestors who helped slaves escape and who had stood up and bludgeoned "the problem of slavery out of history."[53] These stories served the same purpose as the monuments to enslavers appearing along the streets of cities on the East Coast and the flags recalling the Confederacy that would soon fly over southern capitol buildings. They represented a refusal to face slavery's long aftermath.

✦

To be sure, the aging veterans of Battle Creek's antislavery community, those who had helped Emeline and many others to escape, earned the right to some self-congratulation. A few months before the story of the reunion ran in the local paper, residents held a celebration marking the fiftieth anniversary of British West Indian emancipation (August 1, 1834), an occasion to revisit the town's antislavery history and to recall how it had once been a haven for fugitive slaves. Frederick Douglass spoke to the crowd, a fitting choice, as he himself had escaped slavery nearly fifty years earlier. Among the local heroes recognized that day was eighty-three-year-old Erastus Hussey.

For fifteen years, Hussey ferried freedom seekers from Battle Creek on a circuitous route to Canada. "[Z]igzag was one of the regular devices to blind and throw off pursuit. It served moreover to avoid unfriendly localities," Wilbur Siebert, the first historian of the Underground Railroad, wrote of the escape routes that went through Battle Creek, "for slave-owners and their agents were often known to be on the lookout."[54] His history was about white men like Erastus Hussey who had worked the railroad's various stations.[55] Siebert omitted reference to the underground's more numerous and significant Black "agents," enslaved and freed people like Joseph Skipworth, a refugee from slavery in Tennessee, who helped Emeline. Hussey featured prominently in the local news story about Julia and Emeline's reunion. "She heard at every place," it said of Emeline's escape, "of Erastus Hussey at Battle Creek." Stories like hers helped put Battle Creek on the map and to ensure Hussey's place in Siebert's history.

On two occasions, the paper interviewed former freedom seekers who remained residents of the town, Perry Sanford and Emeline. In both cases, the reporter steered the story to a happy ending. "Did you ever expect to live to see the slaves emancipated?" the reporter asked Sanford, to which he obliged with "No. I could not believe such a thing possible. The Quakers had great faith in a time coming when slavery would be abolished, and always told us so, but I could not realize or imagine a thing. But, thank God, it is now a reality."[56] Sanford did not mention the family and kin he had left behind, or those details did not make it into the story.[57] Slavery appears as a quaint bit of nostalgia. "The sisters have been busy recalling old plantation times," read the closing lines of the article about Emeline and Julia, "and reflecting on the great changes that have since taken place. Verily, 'truth is stranger than fiction.'" Among the residents of Battle Creek were people for whom slavery was not a distant memory but as close as the sister or brother they still hoped to find.

◆

Emeline died sixteen months after she rushed into Julia's arms for the first time in forty years. She had been ill for some time before her sister's visit. In her final years, Emeline enjoyed the company of her daughters and granddaughters, surely taking comfort in how her courage had made possible a life for them that she had not had. Family and friends gathered for her funeral at Second Baptist, half a mile from her house; Emeline was buried at Oak Hill Cemetery next to Joseph and Carrie.[58] Visitors can easily find the well-marked graves of Sojourner Truth, cereal magnates C. W. Post and William Keith Kellogg, and James and Ellen

White, founders of the Seventh-day Adventist Church, located near the entrance. But, except for Emeline's daughter Rebecca, the Skipworth graves are unmarked, because even after forty years of working for the town's white elite, Joseph and Emeline had been unable to put away the money for headstones. Battle Creek's "leading citizens" for whom Emeline had washed clothes—those who celebrated their antislavery ancestors, mourned the death of Sojourner Truth, and rushed to witness Emeline and Julia's reunion—did not think to buy a stone for her grave.

At seventy-three, Julia applied for a mother's pension after her son Henry died. When her application was rejected, she spent three years appealing the decision, calling on friends and neighbors in Troy to file affidavits confirming the deaths of both of her husbands and assurances that she was dependent on Henry. Julia Lyons died never having received the pension to which she was entitled.[59] These details were lost on the reporter who described Julia as "well to do."[60] But Emeline and Julia knew how they got together, who had helped make it possible, and how they had never stopped hoping that they might someday see each other again.

CHAPTER EIGHT

Henry Saffold's Chain of Evidence

> Henry Saffold, formerly of Company E. 135 Regiment U. S. C. T. is applying for a pension and needs identification. He is now residing at Penfield, Ga. He knows the following men and would like to hear from them: Joshua Hull, Thomas Smith, Jasper Hayes, Osborne Boler, Sam Eungin, Raif Strainer, Harrison Strain.

Savannah Tribune (Savannah, GA), November 17 and 24, 1888

Other than his wife, Dinah, Henry Saffold did not have any family to turn to for help in 1886 when he applied for a federal pension. Even if he had, they would not have been able to furnish the information he needed, evidence that the disability he suffered resulted from his service in the U.S. Army. Dinah described his symptoms and told the agents that, since he returned from the war, he had often been unable to work. Everyone who knew Henry or who was familiar with his case knew the pensioner was not well. But only old soldiers could help him to build a chain of evidence linking the swelling of his hands and arms to the weeks he had spent in the winter of 1865 building roads in the swamps between Savannah and Charleston.

The roads Henry Saffold and others built carried the men and matériel of U.S. general William Tecumseh Sherman's armies from Georgia into South Carolina in January—and through the Carolinas that spring—in what turned out to be the final months of the Civil War. Heavy rains caused South Carolina's Salkehatchie and Coosawhatchie Rivers to overflow their banks, turning the land in between into a swamp more than a mile wide and twenty feet deep in some places and washing away bridges and roads. Sherman sent Black men into the swamp to repair the roads and bridges so that he could continue his advance to Columbia. Henry Saffold was among these men who remained out in front of Sherman's armies as they made their way through South and North Carolina. When he was finally enlisted into Company E of the 135th United States Colored Troops at the end of March in North Carolina, Saffold had been with the army for four months, and as part of the pioneer corps, he'd helped to build more than four hundred miles of roads.[1]

By then, Henry was sick. "While in the swamps of South Carolina I was poisoned by some kind of vine that disable me ever since," he explained. "My arms and hands swell up and bleed until I am a misery to myself." Saffold struggled with his condition for the rest of his enlistment as well as after he mustered out. The agent sent to investigate Henry's claim was not convinced. "The trouble seems to be that I can not establish a chain of evidence by Physicians of my condition ever since surrender," Henry explained, "and that I can not establish the fact by a commission officer of my regiment or company that I contracted this poison while in service."[2]

When the medical records office failed him, Henry wrote to newspapers for help. "I wish to get the name and postoffice address of any officer or man of Company E, 135th Regiment colored troops," read the brief advertisement he posted in the August 4 and 5, 1888, issues of the Savannah *Morning News*. "Any person who served with that company will confer a favor on an old fellow soldier who is trying to get a pension."[3] A few months later, Henry's search appeared in the Black-owned newspaper the *Savannah Tribune*; in it he named some of the men he was looking for. The notice appeared in two consecutive issues of the weekly, November 17 and 24, 1888.[4]

His ads were successful. Henry found a number of men to step forward for him, comrades and white officers who served as links in a chain of evidence that was otherwise missing from the records of his enlistment. With their help, he secured a pension of $8 a month, which eventually increased to $10.

Tens of thousands of USCT veterans like Saffold faced the challenges of growing old in bodies that had suffered both the unique injuries and illnesses related to their military service as well as the debilitating effects of slavery. Federal pensions could make the difference for veterans who started their lives as free people with nothing—no savings, no inherited wealth, and no compensation for years of hard labor done in slavery. Black veterans struggled to meet the burden of proof, which included tracking down evidence of one's enlistment, discharge, and disability, among other things. Many could not read or write, nor pay for the required medical examinations or for lawyers to prepare the paperwork. And there were opportunists everywhere looking to take advantage of them. Going to the newspapers allowed veterans and their widows to cut out the middlemen and to steer clear of people who would steal their pension checks.

The Last Seen Collection includes 146 advertisements placed by and about Black veterans; fifty-five specifically mention pensions. Women placed fifteen of the latter; most of them were widows looking for information about their deceased husbands' enlistments. The rest were taken out by veterans looking for one another. Black veterans advertised for reasons other than help with their pensions—companionship, for instance, or simply to find out how their friends and fellow old soldiers were coming along. They turned to the papers because they did not have veterans' organizations to help them; the large community of newspaper readers included Black and white veterans whom they had once trusted with their lives and who could perhaps help them recall details and provide documentation.

These veterans acted with a different urgency than did those who used ads in their search for family; they did not rush to the papers in the immediate aftermath of the war. The pace of these advertisements picked up late in the century as surviving veterans responded to expanding pension eligibility, their advancing age compounded the effects of other chronic conditions, and the federal abandonment of civil rights protections restricted their access to other government entitlements.[5] Black veterans like Henry Saffold called on each other to provide proof that they were who they said they were and that they deserved the government's support. Their advertisements help us see the bonds that had developed between the men during their service, and why veterans hoped those bonds could now help sustain them in their old age.

✦

For twenty-five years, Henry Safford fought with agents of the U.S. Pension Bureau, filing repeated claims and sitting for depositions. He could not read the claims form, but others had read it to him, and he'd answered the same set of questions so many times that he was ready with answers. Each time, he said things a little differently than the last.

"Do not know the exact date when I was born nor the year," he insisted in 1905, "as I was a poor ignorant slave and could not keep any records." The year before he'd said it this way on the same form: "At the time of my birth, I was a slave. My old master and his wife are both dead and their family Bible and History cannot be found. My father and mother are also both dead and as they could not read nor write, they had no record of my birth."[6] After decades of dealing with the bureau, Henry Saffold knew the importance that white men placed on written records, and he tried to explain why could not provide them.

Henry was born in Georgia, around 1835 or 1836. By then, white men had been driving coffles of enslaved people from Virginia and Maryland into Georgia for years. "Georgia men" is what enslaved people called those who bought and sold them. Among them may have been Henry's parents. Historians have documented two million transactions made through the Second Middle Passage through bills of sale, auction broadsides, ship manifests, and insurance claims. These records are full of names but not of enslaved people.

Henry recalled how he had changed hands among these Georgia men. "I once was a slave of a man by the name of Nelson and I am sometimes called Henry Nelson." But, he assured pension agents, "I will also state that my right name is Henry Saffold."[7] Thomas Saffold, the last man to own Henry as chattel, was a lawyer and circuit court judge who produced mountains of records about the land he owned in Morgan and Greene Counties and the slave-owning defendants he represented in property disputes. But of the ninety-five people who picked cotton in his fields, we can learn very little.[8] Among them were mothers and children, wives and husbands, *families*. Henry Saffold was among them; perhaps, at one time, his mother and father had been, too. Thomas Saffold may have addressed his slaves as "family," and that's why Henry wondered about the family Bible. But every one of the people Thomas Saffold owned knew he was not family.

Dinah and Henry married sometime around 1860. She already had two children by then, a six-year-old daughter, Catherine, and two-year-old son, Daniel. Both of them went by the last name Reid, as did Dinah sometimes. She had likely come to the Saffold property in Buckhead when Thomas Saffold married his second wife, Sarah Reid. Dinah and her children may have been part of Sarah's dowry, a gift to sweeten the deal for a potential suitor like Thomas.[9] The legal details of that exchange of "property" were recorded and filed with the state, as was their marriage. But no record was ever made of Dinah and Henry's marriage.

Dinah and Henry's family grew to include at least two other children whose birth parents remain a mystery: Elizabeth was the same age as Dinah's daughter Catherine, and Celianne was born in 1860, the same year that Henry and Dinah were married.[10] Throughout their marriage, Dinah and Henry made and remade their family to include children and grandchildren, orphans and adoptees, as the need arose. This adaptability and improvisation ensured the children's survival in slavery and during the Civil War, and it was a hallmark of the families Freedom Generation sought to rebuild afterward. When the war began, Dinah and Henry and the children had not been a family for long. The war would test the ties that bound them.

✦

Georgia slaveholders did not rush to secede in the immediate aftermath of Lincoln's election victory despite the dire warnings of some. Governor Joseph Brown warned in November 1860 that, unless they moved quickly, the Republicans would "corrupt our slaves, and engender discontent among them" in order to start "a war of extermination between the white and black races." Others were concerned that secession would *bring* the destruction that the governor warned of, rather than prevent it. Thomas Saffold was among the latter, at least at first. But when white men in Morgan County elected the judge to represent them at the secession convention in January 1861, he voted to secede. The secession order Thomas and the other delegates signed spoke of the men's desire to protect their property in enslaved people and "our wives, and our children . . . our homes, our altars and our firesides" from destruction.[11] Thomas would later insist that he was a Unionist, that he deserved special consideration from the U.S. government because of his loyalty, but it's hard to reconcile that story with the evidence. When the war that began that April came to Georgia three and a half years later, it exceeded the worst fears of those who had been eager to bring it on, and also men like Thomas Saffold.

Thomas joined the Georgia State Guard, later he would say out of "necessity," and when Sherman's armies swept through Morgan County in the fall of 1864, his wife, Sarah, was the one who managed the disintegration of slavery on their Buckhead plantation.[12]

Sherman and his men occupied Atlanta on September 1, 1864. As they prepared to leave the city two months later, the general ordered his men to burn everything of military significance. The fire spread around the city, burning private homes in nearby neighborhoods. When it was over, much of Atlanta lay in ruins.[13] Sherman's sixty thousand troops set out across the state in two columns with orders to eliminate resistance and make civilians feel the sting of war. The fast-moving army brought opportunities for self-emancipation to enslaved people from one end of the state to the other.[14] Slaves fled plantations when the army moved through. Some headed to Atlanta, others went looking for family members, and thousands followed the army hoping that Sherman's men would protect them from whatever lay beyond the plantation.[15] Anticipating this, the general instructed his commanding officers that "Negroes who are able-bodied and can be of service to the several columns may be taken along, but," he added, in a statement that left room for a great deal of discretion, "each army commander will bear in mind that the question of supplies is a very important one, and that his first duty is to see to those who bear arms."[16]

Although freedwomen repeatedly provided crucial intelligence for the federal army and even bore arms in Georgia as elsewhere, the reference to "able-bodied" freed people signaled that it was only the men who would be taken along.[17] Sherman insisted that women, children, and the elderly would slow the progress of the army, that they could not feed or care for these people. The decision made tactical sense, but the effect was the separation of Black families. Once Henry Saffold was identified as "able-bodied," his fate and Dinah's and the children's diverged. With no documents proving their marriage or the status of their children, no chains of evidence connecting them to one another, Henry and Dinah, like so many other mothers, fathers, husbands, wives, and children, were uprooted and sent away, often in opposite directions.

Thousands of men who presented themselves to Sherman's soldiers learned the hard way that to be taken, or even to go willingly, was not the same as enlisting. Before he began his Georgia campaign, Sherman forbade officers from enlisting Black Georgians because, as he said, he did not want to offend whites in the state who might be loyal to the Union.[18] This decision went against what had been established policy in the U.S. Army for more than a year—that is, that Black men were to be enlisted into the ranks, organized into segregated units, and led by white officers. It also cleared the way for Sherman to make use of the labor of Black men however he saw fit. The general ordered his officers to organize "a good pioneer battalion for each army corps, composed if possible of negroes" who would build roads and bridges to carry army wagons filled with all of the supplies necessary to fight a mobile war inside enemy territory.[19]

Sometime that November, Henry Saffold left Buckhead with the U.S. Army destined for a pioneer battalion. He may have not gone willingly, or else he came to regret the terms under which he had agreed to go. I was "forced with others to go with the Army to cut roads for the Army" is how he recalled it. "(I did not however object to go as a regular soldier.)"[20] He was not alone. Reports circulated of men and boys being snatched from their beds and dragged away by Sherman's men.

Most of these stories come from the pens of white women who, years later, fancied themselves the brave protectors of their enslaved people. Twenty miles west of Buckhead, Dolly Lunt Burge wrote about how she stood up to the Yankee "demons" who "were forcing my boys from home at the point of the bayonet."[21] Sarah Saffold's white descendants tell a similar story about how Sarah—tiny, red-haired, and pregnant—stood with an infant in one hand and the hand of her toddler in the other and dared Sherman's men to burn down her house. Behind her stood the Saffolds' "loyal house servants," who refused to go with Sherman and who, in the white supremacist logic of the Lost Cause, preferred to remain Saffold family slaves rather than embrace the uncertainties of the freedom that came with the Union Army.[22] That likely wasn't true; Henry Saffold surely was not the only one who went with Sherman's men as they passed through Morgan County.

The truth is that Sarah could do little except plead with Henry and the others to stay and to work; perhaps she tried that. Maybe she offered to pay wages to those who stayed, reminding them of past kindnesses. She resorted to threats at least once. "I had a great deal of trouble with him," Sarah reported to Thomas about an enslaved man named Ben, "he was unwilling to exert himself in the least. I had to threaten to have him dragged out of the bed feet foremost or head foremost right on the floor before I could bring him to his senses."[23] When the war began, Thomas owned $75,000 in property, $50,000 of which was enslaved people like Henry.[24] It is easy to see how shocking it was for them to accept the abrupt loss of two-thirds of their worth, how Sarah might have recalled that she protected her house when she tried to stop her slaves from abandoning her, why so many white women churned out Lost Cause memoirs recalling houses full of "loyal servants."

The enslaved people who stayed at Buckhead no doubt had their reasons. Dinah had at least four reasons for staying, if that is what she did: Elizabeth and Catherine, both ten years old, six-year-old Daniel, and four-year-old Celianne. Following the army was dangerous, particularly for women and children.

Henry Saffold was with the U.S. Army in late November 1864 when Sherman's men fought a number of small skirmishes, mostly with state militiamen and small contingents of Confederate raiders, but nothing that slowed their steady progress toward the coast. With each passing day, the crowd of freed people who followed the army grew. From eighty miles outside of Savannah, a white soldier wrote to his sister that "an immense number of 'contrabands' now follow us, most of them able-bodied men, who intend going into the army."[25] For weeks the army had made clear their growing impatience with the women and children who followed them, and early in December, U.S. brigadier general Jefferson C. Davis (no relation to the Confederate president) decided to rid himself of them. As his troops prepared to cross Ebenezer Creek, a river outside of Savannah, Davis ordered the freed people to wait beside the river until his men had crossed over the pontoon bridges.

Henry and the others worked all night to clear a way through the swamp for the army to pass and built a bridge that could be pulled up to prevent the enemy from following in pursuit. They did all of this in sight of Black people who trusted that, when the time came, they, too, would cross the bridge.

Then, as Confederate troops closed in on them from behind, Davis ordered the bridge pulled up, stranding thousands of freed people, most of them women, children, and old men, on the banks of the river that was swollen from winter rain and clotted with rafts of ice. "With cries of anguish and despair, men, women, and children rushed by hundreds into the turbid stream, and many were drowned before our eyes," recalled one of Davis's men. Of those who managed to swim to safety, a few were women with children in their arms. Many drowned in trying; others who stayed on the far bank were murdered or re-enslaved. Witnesses and survivors never forgot what they saw. "It was claimed that this was done because rations were becoming scarce," Colonel Charles Kerr of the 16th Illinois Cavalry recalled twenty years later, but "[t]here was no necessity about it."[26]

We have no record of what Henry saw and heard that day, if he had second thoughts about serving with an army that allowed women and children to drown in an icy river. How his thoughts may have raced to Dinah and the children, wherever they were. We do know, however, that Henry stayed with the army even after Ebenezer Creek. By then he'd already marched more than two hundred miles, seeing something in where it was headed that could make up for where it had been.

The informal way in which Henry and the others became part of the army was formalized in Savannah, but not in the way they had expected. Instead of blue U.S. Army uniforms, they were issued "spades, shovels, and axes" and informed that they were part of the pioneer corps. As they prepared to move out to South Carolina, their enlistment as soldiers was still in question. "I was not out of the state of Georgia at any time before I became free," recalled Solomon Gardner, who left with the army from a neighboring county right around the same time as Henry. On January 1 and 2, the men boarded steamers and headed for Beaufort, where they resumed the work that had helped make possible Sherman's successful March to the Sea. They headed back into the swamp, this time near the Salkehatchie River, "corduroying roads, and doing what work was to be done."[27] To corduroy a road, the men cut down trees and then laid the logs next to one another on unstable or saturated soil, creating a rough road. Crushing injuries were not uncommon, and as the men worked nearly constantly in standing water, they endured hypothermia and frostbite. They were also exposed to waterborne illnesses and to poison ivy, oak, and sumac.

The pioneer corps having done their work, the regular army left Georgia, too, and followed them into South Carolina. Before he left, Sherman issued an order setting aside land in coastal Georgia and South Carolina for the settlement of freed people—a face-saving measure after Americans learned of atrocities like the one at Ebenezer Creek.[28] Special Field Orders, No. 15, raised the hopes of displaced freed people everywhere, who, once they heard that the government was giving freed people "forty acres and a mule," could not be convinced to retrace their steps back to their former enslavers' cotton fields. Once established on their government-issue plots of land, freed people in these coastal communities would be able to support themselves and sustain communities, reunite their families, and give the land they'd worked and improved to their descendants. Surely men like Henry Saffold could expect something similar from the government for enlisting in the U.S. Army.

Enlistment did not come for a few more months. Solomon Gardner explained the delay as a problem of supplies: the army did not have uniforms for the men, officers claimed. And once they had uniforms, they did not have guns. Maybe that's what they were told. But Sherman benefited from stringing these men along, appealing to them with a promise of enlistment while extracting hard labor from them that he hated to ask of soldiers. "These pioneer detachments became very useful to us," he wrote, "for they could work at night while our men slept."

Members of the pioneer corps received $10 a month plus army rations. Once enlisted, the officers promised, the men would draw $13 a month, the same pay as a white private.[29] As soldiers they would be supplied uniforms and sidearms, receive instruction on how to march and shoot, expect to sleep regular hours, and be expected to fight in battle. At each stop, they were told that their enlistment would come at the next one—maybe in Savannah or Columbia?

In the end, they had to wait until Goldsboro, North Carolina. In March 1865, Henry Saffold and Solomon Gardner and three to five thousand other men like them were finally officially enlisted into the 135th USCT. Saffold had come along with Sherman's men in November; four months and more than six hundred miles of marching later he became a U.S. soldier: "We left the spades and shovels and axes in Goldsboro."[30]

The army clerks processing their enlistments recorded a few details about the men, including their names, ages, occupations, and places of birth; their heights were recorded as were one-word descriptions of the color of their eyes and complexions. Henry was: "Henry Suffold," farmer, born in Athens, five feet six and a half inches, black eyes and hair, complexion: "dark."[31] Other men were not so lucky to have their personal details recorded. Gardner, who was enlisted under the last name Monroe, described a perfunctory process: "I was not asked where I was born, at the time I was made a member of Co. B., 135th; nothing was said about my birthplace. I was asked who I belonged to. I don't recollect having been asked any other question."[32]

After the war, they would learn how much it mattered that there were few records of their enlistment, that their names had been misspelled, and that they were hundreds of miles away from people who could testify to who they were and where they'd come from. As an applicant for a disability pension, Henry Saffold would be subjected to repeated, intrusive medical examinations; at enlistment, there seems to have been little to none of that. If the doctor had examined him, he would have found Henry's hands bleeding and swollen and nearly useless. Henry may have hidden the condition, for fear it would disqualify him, or the recruiter ignored it.[33]

Two officials signed their name to a certificate stating that Henry was "free of all bodily defects" and "qualified to perform the duties of an able-bodied soldier." One of them was George W. Johnson, Captain, Company E, 135th USCT, Henry's commanding officer, who would later claim not to know anything about Saffold's injury. The other one was a doctor. The following day, Henry Saffold was promoted to corporal.[34]

From Goldsboro, the 135th headed north to Virginia, arriving soon after Confederate troops there surrendered. The men spent several weeks in camp in Washington, before they were assigned to garrison duty in Louisville, Kentucky. Henry was admitted to the hospital there, suffering from an itchy, burning rash on his hands and arms. His symptoms were consistent with exposure to the poisonous plants that were abundant in the swamps where Henry had been working corduroying roads in the pioneer corps. The blisters on his hands made it painful for him to grip the handle of a shovel or an axe; when he did, the blisters burst, emitting a watery fluid. Sometimes they bled.[35] Yet Henry had continued working for months, despite the pain, because ahead of him lay the promise of enlistment, and behind him was slavery. The army doctors in Louisville may have treated the pustules with an arsenic solution or sulfur, silica, or phosphorus, all of which were commonly prescribed for rashes like his, and none of which would have offered Henry Saffold relief.[36]

The army surgeon who treated him there did not keep a record or, at least, no one could find it. Henry insisted that the injury had first appeared in Louisville, after his enlistment. His comrades had noticed that his hands started bleeding while they were working near the Salkehatchie River in South Carolina.

When the 135th mustered out at the end of October, the men left the army after an enlistment of only seven months, although they had been with the army much longer. Some went back to where they had come from—Georgia, North Carolina, South Carolina, Tennessee—returning to home places to rebuild families and communities. Others moved on.

Corporal Henry Saffold went home to Georgia to a slow and incomplete recovery. "I knew him to be sound and healthy up to the time of his enlisting in the US Army," Dinah explained to the pension bureau agent. But when he returned home "Henry Saffold was in bad health."[37] Surely it was a shock for them both to begin their lives in freedom this way, with four children to feed and Henry unable to work. But surely Dinah was relieved that Henry had survived the war and returned to Buckhead, where they could begin to imagine a time when he was well again. They would be paid for the work that Dinah and the older children did—Henry, too, when he was able to. In the meantime, Dinah and Henry made do with the money he'd managed to save from his army pay.

The year Henry Saffold had been in the army had brought momentous changes. As he was making his way home in October 1865, Thomas Saffold was in the capital in Milledgeville, casting a vote to end slavery in the state.[38] With the stroke of a pen, an assembly of white state representatives accepted emancipation as an established fact, ushering in a new day for the half million freed people in the state. And for white Georgians, too, who had gone to war four years earlier to defend an institution that heaped lavish financial rewards on a few and delivered an emotional payoff to poor whites in the state.[39] It may have once meant something when slaveholders reminded poor whites that they were not slaves, but this did not put food on their tables before the war. And now there was no food.

Many Georgia residents, both Black and white, were starving. Sherman's troops stripped the countryside of food and the means necessary to produce it. Hunger spread along the paths that the army had traveled and then outward to places that they had not touched but that were overrun by refugees. Traveling around Georgia in the summer of 1865,

Illinois journalist Sidney Andrews noted that poverty and hunger "falls most hardly on the negroes."[40] When the Freedmen's Bureau finally began distributing food aid the following summer, agents were under orders to issue rations only to the most destitute. Only a fraction of those who needed help received it.[41] "Able-bodied" men like Henry, despite his illness, were not qualified to receive aid, and, by extension, Dinah and the children weren't either.

Eager to relinquish responsibility for freedmen's relief, Freedmen's Bureau agents pushed freed people into labor contracts with former enslavers. The bureau evicted freed people who had been working land under Sherman's Special Field Orders, No. 15, ending any lingering illusions that they could expect justice from the federal government.

But Black farmers did not cede their land without a fight. Led by USCT veterans, freed people on Georgia's Sea Islands resisted federal authorities' efforts to seize their land, and, when they lost that battle, they fled the islands rather than be subject to the authority of the ex-Confederate whites who returned.[42] Some Black Georgians did become landowners, although never as many as in other southern states, and nearly all of them owned fewer than forty acres.[43] Landownership offered Black Georgians autonomy and protection from whites, but there were other ways to achieve those ends. Working for the railroads, for instance. That's what Henry Saffold did.

As part of the pioneer corps, Henry had cut down trees to build roads; now he would be laying track. It was fitting that he would do so. Colonel Orlando M. Poe, Sherman's chief engineer, who commanded the pioneer corps, had overseen the destruction of the South's railroad lines; Poe designed special tools and processes for ripping up rails, heating them, and twisting them until they were beyond repair or reuse. The track that remained was dilapidated and dangerous for travel.

Perhaps it was Corporal Henry Saffold's experience working in Poe's pioneer corps that recommended him to the railroad, if they recognized his skills as an asset. It is more likely that the company reserved dangerous work for men they thought were expendable. And because Poe's engineers had planted mines in the railroad cuts, men who worked the lines after the war took their lives into their hands.[44]

Money from northern investors fueled the rapid growth of railroads in the postwar South, and between 1865 and 1872, the miles of tracks running through the state of Georgia doubled. Labor everywhere was at a premium.[45] White planters complained of shortages of field hands, but railroading work paid better than field labor and offered men the opportunity to get out from under the thumbs of their former enslavers. "I left the farm then and went to work on the railroad," Frank Magwood recalled his decision to leave the fields. "I thought I was the only man then. I was so strong." When a government interviewer caught up with Hilliard Yellerday in the 1930s, the old man still lived in the five-room house he had bought around thirty years before for $1,000, money he'd earned working for the railroad after the war. "There was a story going that each slave would get forty acres of land and a mule at the end of the war . . . but the mule and land was never given and slaves were turned out without anything." What the "Yankees" did not deliver to Yellerday, the railroad did.[46]

When Henry had recovered enough from the infection in his hands and arms, he, Dinah, Elizabeth, Catherine, Daniel, and Celianne—aged sixteen, sixteen, twelve, and ten, respectively—moved from Buckhead to Madison, where he could pick up work on the Georgia Railroad. The station there and part of the tracks connecting Atlanta to Augusta lay in ruins. Railroad work offered Henry the opportunity to save some money, to buy the house they lived in and some land and, maybe, feel the sense of accomplishment he'd felt when he'd discarded his shovel for a U.S. Army–issue sidearm.

✦

In those first few postwar years, it was clear that white Georgians' limp acceptance of emancipation—the "emancipation" order Judge Thomas Saffold had endorsed—would not prevent a return of slavery in different forms. "He has freedom in name," Sidney Andrews wrote about freed people in Georgia, "but it will be some time before he gets it in fact."[47] Only a sustained military occupation could compel former Confederates to share power with formerly enslaved people, guaranteeing their freedom and equality before the law. When federal troops arrived in Georgia in the spring of 1867, once again they fanned out across the state, this time in support of an ambitious Black voter registration drive. The troops were there to ensure that Black men voted, to protect them from white violence.

Perhaps Henry wore his U.S. Army uniform when he appeared in June before a three-man board—two white and one Black—to register to vote.[48] If so, the board members might have dispensed with the formality of asking him to swear that he had not "engaged in insurrection or rebellion" against the United States government. Henry placed his mark on that oath, and his name was added to the list of registered voters for the election that fall.[49] It was only the second time his name—Henry Saffold—appeared in official records, the first being his enlistment.

Thomas Saffold may have sat out that fall's election, as did many former Confederates, or, perhaps, when asked to swear the oath, he repeated the line that he used in his application for a presidential pardon: that he had been only a reluctant secessionist.[50]

We can imagine the pride Henry Saffold felt voting that fall in Morgan County, where he had been born and raised a slave. Now he cast a ballot for a new state constitution recognizing his freedom, and Dinah's and the children's, and that would protect the integrity of their family. The interracial convention Henry Saffold helped vote into power ratified the Fourteenth Amendment that guaranteed Black Georgians legal equality with whites, fulfilling the requirements for the state to be readmitted to the Union. The army pulled out their troops, and the Freedmen's Bureau recalled their few remaining agents.

Four months later, the Republican-dominated legislature expelled its thirty-two Black legislators, and in the town of Camilla, whites shot and killed unarmed Black Georgians on their way to a political rally. Once white Georgians showed with brutal clarity that they had no interest in respecting the rights of freed people, their representatives' return to Congress was delayed and federal troops arrived again, staying long enough this last time to see the Black lawmakers restored to their seats.[51] But it wasn't enough. Black men retained the right to vote and to serve in public office, on paper, but white intimidation kept them from doing so.[52]

Still, Black Georgians were determined to claim their rights as United States citizens. Led by men like Rev. Henry McNeal Turner of Macon and Tunis Campbell of the Sea Islands, they sustained the political organizations that began in those first few postwar years, including union leagues and the Colored Conventions meetings. Both men, but Turner in particular, helped to foster the rapid growth of independent Black churches in the state and made use of the pulpit to demand rights that had been granted to Black Georgians in the postwar amendments.[53] Pockets of Black political power remained in Atlanta and Savannah. In the end, however, these efforts were inadequate to combat the slide toward Jim Crow, tenant farming, and convict leasing.[54]

Henry and Dinah arrived in Greene County around 1878, soon after the white minority there drove Black state representative Abraham Colby from office.[55] There were more than twice as many Black residents of the county than whites, so the threat posed by Black political participation was real and could not be completely eliminated by white violence.[56] The Saffolds were part of a rapidly growing Black community that saw opportunity there that they did not find elsewhere. The cotton Dinah and Henry picked now, as tenant farmers on the rich bottomlands near the river, was ginned in the Powell Mills, packed, and sent south via the Oconee River to Savannah. No train passed through Scull Shoals, where the Saffolds lived, but the town was located at the intersection of roads leading to Athens, Penfield, and Madison.[57] Next to their cabin, the Saffolds grew food in their garden to supplement what they bought, on credit, at the shop near the cotton factory.

Even with two of them working, the tenant-farm system was designed so that Dinah and Henry would not have money at the end of the year that they could put away to purchase land of their own, or to pay for such things as doctors and medicine. "[When] I came to Green[e] County," Henry explained, "I relied on my own race to Doctor me. Had no money to pay a doctor." The only doctor in town was an Englishman and former enslaver, Dr. Lindsey Durham. Purportedly Georgia's first millionaire, Durham lived in a lavish home at the end of a drive lined with crepe myrtles; his home doubled as an infirmary.[58] For more than thirty years, Henry lived nearby but could not afford to see Durham, if the wealthy English doctor would have agreed to see him.

When they were first married, Henry and Dinah had made a family together of children who were displaced by the slave trade and the war; they did the same now in Greene County when they took in their grandchildren even as they struggled to support themselves. Their daughters, Elizabeth, Catherine, and Celianne, disappeared from the written record when they became adults. If they did. This left Henry and Dinah with no adult children in their household to care for them or to help with their support.[59] Daniel eventually followed his parents to Greene County and lived nearby; he helped when he could, but by 1900 he had six children to feed, and so that help was likely infrequent.[60] Around the time Henry's condition seemed to worsen, Dinah and Henry adopted three of their grandchildren after their mother(s)—whoever they were—died.[61]

Henry's hands and arms continued to swell and bleed. A Greene County neighbor said that he had "often seen the handles of the plows and hoes he was using besmirched with blood that came from the discharged of his hands." Henry wrapped his hands in old clothes and kept working. But the condition got worse, until he could work very little. Dinah measured his decline by fractions. At first, he was only able to do "half of a man's work"; then it was less. His growing weakness may indicate that Henry suffered from other chronic conditions—such as heart or kidney disease—that were common among freed people. Their Scull Shoals neighbors pitched in to help, arranging for Henry to have "light duty" ginning cotton at the public gin, for instance. Eventually, Henry and Dinah could not pay their bills and so they lost the land they were leasing.[62] It wasn't clear what lay ahead for them and their grandchildren.

By the mid-1880s, Georgia's Black newspapers spread the word about expanding access to U.S. Army pensions. Black editors filled the pages of their papers with ads from pension agents and news stories following congressional pension debates. White papers in the state often portrayed the work of the Pension Bureau negatively, insisting that pensions were the result of a corrupt Republican Party sinking the treasury into debt in order to buy votes.[63] Black-owned papers supported the expansion of pensions and offered practical help to potential applicants. The *Savannah Tribune* invited readers to meet with agents in their offices and celebrated pensioners' cash awards, sometimes even comparing them to reparations for slavery. "An Ex-Slave's Pension" was the headline on a story about a New York woman who received $500 in back payments, or arrears, for the wartime death of her soldier son.[64]

In April 1886, encouraged by stories like these, Henry applied for a U.S. Army pension. Before he affixed his X to the application, Henry asked the agent to append a note indicating his proper rank.[65] "I will also inform you that I was a corporal," he explained, "as there was no place in the blank application to put it I [include it] in this letter [to] make that fact be known to the department." As a private he was qualified to receive only $8 a month; as a corporal he could get $10. Henry had gathered information about pensions while he was in the army and followed the talk swirling about lately, in the papers and by word of mouth. He knew pensions were awarded on a sliding scale, and that it mattered that he had left the army as a corporal.

Henry also knew that he would have to provide the bureau with a chain of evidence proving that his disabilities were a result of his time in the army. This would be difficult, because technically he had contracted the infection in his hands and arms before his enlistment, when he was in the pioneer corps. There were few records of the work these men did and no register of their names or their injuries or illnesses until they were mustered into the 135th USCT.

When the bureau office in Knoxville replied that they could find no record of Henry's illness, he sent sworn statements from Dinah and her son Daniel, the Saffolds' white landlord, and from Black and white neighbors, all of whom confirmed the nature of his illness and how it incapacitated him. Henry enlisted the help of the local justice of the peace, a white man named John Colclough, to write to Henry Hull Carlton, a U.S. congressman and former Confederate from a nearby county, recounting the story of how he came to lay roads and build bridges for the U.S. Army and how he was enlisted months later and hundreds of miles from his home.

"The trouble seems to be that I can not establish a chain of evidence," read his letter to Carlton. "I can not establish the fact by a commission[ed] officer of my regiment or company that I contracted this poison while in service . . . [T]he officers of my regiment the men are northern men and I do not know where one of them are which you see shuts me out."[66] When Henry did reach one of these northern men, George W. Johnson, captain of Company E, at his home in Illinois, Johnson said he did not recall the particulars of Saffold's illness. None of this satisfied the bureau, and they continued to decline his applications.

So, after two years of trying, in 1888, Henry placed ads in two newspapers, one white and one Black, calling on the officers and men of the 135th to come to his aid.

Placing Information Wanted ads in Black newspapers offered veterans and widows the opportunity to build social networks that would help them meet the steep evidentiary requirements of the Pension Bureau. The wives of USCT soldiers did so first, writing to the papers to ask if soldier-husbands had survived the war. Widows followed, seeking people who could vouch for their marriages and who could provide information about their husbands' enlistment. The bureau subjected Black women applicants to extraordinary scrutiny and surveillance; agents distrusted their every word and sought to deny or suspend their pensions with what seems like petty cruelty.[67] Their advertisements illustrate the unique challenges Black widows faced meeting the bureau's demands for written records. Veterans used their membership in the Grand Army of the Republic, when possible, in place of lost discharge papers; their widows went to the newspapers.[68] Concerned that he would die before Dinah, Henry completed a form indicating when and where they'd married and that they had done so "by consent of her owner."[69]

More than half of the pension-related advertisements in the Last Seen Collection were placed after the new 1890 Disability Act made pensions widely available to disabled veterans. The pension program, which expanded to include aging veterans, their wives, parents, and dependent children, was the closest the United States government ever came to paying reparations to formerly enslaved Americans. But the bureau rejected many more Black veterans and their survivors than whites. One study showed that between 1862 and 1890 the bureau awarded pensions to 39.5 percent of Black applicants and 77.9 percent of white applicants; from 1890 to 1907, 45.7 percent of Black applicants received pensions while the percentage of white applicants was 72.5 percent.[70] USCT soldiers did not live as long as white soldiers, Union or Confederate, and so there were fewer of them around after 1890 to apply. Yet, they were still much more likely to be denied, as were their surviving family members.

Black veterans like Henry Saffold more often returned home sick rather than with battle-related injuries, and it was more difficult to prove that chronic heart or lung conditions originated in the war than a bullet wound or amputation. But even after this form of evidence was no longer required, Black pensioners were turned away. "It is a disgrace to the government that excepted [*sic*] his services," an essay in one Black newspaper remarked, that "[c]olored soldiers have more difficulty today in establishing a pension plain that [*sic*] any other class."[71]

Henry Saffold's brief advertisement appeared in Savannah's *Morning News* on two consecutive days, August 4 and 5, 1888. Owned and edited by an ex-Confederate, the daily charged a cent a word for personal ads; it's no wonder that freed people did not write to the paper with Information Wanted ads looking for their family members.[72] The *Savannah Tribune*, on the other hand, was owned and edited by John Deveaux, a Black man and Republican Party organizer.[73] The *Tribune* did not run a column of Information Wanted ads taken out by freed people looking for their families. But Deveaux made an exception for Henry Saffold.

In fact, only two Georgia papers ran ads. A short-lived Black newspaper in Augusta, first called the *Colored American* and then the *Loyal Georgian*, published ads until it shut down in 1868, and the *Atlanta Constitution*, a paper resolutely associated with white supremacy, published a limited number of advertisements.

Because they had few options and those options were expensive, more Black Georgians took their ads to newspapers published out of state and those associated with the African Methodist Episcopal Church, like Philadelphia's *Christian Recorder* and New Orleans's *Southwestern Christian*

Advocate.[74] Henry may have had a number of reasons for addressing his search for members of the 135th USCT to two Savannah papers, one white and one Black; surely one of them was because he had reason to believe that they read these two papers. Readers of the *Morning News*, he may have reasoned, could get word out to the white officers, whom he didn't know, whereas he'd write to the *Savannah Tribune* for the people he knew and that he figured would know him.

Henry's August ad was an open plea for the names and addresses of the officers and men of the 135th. His November query in the *Savannah Tribune* named seven men—Joshua Hull, Thomas Smith, Jasper Hayes, Osborne Boler, Sam Eungin, Raif Strainer, and Harrison Strain—and within a few months, he heard from two of them.

Jasper Hayes submitted an affidavit in support of Saffold's claim from Savannah, and Joshua Hull sent one from Knightsville, Indiana. Two others wrote, too, although he had not named them: from Savannah came a statement from Brutus Butler, and Stephen Bookhart submitted one from Columbia, South Carolina. Perhaps the word had gotten to them through the others. Each confirmed Saffold's accounting of the events.

Bookhart recalled the first appearance of infection in "Comrade Henry Saffold's hands" when the men were building roads and recounted how they suspected that his promotion was an attempt to give him lighter duty while they healed. "I was in charge of Henry when he received his affliction," Joshua Hull explained, and "I told him that I believe he was poisoned [and] to get some sweet milk and rub them. I told him not to scratch them."[75] Hull was twenty-one years old, a couple of years younger than Henry, when he became 2nd Sergeant, Company E, and saw to the care of men who'd been at work for the army for months. Brutus Butler, 1st Sergeant, Company F, 135th USCT, was denied a pension for injuries he sustained when he was run over by a wagon while corduroying roads with the pioneer corps, but the statement he sent in support of Henry's claims helped his former comrade get a pension.[76] Henry began drawing a pension in his late fifties. By then, his heart was failing.

Doctors who examined Henry for the bureau noted swelling in his ankles and knees, his irregular and rapid heartbeat, and the difficulty he had breathing, symptoms commonly associated with heart disease. Early on, a panel of physicians declared Henry totally incapacitated and recommended that he be awarded $30 a month.[77] That never happened. Other doctors had less sympathy for Henry when they turned their attention from his hands to his feet, noting that his condition was chronic and therefore, they believed, not war-related.

Even as pensions became more generous and access widened, doctors routinely dismissed Black veterans as dishonest and discounted the severity of their disabilities. White doctors' examinations of Black veterans were often shaped by scientific racism.[78] What else explains how a panel of examining doctors who noted extensive scarring on Henry's hands causing his fingers to contract, weak and irregular pulse, and swollen knees and legs nonetheless concluded that the old soldier did not deserve an increase? That was in 1905. Henry was seventy years old. It was the last time Henry Saffold took his case to the Pension Bureau. "I am about 70 years of age," he explained on the form.[79] It is easy to read exasperation into his responses to the same questions he had answered so many times, the request for records that did not exist, the seemingly endless search for a chain of evidence that could satisfy federal agents. What else besides lack of interest or racism explains their stubborn insistence that Henry Saffold was a private despite his army service records indicating that he was, as he said, *Corporal* Henry Saffold? Including a letter in his file from Captain George Johnson confirming that fact?

Henry Saffold was admitted to the pension rolls in January 1890. The bureau approved his request for an arrears payment dating to his original April 1886 application. That meant that sometime in 1890 he received around $264 in back pay. Some of that went to the lawyer who filed his claim, but Henry still had enough left over to go to the doctor. The money could not bring back his health, and it wasn't the forty acres enslaved Georgians believed Sherman was going to deliver to them, but it was a good deal of money for the couple, who were used to having none. Henry put a little away to help pay the future costs of applying for an increase to his pension.

A few months after Henry and Dinah received the good news from the bureau, Congressman H. H. Carlton wrote to the paper to take credit for Henry Saffold's pension. "A Georgia negro, Henry Saffold, of Greene county, draws a pension of $25 a month from the national government," read the announcement in the *Morning News*, the same paper to which, three years earlier, Henry had appealed for the names and addresses of the officers and men of Company E, 135th USCT. "Henry went into the army as the servant of a union soldier, and contracted a disease which incapacitates him for work. The application for a pension was looked after by Congressman Carlton, who, after two years' work . . . succeeded in getting it granted."[80] There is no evidence in Saffold's pension file that Carlton interceded on his behalf, that he was responsible for "getting it granted." The congressman got few of the details correct—Henry was awarded $8 a month, not $25, for instance, and he did not enlist as a servant but as a soldier. Perhaps Carlton had not made an error when he claimed that Henry was pensioned for having been a loyal servant. Such a lie played into the Lost Cause's "loyal slave" narrative and covered over the inconvenient truth that white Democrats like Carlton had been unable to eliminate Black political power in the state.

That didn't happen until 1908, when an amendment to the state's constitution disenfranchised Black men and added a number of other disqualifiers for good measure, such as a poll tax, education and property requirements, and a stringent new system of voter registration.[81] Until then, with the federal pension program poised to undergo an ambitious expansion, even Democrats like H. H. Carlton recognized the political capital to be gained in boasting about having secured one for a Black man.

◆

Henry Saffold died on July 15, 1911.[82] Sometime that spring, the town's white doctor, Lindsey Durham, provided Saffold with medication to relieve the pain he felt in his hands and arms—and in his legs and chest. Durham may have been moved by Saffold's discomfort, but, just two weeks after Henry died, Durham submitted a bill to the Pension Bureau requesting payment of $9.75 for the medicines that one hopes brought the old soldier some comfort.[83]

Henry's pension file lists his official cause of death as "dropsy of the heart," or heart failure. He was about seventy-seven years old.

As a young man, twenty-two or so years old, he had gone with Sherman's army as it began its March to the Sea. He'd stayed with that army as it made its way through Georgia, striking at the heart of slavery, and when it arrived victorious at Savannah. "I beg to present you as a Christmas gift," Sherman wrote to President Lincoln a few days before Christmas, "the city of Savannah, with one hundred and fifty heavy guns and plenty of ammunition, and also about twenty-five thousands bales of cotton." Newspapers in the North rushed to calculate what the seized cotton was worth; the *New York Times* put it at $7,821,000.[84] That cotton, some of it picked by Henry's and Dinah's own hands, became the property of the U.S. Department of the Treasury. Treasury sold it to pay down the war debt, which by 1865 included the government's promise to pay pensions to the families of soldiers who died in the service of the country, including, at least nominally, the widows and dependent children of USCT soldiers.[85]

When at the end of April 1865 Sherman accepted the surrender of Confederate troops in North Carolina, Corporal Henry Saffold could take satisfaction in having helped to make that victory possible. From North Carolina, the 135th went to Virginia, and then to Washington. Henry, who just a few months before had never left Georgia, arrived in the nation's capital dressed in a U.S. Army uniform. Surely not even the discomfort in his hands could detract from the pride he felt when he saw the capital streets filled with troops cheered on by jubilant crowds of onlookers. Henry returned to Dinah just before Christmas 1865, having been told by the army doctors in Louisville that the rash on his hands and arms would go away with time.

It is not difficult to imagine what Henry might have done had his pension allowed him to take care of his hands and his heart: buy a small house for him and Dinah, one that he might have passed along to one of his grandchildren or to Daniel Reid and his wife, Sandy, and their children. Dinah died five years before Henry; perhaps he was relieved that she would not have to endure the scrutiny of the Pension Bureau on her own. It was surely a comfort to Henry that Daniel and Sandy attended to him in his final illness.

It was a comfort, too, for men like Henry to hear from their comrades, to have their stories confirmed, perhaps even to share memories. It is no wonder, then, that old soldiers continued to write to Black newspapers late in the nineteenth and into the twentieth century with lists of names of men they hoped to find.[86] As they did, they built a public record of their time in the U.S. Army that reads like a final roll call of Freedom Generation's soldiers.

CHAPTER NINE

Husbands and Wives

Americans in the post–Civil War era could not get enough of *Enoch Arden*. Tennyson's 1864 poem hit the country at just the right time to become something of a phenomenon. The poem's protagonist, Enoch Arden, returns from a decade at sea to find his wife, Annie, married to another man. After Enoch was shipwrecked, a heartbroken Annie struggles to accept that her husband and the father of her children is likely dead, and, facing a future of destitution, she remarries. When Enoch finally returns and sees her contentment, he does not reveal himself to her; instead he slips away quietly and dies of a broken heart.[1] *Enoch Arden* was read out loud before rapt audiences and performed as a play; it so saturated American popular culture that the term was regularly attached to stories of "wandering husbands" returning from the war or the West to find themselves replaced. Readers found Annie to be an infinitely sympathetic character, the perfect "pure, loving, faithful, and pious woman."[2] At a time when no one knew how many men had died in the war—and when everyone seemed to know one who was supposed to have died—lawmakers revised state marriage laws to protect women in Annie's situation, shortening the time from seven years to three that a spouse had to be absent before a marriage was considered dissolved and easing the way for abandoned spouses to remarry.[3] The principle behind these laws is called the Enoch Arden Doctrine.

Of course, Tennyson wasn't for everyone. Critics liked to poke fun at Enoch, dismissing the sentimentalism that would drive a man to sacrifice his own contentment for his wife's. Instead of gazing at their wives through windows, complained one newspaper about Tennyson's "preposterous teachings," returning husbands should walk in and ask "whether they were ever to have any supper." Another pointed out the absurdity of sympathizing with wandering husbands who were a burden; they did not "come back rich; none are handsome, strong or useful; all are in a condition that would justify a poorhouse or hospital."[4]

When white newspapers discovered the comic potential in attaching the Enoch Arden label to formerly enslaved people's efforts to find missing spouses, stories ran in papers across the country about "colored Enoch Ardens" returning to their wives—each article trying to outdo the other in melodrama and condescension. "Chattanooga has a colored Enoch Arden case," declared a California paper; "The latest Enoch Arden is colored," announced a paper in Detroit; and a Minnesota paper ran one piece about "Chicago's pet Enoch Arden."[5] "Colored Enoch Arden" stories dripped with racism and slavery denialism and reveled in the anguish formerly enslaved people felt when their searches ended in the discovery of a remarried former spouse. When an aging and remarried South Carolina freedman discovered the woman he had married in slavery living nearby, a newspaper account laughed at the "old man's bad predicament . . . one calculated to put wiser men than the old darky to thinking."

A reunited couple's joy became the subject of ridicule under the "Colored Enoch Arden" headline, even when neither partner had remarried. Such was the case with Peyton Hemingway's reunion with his wife that resulted in the couple losing their footing and rolling down a hill locked "in each other's dusky arms . . . their children on top of them uttering what the darkeys call 'loud lamentations ob joy.'"[6] Often the subjects of these stories remained unnamed, as the aim was not to acknowledge the pain of losing a spouse but rather to amuse readers with accounts of hapless and lovesick ex-slaves, plantation love stories set in the modern day. The poem *Enoch Arden* was romantic tragedy, but the reunions of formerly enslaved people were portrayed as comical.

Slavery's defenders had always insisted that marriage between slaves did not carry the same meaning or expectations as marriage did for their white enslavers. They told themselves this as they wrote laws banning slaves from marrying, forced men and women into "marriages," and sold wives and husbands away from one another. They repeated the explanation despite what they saw with their own eyes, the way enslaved spouses escaped to be with one another or negotiated their own re-enslavement rather than live apart. That apology for slavery was taken up again early in the twentieth century by scholars who were deeply committed to the Lost Cause. "[N]egro domestic ties were weak at best," historian U. B. Phillips wrote, and American slaveholders were, in general, nice white people who "deplored" the breakup of families.[7] This thread ran through white newspaper stories about the happy reunions of long-separated husbands and wives. Appearing under headlines like "Romantic Lives of Slave Couple" and "A Romantic Meeting," these accounts spoke the language of the Lost Cause, about how slavery had not been all that bad, that old slaves found each other again before they died.[8] Casting freedmen in the role of Enoch Ardens continued this casual dismissal of the violence done to Black domestic ties in slavery and afterward.

Against this backdrop, freed people resolutely searched for their former lovers, husbands, and wives, so that they could legitimatize these unions under the law or simply live together as they once had. Sometimes they found one another, but, of course, reunions like these were fraught and not always happy. Despite what white people thought, Freedom Generation told the true story in the ads they sent to the papers describing marriages that had never been recorded, or perhaps only by a slaveholder, but that had nonetheless been celebrated and that once brought comfort and perhaps joy. Once married freedwomen and -men followed no one path as they searched for one another, and each search took as many turns as there were types of relationships. What follows are profiles of several people as they tried to find missing spouses, mend marriages, and live together in dignity.

✦

Slaves were prohibited from marrying throughout the antebellum South. Yet in rituals of their own making enslaved people married, and they recognized marriage as a foundation on which families were built. The same slaveholders who wrote the laws banning slaves from marrying sometimes consented, seeing the value in a contented workforce and the payoff in the children a marriage would produce. But enslavers thought nothing of breaking them up when it suited them, by sale or forced migration or via any number of coercive moves, such as forcing slaves into a relationship with one another or assaulting a married woman. "Slave marriage," historian Tera Hunter says, "was by design an oxymoron." Scholars estimate that a third of first marriages were broken up by the slave trade; more were disrupted through other arrangements, such as hiring out and forced migration.[9]

The advertisements in the Last Seen Collection document the violence that enslavers and slave traders perpetrated against Black marriages. Of the more than 4,500 ads in the collection, 490 were placed by husbands looking for wives and 382 by wives looking for husbands. If the success rate was the same as in other types of searches—2 percent—then seventeen of these separated spouses found one another. Of course, unless they announced their reunion in the paper or we find them in the available records, we cannot know for sure. Ads searching for husbands and wives tended to be shorter, less full of crucial information that might have been used to find one another, maybe because they described people who were separated as adults and searchers hoped that names alone would be sufficient to find them. At just 19 percent of the collection, spousal searches are the least common type.

It's difficult not to read into the brief ads a sense of practical defeatism about the impermanence of marriage relative to one's relationship to one's parents, children, or siblings. On the other hand, nearly half of all the reunion accounts in white newspapers (fifteen of thirty-four) describe the remarriages of "old slave" husbands and wives, indicating that white audiences loved their slavery stories to be about romance. No wonder freed people rarely turned to white newspapers for help in locating loved ones. Formerly enslaved husbands and wives searched for one another despite the environment of continued disregard for Black marriages.

Pottstown has an Enoch Arden in the shape of a colored man named James Dogan, who was a slave prior to the rebellion, and, escaping into the Union lines, afterwards became a soldier and fought all through the war. He became separated from his family, and not hearing from them for several years, subsequently married again. Recently he learned of the whereabouts of his first wife and family, and is about to return to them, his second wife giving her hearty consent.

James Dogan [*sic*], *Reading Times and Dispatch* (Reading, PA), July 26, 1871

James Dogans did not write to the papers for help finding his wife and children. Dogans separated from his family in June 1864 when he slipped across Union lines in Bedford, Tennessee, and enlisted in the United States Colored Troops.[10] Seven years later, Dogans was living in a small town outside of Philadelphia when he found them. Somebody tipped off the local paper, and a brief story appeared in the *Reading Times and Dispatch* announcing the happy result of his efforts. The editor knew a good human-interest story when he saw it, and he saw one in the story of James Dogans finding the wife he had had in slavery.

But there was another angle, too, that the paper hoped to exploit: James Dogans already had a second wife. What would he do now, with two?

"Pottstown has an Enoch Arden in the shape of a colored man named James Dogan," the paper said of Private *Dogans*, as his name was spelled on his enlistment papers. "He became separated from his family, and not hearing from them for several years, subsequently married again. Recently he'd learned of the whereabouts of his first wife and family" and was returning to them. The *Dispatch* seemed not to care that in the poem Enoch Arden did not have two wives. The paper offered no details about Dogans's search for his family, how he had found them and decided to go to them. Neither did it explain Dogans's decision to leave his current wife, only that she'd given "her hearty consent." We don't even get their names.

That's because the story was not about how James Dogans rebuilt his first marriage. It was about the easy dissolution of his second. The paper, which served rural counties northwest of Philadelphia, was strongly supportive of the Republican Party's policies toward emancipation and civil rights, but it did not publish advertisements and it showed little interest in matters related to African Americans. When attached to Tennyson's words, a formerly enslaved man's search for his wife became absurd; Dogans appeared a fool.

Like most of the 180,000 men who enlisted in the USCT, Dogans beat his path to freedom through military enlistment, leaving his wife and children behind. In Union-occupied West and Middle Tennessee, including Bedford County, where Dogans was from, the U.S. Army was charged with protecting the property rights of enslavers who pledged their loyalty to the U.S.[11] This situation left the fate of freedom seekers like James Dogans uncertain. If Dogans's wife's enslaver convinced federal officials of their loyalty, then she and their children may have remained enslaved even after James enlisted, or they went to a refugee camp, perhaps nearby in Nashville.[12]

James made his way to Pennsylvania, where, on June 28, 1864, he enlisted in Company K, 43rd USCT, a Philadelphia regiment. He fought at and survived the Confederate massacre of Black soldiers at the Battle of the Crater, near Petersburg, Virginia, and served with the 43rd in occupation in Texas's Rio Grande Valley. There Dogans and his comrades oversaw the emancipation of enslaved Texans in the summer of 1865. When the men mustered out in Philadelphia at the end of October, James Dogans did not go far, settling in the small town of Pottstown, forty miles to the west.[13] He married a woman named Harriet, who was ten years his senior.[14] The trail leading to his first wife had gone cold, perhaps.

Pottstown's claim to having an Enoch Arden among the town's residents was intended to get tongues wagging among *Dispatch* readers who would have otherwise not had reason to pay the town much attention. Pottstown boasted a total population of only 4,125 in 1870; among their number were twenty-nine African Americans, including Harriet and James.[15] Black residents of the town surely knew about the story before it caught the attention of a white reporter. They knew James's wife's name was Harriet; some perhaps also knew the identity of his first wife and their children. Someone helped him address inquiries after them to Tennessee, because neither he nor Harriet could read or write. Maybe it was the pastor of Pottstown's Bethel AME Church.[16] Or another USCT veteran with whom James had served. And James likely counted on neighbors for help raising the money he would need to get there. It may be that no one in the small town was privy to the conversation between Harriet and James when he told her he was going to his first family, but the word spread to someone at the paper who was only interested in why James's wife in Pottstown was eager for him to go. The *Pittsburgh Commercial* ran the same story ten days later, adding no additional details, but, unlike some of the other "colored Enoch Arden" accounts, Pottstown's was never picked up by out-of-state papers.[17] The town's attempt to share some of the Tennyson limelight ended there.

James and Harriet's story did not end there. After the white papers lost interest, the couple worked to untangle the bonds of affection they shared with one another and those that had bound them to others in slavery.

That no record of their marriage could be found might indicate that James and Harriet married by mutual consent; they did not apply for a license or register their marriage with local officials. At fifty-five years old (in 1870), Harriet had likely been married before; perhaps she found James wanting as a husband and gave her "hearty consent" to his departure because she was happy to be rid of him after a few years of marriage. Or she consented because she understood all too well the pain that slavery inflicted on enslaved couples and recognized that James could not start again even though he had tried with her. Their negotiation and the considerations on which it was based went unrecorded. Difficult decisions like theirs took place all over the country after the war. "Every time I gits a letter from you it tears me to pieces," Laura

Spicers's first husband wrote to her in a refugee camp, explaining that he had remarried. "I do not know which I love best, you or Anna."[18] Maybe James felt that way, too, and Harriet did him the extraordinary generosity of letting him go.

James Dogans's evidentiary trail disappears after he left Pottstown. He did not apply for a pension, and neither did any of his dependents. Harriet surely knew of James's war service. Had they remained married, Harriet would have qualified for a widow's pension, although without a marriage license she would have faced resistance in defending that claim. So, too, would his first wife, unless their reunion was followed by a registration of their marriage before federal or local officials in Tennessee.[19] That none of this happened could be explained in a few ways, including that James Dogans died before he reunited with his first wife or soon thereafter—or that there was no reunion. A pension application would have offered more clues about what happened after Dogans left Harriet.

James's marriage was disrupted not by sale or forced migration or by a "slave marriage" made at the command of an enslaver. But all these experiences were common among enslaved people and any of them might have been the experience of the wife Dogans left behind in Tennessee. She may have married again when he left her, seeking a way to ensure her survival and that of her children. Historians use terms like "serial monogamy" to describe the intimate relationships that enslaved people had over their lifetimes—how, out of necessity and desire, they began new relationships when previous ones came to an end. The term seems not quite to capture the trauma of these repeated losses and what it took to hold on to the hope that they might be reversed. It took years for Freedom Generation to sort through these relationships. It wasn't over when they were free or even when sometimes they found one another, as had James Dogans and the wife he'd lost in slavery.

Neither was that work complete when his white neighbors lost interest and moved on to the next "colored Enoch Arden."

✦

INFORMATION WANTED.

John Walker, a servant of Dr. E. M. Patterson, in 1850, wishes to know the whereabouts of his wife Peggie, and his three sons William, Samuel, and Miles, who were also slaves of Dr. E. M. Patterson, of Nashville, Tennessee. Dr. Patterson lived at a place called Flat Rock, about three miles from Nashville. And also the whereabouts of my last wife, Cornelia, who was a slave of Lee Shoot, a negro trader, in Nashville, Tenn. Any information of the above persons will be gladly received by John Walker. Ministers in charge will please read this to their congrgations. Address letters to JOHN WALKER,
No. 114 P St., betw'n 4th and 5th Sts,
Sacramento, Cal.
Feb. 27—1mo.

John Walker, "Information Wanted,"
Christian Recorder (Philadelphia, PA), February 27, 1869

John Walker's advertisement appeared in the paper on February 27, 1869. Sixteen months later, he was living in Nashville with Peggie, their son Miles, Miles's wife, Amanda, and the younger couple's three children. John's success in finding his wife speaks to the great power of Black newspapers and the network of communities they served. From Sacramento, California, John Walker wrote to Philadelphia's *Christian Recorder*. Pastors throughout the country read his plea to their congregations: John Walker was looking for his two wives, Peggie and Cornelia, who had come after Peggie. When word got back to him that Peggie was in Nashville, John headed there. By the following June, more than twenty years after they had been separated, John and Peggie were living together again as husband and wife. Peggie was fifty-five years old, and John sixty-three.[20]

Their reunion was the sort that white papers loved to cover, one of romance and happy endings. But no white paper in Tennessee or elsewhere took note of John's epic trek back to Peggie across thousands of miles, their (re)marriage, or the way they lived out their days together. Without attracting the attention of their white neighbors, John and Peggie Walker found one another again and repaired the ties of affection that had bound them together in slavery. Those ties held, even as they were sold away from each other, and John was taken to California and married again. When John Walker died sometime before his seventy-third birthday, Peggie was beside him, and perhaps his son and grandchildren; there were five or six by then.[21]

Like James Dogans, John Walker began his life in freedom far away from the family he had made in slavery. The *families* he had made in slavery. For a minute, the town of Pottstown paid attention to James Dogans and his two wives because it was an Enoch Arden story in reverse and because it came "in the shape of a colored man." But the work Dogans did to find his first wife took place beyond the scrutiny of readers of such white papers. James and Harriet Dogans alone engaged in the intimate and painful work of negotiating their way out of a marriage. When John Walker placed an ad looking for two wives, he called on Nashville's Black community for help sorting out his marriages. "John Walker, a servant of Dr. E. M. Patterson, in 1850, wishes to know the whereabouts of his wife Peggie, and his three sons William, Samuel, and Miles, who were also slaves of Dr. E. M. Patterson of Nashville, Tennessee," his ad began. Walker continued: "And also the whereabouts of my last wife, Cornelia, who was a slave of Lee Shoot [Shute], a negro trader, in Nashville, Tenn." He may have hoped to find one wife, Peggie *or* Cornelia, or perhaps he meant to find them both, as he said.

Walker's was not the only advertisement to mention more than one wife, but ads naming two or more spouses appeared infrequently—and none were placed by women. Some remarried freedmen who carried with them into freedom a sense of obligation to a previous wife or wives placed ads in the papers offering their material support.[22] Freedwomen caring for dependent children were in no position to make a public offer of support. And, having survived enslavers' obsessive focus on and repeated violence to their reproductive lives, they had everything to lose by going to the papers to describe the various paternities of their children. Ads like John Walker's document the long-term consequences of America's domestic slave trade to Black marriages and the extraordinary effort required to mend even one.

John and Peggie had married on Dr. E. M. Patterson's place, outside of Nashville, where enslaved people grew corn, wheat, and tobacco and raised livestock. On their small holdings, Patterson and his white neighbors entertained one another in imposing manors and sought strategic marriages for their children. The nine souls that Patterson counted as his property were hardly enough to support the social aspirations of his six teenage children. To marry his children well, Patterson sold Peggie and hers.[23] He "put them in his pocket," as they called it, because doctors and gentlemen did not *sell* wives and children; that was the business of men like Lee Shute, the Nashville slave trader Walker named in his ad. Patterson may have told John that he had no choice but to do so; maybe he promised to keep them together or sell them to someone nearby. But the doctor wasn't done making promises. He had big plans for the cash in his pocket, and they included John Walker.

Late in April 1850, E. M. Patterson joined a company of Nashville investors, the Nashville and Clarksville Havilah Mining and Trading Company, headed to California to mine for gold.[24] John Walker was to accompany him as his "personal servant," a title that signaled Patterson's thinly veiled evasion of the state's prohibitions against slavery. California lawmakers looked the other way when men like Patterson migrated to the state and brought their "servants" with them, making the state functionally a slave state—perhaps, rather than Texas, California was the westernmost terminus of the Second Middle Passage.[25] It was risky for a man as old as the doctor (fifty years old in 1850) to make the dangerous overland trek to California, to liquidate his property in slaves to fund the trip. There was no guarantee that Patterson and his associates would find gold or that the two enslaved men they brought with them—John Walker and one other—would not escape on the way. Or, with the help of Sacramento's free Black community, they'd escape when they got there.[26] If Walker walked away from the company of Tennessee gold miners, Patterson would lose twice, once in the loss of his enslaved "property" and again in the loss of stock in the company. Even after he sold Peggie, Patterson was short on the cash necessary to be a full partner in the company, so he put in John Walker as the remainder of his stock.

In the moral universe inhabited by American enslavers, Patterson sold a man's wife and used the proceeds to take her husband across a continent to dig for gold—which could be used to buy more people's wives and husbands. If they never struck gold, or some tragedy befell them, then he'd sell the woman's husband to pay his debt to the other investors. It didn't matter if he'd promised to free that man. It was just bad luck, the kind that could hit a white man in California's goldfields or in the cotton fields of the Mississippi Valley.

Perhaps Walker and Patterson struck a deal before they left: in return for Walker's word that he would help the doctor survive the long journey and would remain with the company until the men struck gold, Dr. Patterson promised to free John Walker. Such deals were common during the gold rush, but they angered resident whites who saw the free Black population as a threat to their racial dominance. A few months before the men left Nashville, the California legislature tried to pass a law banning Black migration to the state, but it failed because lawmakers remained keen to welcome the South's many Pattersons—just so long as when they left, they took their John Walkers with them.[27] Once free, Walker may have hoped to make some money for himself in California's goldfields before returning to Tennessee to buy his family's freedom.

For four long months, John Walker walked behind a wagon train carrying men and supplies, a journey of more than twenty-three hundred miles. Leaving Nashville at the end of April 1850, the men boarded a steamboat to Independence, Missouri. From there they struck out on the California Trail; their eight horse-drawn wagons made their way to Fort Kearny, Nebraska, and then followed the North Platte River as it snaked northwest to Fort Laramie, in present-day Wyoming. From Fort Laramie to the Great Salt Lake, the men proceeded through southern Wyoming's high desert, where many in their party became ill with cholera and measles, and supplies ran short for both the men and the horses. They left Salt Lake (Utah) at the end of July, crossing the Nevada desert via the Humboldt riverbed to the foot of the Sierra Nevada mountains one month later. Abandoning the wagons full of heavy mining equipment at the base of the mountains, Walker and the others hiked up steep mountain passes and through river canyons, reaching the goldfields in September.[28]

How strange the wide expanses and snowcapped mountains must have looked and felt to a man like John Walker who had never left Tennessee, had seldom been off Patterson's property in Flat Rock, and then only with a pass restricting his travel to a few miles, perhaps to Nashville and back. After mounting a summit in the Black Hills late one June afternoon, a white man in their company described what he saw: "The last rays of the cloudless, setting sun tinselled this romantic and sublime spot of nature, that seemed adorned with a fringe of gold—while the dark, dense shadows of the innumerable evergreens made all beneath as black as Egyptian darkness—presented a scene too beautiful—too grand and too sublime to pass unnoticed."[29] One wonders what John Walker thought about as he stood on top of that hill. Did he consider slipping away into the shadows and turning back? Did he see gold in the sunset? In the months he had been walking the trail, Walker had no doubt heard stories about Black men striking gold in California. "The whole country . . . is filled with gold," a correspondent to Frederick Douglass's *North Star* reported, and "there are but three classes of individuals that can even work these mines, Negro, Indian, and Irish." Abolitionist papers on the East Coast reported on Black men's luck in the mines, and word spread quickly when an all-Black mining company hit the Mother Lode.[30] The white men he traveled with imagined they'd transplant their old ideas about slavery and white supremacy to this strange and beautiful new place, but from where Walker stood, it may have looked like the whole country was "filled with gold." There was plenty to go around and enough for a man like him.

Luck, as it turned out, was in short supply among the men of the Nashville and Clarksville Havilah Mining and Trading Company. In a few short months, the company dissolved, and the men went their separate ways. Dr. Patterson headed back to Nashville but returned a few months later with his family, having sensed other opportunities in California. He tried his hand in politics as a Democrat when the party was shepherding a new fugitive slave law through the legislature that gave slaveholders broad powers to seize and re-enslave Black Californians and deport them to the South.[31]

It is not clear what became of John Walker and the other "servant" when the company dissolved. Patterson may have stuck to his word and freed Walker, or he hired Walker out to someone. Walker may have freed himself and sought help from Black activists who sheltered freedom seekers like him.[32] As a free man, Walker likely kept a low profile. White men continued to exercise unchecked authority over enslaved people and free Blacks, including over their marriages. A newspaper in San Francisco reported that when a white man named William Marr learned that his enslaved woman Margaret had married, he dragged her away at gunpoint. It didn't matter that Margaret's husband may have been a free man or that what Marr did was illegal.[33] If John married a woman in California, Dr. Patterson might have done the same; he would not have been compelled to respect Walker's marriage to her any more than he had his marriages to Peggie and Cornelia.

So long as Patterson remained in California, the doctor could re-enslave Walker and send him back to Tennessee. Maybe that explains why we can find no trace of Walker in the census or elsewhere. Maybe that's why when E. M. Patterson headed back to Nashville in 1857—for good this time—he did not bring John Walker with him. Walker may have hidden himself so well among Sacramento's free Blacks and other groups that Patterson could not find him—and neither can we. By then, the political winds had shifted in favor of Republicans, whom men like Patterson expected to enforce California's ban on slavery. Back in Tennessee, Patterson invested his mining proceeds into the purchase of more slaves, confident that this investment would provide for him and Elizabeth and for their children and grandchildren. When the Civil War came to Tennessee in 1862, E. M. Patterson owned twice as many enslaved people as he had in 1850.[34]

U.S. Army forces led by Ulysses S. Grant, fresh off stunning victories at Forts Henry and Donelson, seized Nashville late in February.[35] Reeling from these defeats, the Confederacy instituted a draft, pulling into the army white men between the ages of eighteen and thirty-five; later that year, they extended the age to forty-five, and two years later, to fifty, in response to a worsening manpower problem. At sixty-two, Dr. E. M. Patterson was well beyond the age in which he would be forced into the army. He enlisted anyway and died fighting outside of Murfreesboro, Tennessee, thirty miles south of Nashville, early the next year.[36] By then, due to the U.S. Army's recruitment of Black men and enslaved people's self-emancipation, there wasn't much slave-ownership left in Union-occupied Nashville for Dr. Patterson to have died defending. Although still technically legal, as the state was exempt from the Emancipation Proclamation, slavery practically ended in Tennessee by 1864. Peggie and her children were free, as was Cornelia Shute, if that was her last name, early the next year, when legislators approved an emancipation measure.[37] Perhaps, like James Dogans's wife, they experienced their first days of freedom in a refugee camp, hoping to pick up word of loved ones.

John Walker was far away from the people and places he knew, his first wife, Peggie, and his "last wife," Cornelia, cast adrift from their lives by forces he could not control. But he was not alone. He was surrounded by people like him looking for their wives and husbands, children, brothers, and sisters. Walker was part of a vibrant Black community that built and supported institutions that helped collapse the distance between him and them. News about family traveled along the grapevine telegraph with the enslaved and free Black migrants arriving in the goldfields and even when they failed to arrive. The Last Seen Collection includes more than one hundred ads reaching out to and from small Black communities in California. More than half were placed by California freed people; the rest came from family members in the East looking for them.

Once the war got underway, official communication buzzed back and forth between the two coasts via telegraph, and by 1869, mail traveled by transcontinental railroad from California to New York City in just over a week. But when John Walker sent his letter to Philadelphia's *Christian Recorder*, it took longer to arrive. A pastor at Bethel AME or St. Andrews AME, both on Seventh Street, a short one-mile walk from Walker's home on P Street, helped him prepare the ad. Perhaps Walker had heard similar pleas read from the pews.[38] His was unusual in that he hoped to learn about two wives. The ad appeared in the paper late in February. By that June, John Walker was living with Peggie and their son Miles in Nashville.

Traveling on modern roads, California to Philadelphia is a trip of nearly three thousand miles, or roughly forty hours of driving. It of course would have taken a lot longer for John Walker, who may have traveled overland again, or by boat to Panama. With the completion of the transcontinental railroad later that year, passengers could make a trip like Walker's in a couple of weeks. From the window of the segregated train car, if that's how he did it, Walker would have found it hard to pick out landmarks. The landscape had been transformed by the wars—the one fought between the U.S. and the Confederacy and the one the Cheyenne, Sioux, Arapaho, Shoshone, and Paiute people waged to defend their homeland from private railroad companies and the U.S. Army that defended them.

He arrived in Tennessee just as the Ku Klux Klan declared war on Black Tennesseans, aiming to reverse the modest civil rights gains that had been made since May 1866, when, over a three-day period, former Confederates in Memphis murdered forty-six freed people and burned down the city's Black churches and schools.[39] After hearing the testimony of Memphis Massacre survivors, U.S. congressmen moved quickly to pass the Fourteenth Amendment securing to Freedom Generation and those who came after a promise that the federal government had their back, that it would see to it that white men did not murder Black people with impunity in the streets of a city in Tennessee or anywhere else. Lawmakers in Nashville ratified the amendment a few weeks later, securing the state's readmission to the Union—and ensuring that no federal troops would be called into the state to make good on the amendment's promise.[40] In cities and towns, Black Tennesseans nurtured the communities and institutions they would use to protect themselves, creating pockets of Black political power that the Klan could not eradicate.

If John Walker and his son Miles voted in the fall of 1870, they did so alongside other Black Nashville men who went to the polls to vote for candidates who promised to fund Black schools and to support the new civil rights guarantees coming out of Washington. Perhaps they joined other Black men from throughout the state who met at the Colored Convention in Nashville to discuss the Black community's most pressing needs. When David Galloway, a USCT veteran, was incarcerated at the state penitentiary for marrying a white woman, for instance, convention delegates raised money for his legal defense and resolved to fight to "maintain the rights of the colored citizens of Tennessee to the civil rights of marriage with whomsoever they may contract and choose."[41]

Like most Reconstruction-era measures, Tennessee's 1870 marriage law was billed as a civil rights measure, but it acted as a Black Code. The law recognized the marriages of formerly enslaved people, declaring men and women who had lived together as husband and wife in slavery as automatically married. Freed people throughout the former Confederacy demanded these rights and protections. But, in addition to criminalizing Galloway's marriage, Tennessee's law carried forward longstanding prohibitions against bigamy and adultery.[42] Applied now to freed people, these prohibitions ensnared men and women emerging from slavery in the criminal justice system.[43] When they couldn't pay to have their marriages registered or dissolved or when they were not aware that the state recognized their cohabitation as marriage, freed people were found guilty of bigamy or adultery and sent to the penitentiary. Then they were sent back into the fields to pick cotton or, as was the case for Galloway, sent to a chain gang at work on the railroads.[44]

Had Walker returned to *both* Peggie and Cornelia, he might have been suspected of bigamy, even if he considered only one of them his wife—or if he had no intention of marrying either of them. A white newspaper in Ohio referred to a Black pastor who found his wife as a "colored Enoch Arden" and an "unintentional bigamist."[45]

The situation John Walker found himself in was made by the white men and women who had forced enslaved people in and out of marriages and sold away their wives, husbands, and children when it suited them. Now, new laws threatened freed people trying to disentangle these relationships and mend their marriages. When the delegates to Nashville's Colored Convention demanded the right to marry "whomsoever they choose," they had in mind many things, including that freed people alone should determine which relationships they carried into freedom and which ones they did not.

Peggie may have heard John Walker's name read in church. Perhaps she sent word back to him in Sacramento. If not, she learned that he was alive when he arrived at her door.

Cornelia may not have learned his whereabouts at all, and it is difficult now to determine hers. Records for a Cornelia Shute indicate that she married in a town just north of Nashville in 1866 and moved to Indiana sometime thereafter.[46] Hers was likely the most common experience among the freedwomen of her generation: she entered freedom not knowing what had become of her husband. Perhaps, like Enoch's Annie, she waited for a time before she moved on. Maybe she tried to find John Walker first. Lee Shute, the Nashville slave trader, may have commanded Cornelia's "marriage" to John: a man whose business it was to buy and sell people would have seen the value of a union that could produce children. As a freedwoman, Cornelia could have embraced the right to marry "whomsoever" she chose.

After nearly twenty years, how did Peggie feel when John arrived at the door? She was fifty-five years old, living with her twenty-seven-year-old son, Miles, his wife, Amanda, and their children, four-year-old Martha, two-year-old James, and one-year-old Frances. Surely, Peggie was relieved, perhaps happy, to see him again. But, then as now, one did not simply pick up after all those years, move forward as if no time had passed and there had been no other wives or lovers, as if the accumulation of losses over a lifetime did not make it difficult to trust *any* relationship. This was a hard truth about the long afterlife of slavery and the way that enslavers had forced men and women into and out of marriages. Reunions were not necessarily happy—maybe not even most of the time. Surely

John Walker had thought about the possibility that Peggie would reject him or greet him with ambivalence. There was always that chance.

Peggie didn't reject John. She and Miles welcomed John back into their home, and they lived together in a noisy house full of grandchildren. Miles's wife, Amanda, had a child every other year: Annie, Miles, Margaret, and Mary Ellen were all born after John came home. Together they mourned the loss of Frances and James. Those who survived got to know their grandfather and hear his stories about California, the people he had met there and the places he had seen. How he got there and how, although marooned in that faraway place, he managed to get back to them.

John Walker died sometime before 1880. He spent the last years of his life surrounded by the family he had made in slavery. There is no record that he and Peggie registered their marriage, but when the census enumerator appeared at Miles's house in 1870, he recorded their names as John and Peggie Walker. The next time an enumerator came around, Peggie, now widowed, had reverted to Patterson. It may be that after so many years living without John Walker, Peggie never warmed to the last name Walker. Or she preferred to share the last name Patterson with her children, like her son Edmund, whom she lived with in Nashville after John died. Edmund was born a year or two after Peggie was sold away from John. Nothing can be learned about Edmund's father.[47]

Peggie never wrote to the papers looking for John Walker. When freedwomen went to the papers, they searched for their children, not their husbands. Maybe they expected husbands were remarried or worried that men would reject children, like Edmund, born of different fathers. "If you love me you will love my children and you will provide for them as well as if they were your own," a freedwoman wrote to her husband, hoping that he agreed.[48] Women may have wanted to avoid attracting unwelcome attention by writing to the papers, or they could not see how to manage the expense when they had children to feed and shoes to buy. Or they expected not to succeed.

✦

INFORMATION WANTED.

Araminta Turner (formerly Clements), from Mobile, Ala., is desirous of learning the whereabouts of her husband, Alexander Turner, known also as Alexander Thorpe. Before the war he was taken to Texas by his owner, Col. Thorpe. Since that time she has not seen him. Her owner took her to Winchester, Tennessee. Should Mr. Armistead Saxon or any of the friends of the above named see this, they will confer a favor by addressing any information to

Mrs. ARAMINTA TURNER,
Care *Christian Recorder*,
Philadelphia, Pa.

N. B.--Ministers in Alabama, Texas or Tennessee will please read this notice in their churches.

June 12—1mo.

Araminta Turner, "Information Wanted," *Christian Recorder* (Philadelphia, PA), June 12, 1869

Araminta Turner wrote to the papers looking for her husband, Alexander, a few months after John Walker. She had been separated from him when Alexander's enslaver took him from her and marched him hundreds of miles away. Araminta Turner never found him.

Araminta and Alexander had married in Mobile, Alabama, before the war. They were likely migrants to the city, as most enslaved people were, having been force-marched there from Virginia, Maryland, Georgia, or the Carolinas.[49] "Araminta Turner," read her advertisement, "(formerly Clements), from Mobile, Ala., is desirous of learning the whereabouts of her husband." An Anderson Clements appears on the 1850 slave schedule in Mobile, but he owned only one female slave around thirty-five years old—too old to be Araminta and likely too young to have been her mother.[50] As to her husband, Araminta gave readers the following clues: "Alexander Turner, known also as Alexander Thorpe. Before the war he was taken to Texas by his owner, Col. Thorpe." At least fourteen people carrying the last name Turner appear on the 1850 schedule, and they counted sixty-seven people as their human property. Alexander may have been among them at that time. Like most of Mobile's slaveholders, the white Turners were all small slaveholders—owning two or three enslaved people.[51]

Marriages between enslaved people in these small holdings required a negotiation among at least four people—the couple and both of their enslavers. Perhaps Araminta's enslaver conceded to the marriage so long as Alexander's enslaver agreed to respect his claim to her children. And Alexander's enslaver agreed to the marriage to secure Alexander's loyalty and labor. Clements and Turner or Clements and Thorpe may have promised not to sell them away from each other. Consenting to marriages of slaves sustained slave owner paternalism, but there was nothing binding in a promise made by an enslaver to their slave. That's why enslavers who officiated the marriages of enslaved people left out the words "Let no man put asunder." Because, like God, they assumed the right to both join *and* pull apart.

If they made such a promise, Araminta's and Alexander's enslavers did not keep their word. Once Alexander was taken to Texas, Araminta heard nothing further from him. And then Araminta's enslaver took her to Winchester, Tennessee. Married in Mobile, Alexander and Araminta were now separated by more than eight hundred miles. Colonel Thorpe likely traveled via ship from Mobile to New Orleans before making his way to Texas. The colonel and Alexander may have been among the various Thorpes living in Lamar County, Texas, northeast of Corpus Christi, in 1860. The wartime population swelled with the arrival of enslavers and their "slave property" fleeing federal troops.[52] Louisiana native Kate Stone called Lamar County, where her family had taken their slaves, "the dark corner of the Confederacy." Despairing on the long journey, Stone gazed at the sky and thought "of all the dear friends that the waves of Fate are sweeping farther and farther away from us every day."[53] Perhaps when Alexander Turner looked at the stars over Texas, he thought about the loved ones he had left behind—his wife, Araminta, for instance.

The separation may not have meant the same thing for Alexander as it did for Araminta. Alexander Turner did not place an advertisement in the papers looking for her. Alexander may have married again in Texas and may have been concerned about the implications of finding her to his current marriage. Perhaps he suspected that she had died or remarried. He may have missed the ad she placed in a Philadelphia newspaper. It had been at least eight years since Alexander was taken from her. He may not have survived the trip to Texas, the war, or its violent aftermath there.

Or, he may have heard her query and ignored it.

Araminta came to Philadelphia during the war or soon afterward. Once slavery began to fall apart in Middle Tennessee in 1862, Araminta could have made her way from Winchester to the contraband camp in Murfreesboro, fifty miles north, or to Pulaski, sixty miles to the west. At Pulaski, refugees met northern missionaries who supplied them with clothing and staffed freedmen's schools.[54] Perhaps it was here that Armanita first set her sights on Philadelphia; here, too, Araminta tried to pick up any news about Alexander, heard the names of loved ones read from advertisements in the papers, and witnessed the marriages of fellow freedom seekers.

The search for family often began at camps like those in Tennessee. Lucy Chase, a white teacher, reported a conversation among refugee women in Virginia looking for husbands, some casually, others with urgency:

> One of Mrs. Brown's girls thinks, "Perhaps if I go to Norfolk I can get a husband."
>
> "But you have one," says Mrs. B.
>
> "Oh yes, but I have not seen him since last August, and I have not got anyone to take care of me. How'd you like that?"
>
> The cook lays down her fork, and says, "I think if I fall in love, I must marry again. I don't know whether my husband is living or not, he left me in Hampton."
>
> . . . poor Nancy, says, "I've only got *one* man, and he's away; left me here like a rotton stick to drop down and die."

Sometimes finding a husband could be as painful as losing him. Chase witnessed the heartache of a woman who found her first husband among her fellow refugees: "'Twas like a stroke of death to me," she said, rushing into his arms. Both of them had remarried, and she would not leave her new husband. "My husband's very kind, but I ain't happy. White folk's got a heap to answer for the way they've done to colored folks! So much they wont never *pray* it away?"[55]

For some women, shedding a husband was a form of freedom.

Women missionaries and teachers who worked among the refugees were in a position to hear many stories like these, of women making their way to freedom, hoping to find husbands, wondering how they would manage if they didn't. If Araminta spoke of Alexander to someone like Lucy Chase, perhaps the aid worker asked around. Maybe the advice she offered Araminta along with the donated clothing was to find work, that she should not expect the generosity she experienced in the form of a pair of shoes and a clean dress to continue. "We must strive so to regulate our charities," Chase reminded herself while handing out shoes donated by Philadelphia Quakers, "as not to educate paupers."[56] Supplying their material needs might help to keep refugees in the South. Northern whites contributed liberally to freedmen's aid when they saw it as a means of preventing a mass Black migration into their communities.[57]

But aid workers also saw in freedwomen who arrived in camp an opportunity to respond to northern women's insatiable appetite for domestic labor and sent them to the North to work in white women's homes. White northerners who supported abolition saw no contradiction in desiring for themselves a Black woman who would cook for them, wash and iron their clothes, and care for their children—work they did not want to do and for which they hoped to pay little. It may have been through a program like this that Araminta made her way to Philadelphia.

Every Thursday, freedwomen and children arrived at the offices of the Pennsylvania Abolition Society in Philadelphia and were sent to work in the homes of white city residents. "To prevent disappointment," read the society's circular, "we would state that many of these people have little or no acquaintance with housework, and are apt to be slow, though mostly of good dispositions and willing to learn."[58] The program invited white women to guide Black women in their transition to freedom by training them to be maids, cooks, and nannies. White

Philadelphians applied to the society with their preferences. "I would like to have a coloured Girl from 12 to 14 years of age, one that would be well calculated for general housework," wrote an applicant. Another one preferred "a woman who understood cooking, washing and ironing and would be obliging and willing, age between 25 and 35 without a child with her."[59]

That last employer might have had in mind Araminta Turner, who was in her mid-thirties when she arrived in Philadelphia and seems not to have had a child with her. Neither did she come with a husband or other kin with whom she might expect to spend her leisure time. When freedwomen migrated north to take work as domestics, they left one system of human trafficking behind for another.[60]

Araminta found work in the Philadelphia home of Andrew and Henrietta Miller and their four children.[61] Andrew was a grocer, a business that placed him comfortably in the middle class, but only so long as Henrietta was relieved from labor in and outside of their home. That's where Araminta came in. As the Millers' only servant, her work in a household of seven was considerable and likely included cooking, washing, ironing, and caring for the younger children. White women with means complained constantly about domestic servants who failed to live up to their expectations, who worked too little and demanded too much. Maryland-born, Henrietta Miller may have preferred a Black woman in the kitchen and in her laundry; perhaps her own mother had counseled her that the affection that white women felt for the Black women in their homes was reciprocated and compensated for poor wages and overwork.

Araminta had survived the domestic slave trade, made her way to freedom when the war came to Tennessee, and recruited allies who pointed her to Philadelphia and helped her get there. She was courageous and resourceful, and she no doubt knew how to flatter a white woman's ego, appear to be devoted to that woman's family over her own, and keep from Henrietta information about her husband, the family they had once had, and the one she hoped she would have again. The Millers didn't seem to have given much thought to these things, reporting to a census enumerator in 1870 that Araminta was twenty-five, a number that was low by about ten years, and born in South Carolina. She was alone in their household and kept these personal details to herself, but in Philadelphia Araminta found people with whom she shared her story and who steered her to those who helped her look for Alexander.

It was just a little over a one-mile walk from the Millers' to the Seventh Ward, home to a large Black population whose members sustained Black-owned businesses, schools, and churches. Black Philadelphians walked a little lighter now that slavery was outlawed and the state legislature, bowing to the pressure of Black activists and their Republican allies, had begun enshrining civil rights into state law—the right to ride the city's streetcars for instance and Black men's right to vote.[62] Philadelphia had served as a center of United States Colored Troops recruitment and training, and when these men returned to the city to muster out—as had James Dogans, before relocating to Pottstown—they fed a sense of expectation that the war would result in lasting change. In Philadelphia, Araminta joined a vibrant and dynamic Black community.

Even so, the city's reputation for employment discrimination and racist violence held fast, and the Black population grew slower than in other cities with substantial Black minorities.[63]

◆

Every right Black Philadelphians won had to be fiercely and repeatedly defended. On election day in 1871, the second in which Black men voted, white men hunted Black men in the streets determined to drive them away from the polls, and the police failed to respond. Several died that day, including among them Black teacher and activist Octavius V. Catto.[64] Only when freed people began to flee the South en masse at the end of the century did they make Philadelphia their destination. More women came than did men; when they did, like Araminta Turner, they found a community of people and institutions to support them, even when the city was unwelcoming.[65]

The office of the *Christian Recorder* was located just around the corner from Mother Bethel African Methodist Episcopal Church. Pastors there invited freed people to write to the church-owned paper for help finding loved ones. In June 1869, Araminta went there. Someone sat with her as she recalled the facts surrounding her separation from Alexander. Perhaps it was Elisha Weaver, pastor at Mother Bethel and editor of the *Christian Recorder*, who encouraged her to include additional details, such as her maiden name, Clements, and that her husband had once gone by Thorpe. Like most ads for spouses, Araminta's was brief and included only a few names and places, her husband's and a "Mr. Armistead Saxon or any of the friends of the above." Saxon's connection to her was left unclear. The ad instructed readers to contact her at the office of the *Christian Recorder*, which served as a missing persons bureau.

Her call for Alexander was read before AME congregations everywhere, and likely Araminta checked in to see if word from Alexander had arrived from Texas or Alabama or Tennessee. There probably had been no ceremony marking the beginning of their marriage, and now it was unclear if it had ended. As pastors read their names from the papers, they called on their congregations to be witnesses to their marriage. The same thing was repeated hundreds of times over in churches throughout the country. Perhaps there were prayers, a collective acknowledgment of marriages that had not taken place before a county clerk or Freedmen's Bureau agent.

White newspapers covered separations like Araminta's when they could be cast as "colored Enoch Ardens" or when they were resolved in quaint and affecting wedding ceremonies. Readers loved to witness the (re)marriage of old slave couples, in courthouses and in the papers. Under the headline "Two Old Darkies United After a Separation of Twenty-Five Years," a Louisville paper reported on the marriage of John Thompson and Kitty Owens, eighty-five and seventy, respectively. "A curious crowd" looked on as the two exchanged vows at the county clerk's office and Thompson fumbled in his pockets for the money to pay the clerk. (He came up short.)[66] Often, as in the story about James Dogans, papers did not bother to include the wife's name, even when she was responsible for the reunion. Surely, Harrison Bradley's first wife did not come to Yellow Springs, Ohio, "by accident" to find her ex-husband there, prosperous and living "in very good circumstances," as a Cincinnati paper reported. But that version of the story made for good entertainment, as did the paper's description of their marriage in slavery, when the two had "lived and cohabitated together, as beasts of the forest."[67] As if the lack of formality in enslaved people's marriages had resulted from racial inferiority rather than because enslavers denied slaves the right to marry.

Most women didn't find the husbands they sought, and when they did not, they did well to take care what they did next. State laws recognizing enslaved people's marriages and equalizing access to marriage were double-edged swords, as freed people often found themselves in violation of the legal definition of marriage. Enslaved people had developed a number of strategies for coping with the forced dissolution of their marriages. Some remarried. But they also negotiated a variety of temporary unions: "sweethearting," for instance, which historian Tera Hunter describes as "essentially lovers and not necessarily monogamous," or "taking up," which described a monogamous relationship, as did a "trial marriage." These practices that had guaranteed enslaved people's survival were criminalized under the new marriage laws, and freed people were disproportionately prosecuted for fornication, bigamy, and adultery.[68] Some of the newly defined offenses against the institution of marriage might have resulted *from* the process of trying to mend a marriage lost in slavery, from freed people's resolute commitment to the institution of marriage.

Sometime after 1870, Araminta left the Millers and took a position as a cook in the home of Allen Cuthbert, a retired grocer, and his wife, Rebecca.[69] She shared living and workspace with three other Cuthbert servants, a chambermaid, waitress, and gardener; perhaps she enjoyed a bit more leisure time there, though perhaps still not much privacy. The Cuthberts were elderly, and as Allen was deaf, the couple did little entertaining; Araminta's workload likely was predictable and consistent.

She did not remarry. With hundreds of ads searching for missing spouses, the Last Seen Collection can mislead us into concluding that marriage was the only intimate connection that mattered, the only love between adults that Freedom Generation experienced. But of course that was not the case; enslaved and freed people experienced the range of human emotion and connection that people have felt throughout history. They formed relationships of all sorts, most of which were never solemnized, some that served in place of marriage or alongside of it. Women like Araminta were used to forming strong bonds with other women, such as those with whom they lived and on whom they depended in the slave quarters. "If we define a stable relationship as one of long duration," historian Deborah Gray White has explained, "then it was probably easier for slave women to sustain stable emotional relationships with other bondwomen than bondsmen."[70] Perhaps Araminta found a comparable community of women in Philadelphia among the other domestic servants or in the pews and the kitchen of Mother Bethel.

It was not unusual for a woman like Turner to throw her lot in with friends. At least seventy-eight advertisements were placed by people looking for friends. Mrs. Lou Davis in Edwards, Mississippi, placed advertisements looking for three: Lethea Waters, whom she described as "a lady friend"; Irvin Loveless, "a gentleman friend of mine"; and Manda Hester, "an old lady friend of mine."[71] Like theirs, Araminta's life did not end with the loss of a husband.

Perhaps she sweethearted or took up with someone. Unlike in the former Confederate states, Pennsylvania did not pass postwar marriage laws aimed at entrapping freed people in the criminal justice system for unwittingly violating prohibitions against adultery or bigamy. In fact, in 1862, a state court affirmed the right of a woman to remarry when her absent husband was presumed dead, the same principle that would inform similar Enoch Arden Doctrine laws. The case involved a free Black woman, Lavinia Johnson, whose husband went away to sea and was never heard from again.[72] According to Pennsylvania, Lavinia was free to move on. So, too, was Araminta. In the twenty years that she lived in Philadelphia, Araminta had ample opportunity to make connections like Lou Davis's "lady" and "gentleman" friends with whom she could trade confidences and from whom she drew strength. Because she continued to work as a live-in domestic servant, even as women demanded to live with their own families, her personal space was circumscribed. The kitchen was hers, though, and here she greeted friends, told stories about those she had loved and lost, and kept her ear to the ground for word from Alabama, Tennessee, or Texas. When the enumerator attended the Cuthbert home in the Germantown neighborhood of Philadelphia in 1880, Araminta told him she was a widow.

Araminta Turner died two years later at fifty-five; the official cause of death was stroke, or apoplexy. She was buried at Olive Cemetery, a Black-owned and -operated property that also held a school, chapel, and the Home for the Aged and Infirm Colored Folks.[73] Perhaps her friends attended services for her at Mother Bethel AME before her interment; she had a history at that church, having gone to the pastors there for help looking for her husband, Alexander.

✦

Araminta surely knew that the odds were long in finding spouses who had been sold, marched, or driven away. Freedwomen who looked for their husbands were burdened by the same difficulties as men—relying on out-of-date information, for instance, and navigating the new names their spouses had adopted at freedom—and challenges unique to their condition, such as the name changes they themselves had made with each consecutive marriage. They also endured the poverty associated with caring for dependent children. We cannot know if the smaller number of advertisements in Black newspapers indicates that fewer women searched for their husbands than vice versa.

Perhaps they were concerned about sharing intimate details of their marriages with the male pastors whom they relied on to write the ads, men who were their neighbors and whose approval they could not afford to lose. Elisha Weaver, pastor at Mother Bethel, for instance, who, when he wasn't helping women like Araminta write their ads, offered moral advice to them in a column in the paper.[74] At a time when white lawmakers were carefully scrutinizing Black marriages, freedwomen and -men who took these searches public risked inviting trouble. Widely circulating stories about "colored Enoch Ardens" were a distraction from the new campaign of violence underway against Black marriages. They aimed to make light of the efforts of formerly enslaved husbands and wives to find one another despite the odds—and those odds got longer with the Black Codes and the rise of the carceral state.

Reunions could be fraught, uncomfortable, and traumatic and could even end in rejection. Freeborn Black author Charles Chesnutt witnessed reunions like these firsthand while teaching at Freedmen's Bureau schools in North Carolina. He wrote about the trauma of losing a spouse and finding them again in his short story "The Wife of His Youth." When an aged freedwoman, Liza Jane, finds her husband, Mr. Ryder, on the eve of his engagement, like Enoch Arden, Ryder hides his identity from Liza Jane. Not out of concern for her happiness but his own. Ryder eventually reveals himself to her, but Chesnutt pointedly lets the story trail off without a resolution.[75] Real-life reunions were perhaps more likely to end in ambiguity than over a Christmas dinner.

But Freedom Generation's husbands and wives searched for one another anyway, and hundreds took to the papers to tell how they had loved and cared for one another once and how they hoped to do so again.

CHAPTER TEN

Diana Johnson's Hope

Mr. Editor—I desire to find the whereabouts of my mother. sisters and brothers, whom I left in Roan county, North Carolina. My mother's name was Hannah Hilliard; sisters, Jinsy, Flora and Lucy; brothers, John, Benjamin and Milas Calvin. My father, Jack Hilliard, died when I was quite an infant. I was sold from the Hilliard estate to a speculator by the name of Bill Hadin, who brought me to Texas, whom I have been living with ever since. Address Dianah Johnson, Goliad, Texas.

Dianah [*sic*] Johnson to "Mr. Editor,"
Southwestern Christian Advocate (New Orleans, LA), September 3, 1885

From her home in Goliad, Texas, Diana[1] Johnson searched for the family she had last seen forty years earlier in North Carolina. She placed a series of advertisements in the *Southwestern Christian Advocate*, the newspaper affiliated with the Black Methodist church in New Orleans. Next, she wrote to Philadelphia's *Christian Recorder*. Each ad began with a plea: "I desire to inquire for my relatives," "I desire to find the whereabouts of my mother sisters and brothers," or simply "I desire to find my people."[2] Her ads ended with: "Any information concerning the above named persons will be very thankfully received. Address, Mrs. Diana Johnson, Goliad Texas." Or, in this case, simply, "Address Dianah Johnson, Goliad Texas."

> My mother's name was Hannah Hilliard; sisters, Jinsy, Flora and Lucy; brothers, John, Benjamin and Milas Calvin. My father, Jack Hilliard, died when I was quite an infant. I was sold from the Hilliard estate to a speculator by the name of Bill Hadin [Haden], who brought me to Texas, whom I have been living with ever since.

Over the next fifteen years, she placed at least five different advertisements. She updated the later ones to reflect new information she had gathered since the previous one. Nine years after placing her first ad in the papers, for instance, Diana added the names of people who had bought her brother John (William Golden) and her sisters Lucy ("Catherine Hellard, who married John Keller") and Jency (Douglas Haden). She learned the fate of those who had been separated from the family through inheritance: her mother, Hannah, had "fallen heir to" Mrs. Nancy Tar and Flora to Jessie Hellard. Four years later she'd learned that her sold-away sister Jency (after the first two ads, Diana settled on this spelling) had married a man named Harry Galloway. Primed by her ads in the Black newspapers, information reached Diana Johnson that helped her to fill in some of her family story.

The new details she received fed Diana Johnson's hope, or as she phrased it, her desire. And she kept looking.

Then, in 1900, she marshaled all the knowledge she had acquired over fifteen years of searching and wrote to Buffalo and Chicago. Early that year, she addressed letters to local officials there, hoping they would know what to do next. For a few days, Diana's name and her story appeared in newspapers in both cities. The *Buffalo Evening News* ran her story under the headline "Echo of Slavery. Colored Woman from Texas Is Endeavoring to Find Her Family" on January 16, 1900. "Former Slave Writes to Clerk," read the headline in the *Buffalo Enquirer* that same day, followed by "Diana Johnson Is Looking for a Dozen or More Relatives." A newspaper in Chicago published Diana's letter on January 17, as did other Illinois papers. Newspapers in Iowa, Wisconsin, and Nebraska picked up the story and ran it, too.[3] There may have been others.

Appearing alongside front-page news about America's war in the Philippines, Diana Johnson's account of the family she'd lost in slavery was from a bygone era, a distant time in the nation's past. The headlines made the point, as did the commentary. "The letter," said the *Buffalo Review*, "brings forcibly before the present generation the state of affairs which existed in the South before the days of the Civil War."[4] Americans were looking to the new century, having left slavery and the war fought over it behind them. Former Confederate and Union veterans called on their countrymen to fight alongside one another against Spanish forces in Cuba and the Philippines—and then against the people of the Philippines. White Americans embraced a new nationalism based on their racial superiority and on forgetting that they had once fought each other over slavery.[5] An entire generation had grown up mostly untroubled by that past. But perhaps reading a letter "from a former slave now in Texas who is trying to find a trace of her broken up family" could teach younger readers to take pity on those less fortunate. "Recollections of slavery days," explained the *Buffalo Weekly Express* in their preface to Johnson's letter, "and a pathetic picture of those times will be brought to younger minds rather more vividly than story-books convey such pictures."[6]

Diana Johnson's story of love and loss came to white readers as an echo of events that happened long ago and far away. It flitted across the pages of their papers for a few days early in 1900, destined, perhaps, to be read at dinner tables to prick the consciences of young listeners, and then it vanished.

But Diana Johnson kept searching, and hoping, as she had for years, with the help of people near and far away who sent word about what they knew of her sisters, brothers, and mother, Hannah. Help came from teachers and pastors, kin, friends, and neighbors whose searches inspired hers, people who wrote to the papers with the names of the loved ones they hoped to find. It came also from strangers in distant cities who determined to put her name in their papers, although they didn't know her or the people she named. But even as it leapt from one paper to the next, and as others lent a hand, the central facts of her family's story remained the same: she and a brother were sold from their mother and force-marched far away. Her sisters were sold, one by one, and then her remaining brothers and mother. When freedom came, members of Hannah and Jack Hellard's family were scattered across the country, and they remained scattered because there was no nationwide reckoning with the human costs of the domestic slave trade and the violence it had wrought. No program was dedicated to the work of reuniting these families. The facts about her family's separation could not be conscripted to the project of forgetting underway in the white press, the new "research" about the weakness of Black family ties, and the statues commemorating slaveholders as heroes and martyrs with no mention of how they had separated families.

Diana Johnson shared a hope with others of her generation: to see her brothers again, enjoy the company of her sisters, and to know from them what became of their mother. We don't know if she set her eyes on one of her brothers or held a sister in her arms again. But her repeated ads are a measure of the hope that sustained her. We should not discount the power of hope around which communities of freed people were built, all of them searching for someone, because we cannot be sure whether it was fulfilled. Because the evidence of Freedom Generation's searches for family has been lost and because the enduring search for family defies the logic of white supremacy. Hope like Diana Johnson's was infectious, sustaining, enduring. It drove her and thousands like her to commit to the work of reconstituting their families even when the odds were long and the obstacles many.

✦

Either by her choice or theirs, the letter that made it into the white papers was peopled with speculators and references to debt, but nothing about George and Catherine Hellard, who had sold Diana and her brother and sisters.[7] Diana figured she was about eleven when that happened. Johnson was in her mid-seventies when she wrote to clerks in Buffalo and Chicago listing their names alongside hers.[8] Diana was a mother of six children and grandmother to at least fifteen. Her daughters Maria and Kate and her sons Alexander (Alex) and Edward remained in Goliad, living with their mother or nearby. Diana's daughter Lucy, named, perhaps for her own sister, lived two counties to the east, in Edna, Jackson

County, Texas.[9] Sometime after 1900, Kate and Alex and their families relocated to Beeville, thirty miles in the other direction. Close enough to keep an eye on their mother and for her to visit.

It was likely on one such visit that Lucy sat down with her mother and helped her address queries to clerks in Chicago and Buffalo.

Train lines connected Diana Johnson and her children to one another and to Houston toward the northeast, San Antonio to the west, and, through Beeville, south to Corpus Christi. Diana lived her entire adult life on the flat, grassy coastal plains at the center of the postwar Texas cattle industry; she was proficient at riding horseback. In her seventies, she may have preferred the relative comfort of the train's segregated smoking car to the saddle as she made her way the fifty miles to Edna to visit Lucy. Perhaps she shared the car with Black cattlemen and ranch hands or mixed with them at one of the many stations along the way, where they talked of beef prices and slaughtering the stock ahead of the season's ice storms. One of the stops was the station at Cologne, a Black-owned town where freed people built churches and a school and ran a slaughterhouse and other businesses.[10] Towns like Cologne were often called freedom colonies where residents sought safety and protection from hostile white neighbors.

For nearly a decade, Diana Johnson supported her family on the 160-acre tract of land she'd purchased from the state of Texas, near the freedom colony of Cologne. She raised cattle there—Texas longhorn—maybe some sheep or turkeys. Perhaps she supplied ranch hands with horses broken from the wild stock found on the prairie. There was no part of the cattle business that Johnson did not know, but when she decided to take her search for her family to faraway places with unfamiliar place names, she enlisted the help of her schoolteacher daughter.

Lucy had heard her mother speak often of Hannah and how the Hellards had taken Hannah's children from her, one by one, and sold them to men who took them to Alabama and Texas. Diana recalled the names as best she could, having never seen them written down. Hellard appeared in one of Diana's early ads as "Hilliard," and eventually, Diana decided that "Calvern," her mother's new last name, was actually "Garner," or maybe it was "Gardner." Sometime late in her life,

Johnson attended school, learning enough there to read the *Southwestern Christian Advocate*, where her first ads appeared.[11]

About a third of the population of Goliad were freed people. Years before the town was accessible by train, when crossing it required hailing a boatman to cross the San Antonio River, freed people began placing ads in the *Southwestern* looking for their family in Missouri, Alabama, South Carolina, and Tennessee.[12] Freed people in Goliad drew inspiration from their neighbors and recruited allies. Sometimes help came from surprising places.

Diana Johnson wrote to the *Southwestern* four times between 1885 and 1897 and then to the *Christian Recorder*. Determined to find her family members, she enlisted Lucy's help in reaching beyond Black newspapers and the pulpits of Black churches. She focused on two midwestern cities with small Black communities. African Americans accounted for only 2 percent of the population of Chicago, and in Buffalo they barely registered at one-half of one percent.[13] Diana's ads in the Black press reached many more Black readers than the letters she addressed to clerks in two cities she'd never been to. She must have had good reason to go through the trouble.

Diana Johnson was familiar with the clerks at Goliad County Courthouse. She stood before a clerk in Goliad in July 1873, declaring her intent to purchase the land where she lived and worked and that, as head of a family, she was entitled to claim as preemption. Three years later, in August 1876, she filed her application for a title to the land along with a surveyor's field notes, indicating the exact coordinates of her property. Above the mark she made in place of her signature, the clerk confirmed that she was "Head of a family" and "Bona fide settler" on the homestead that she "occupied and improved."[14]

A clerk in Austin issued her a deed to that land in 1881 over the governor's signature, confirming that she had paid for it in full, and a clerk in Goliad registered Diana Johnson's sale of twenty-five acres of that property to Samuel Ware, her son-in-law (Kate's husband).[15] In March 1884, Diana was back at the courthouse, where a clerk registered the conditional sale of the remainder of her original 160 acres; a few weeks later, a clerk recorded Johnson's purchase of a plot of land on

Fannin Street, in the town of Goliad, for $465.75.[16] Clerks recorded the taxes she paid on her property each year. Various neighbors, Black and white, in Goliad vouched for her reputation as landowner and head of a family and signed their names next to hers on her land transactions. Clerks in the courthouse knew Diana Johnson. She expected that the clerk in Buffalo would know his community as well as did those in Goliad, recognize the last name Hellard or Garner, she reasoned, and know how to reach them.

Lucy helped her address those letters, which arrived early in 1900.

✦

Fortunately, Diana's letter landed on Buffalo clerk Otto Wende's desk. The industrious young man opened the letter on January 16 and walked it to the offices of five newspapers. Three published it the same day: the *Buffalo Evening News*, the *Buffalo Commercial Advertiser*, and the *Buffalo Enquirer*. Some of the details were changed, maybe as reporters copied them from the letter. At the *Evening News*, Jency, Diana's sister, became "Jennie," and the *Buffalo Enquirer* decided on "Janey." Both changed the spelling of Diana's mother's last name from Garner to "Gerner." All the papers read Diana's or Lucy's "Rowan County, North Carolina," as "Roman." The *Commercial Advertiser* introduced Diana's letter with a headline reading, "Slavery Days. Texas Woman Tells a Story of the Breaking Up of Her Family." The *Evening News* appended the following to her letter: "The County Clerk will endeavor to learn if there are any persons here in Buffalo who know anything about this family."[17]

Something in Diana Johnson's appeal spoke to Wende, county clerk in Buffalo, Erie County, a city of 350,000, and he decided he would try to help. Maybe it was his German immigrant mother's experience of leaving her family behind that explains why Diana's story struck a chord.[18] Immigrants like Mary Wende posted advertisements of their own in the papers, looking for family and kin who had arrived before them, naming places in Ireland, Italy, Poland, or Germany where they had last seen their loved ones.[19] Finding these earlier immigrants could give them a leg up or, at least, ensure that they did not start from scratch. Nearly three-quarters of the population of Buffalo in 1900 were immigrants; they might relate to Diana's story even if they had never known the violence perpetrated against enslaved people and their families.[20]

What motivated Otto Wende to take such an interest in Diana Johnson's letter, we don't know. But at a time when white Americans were interested only in stories that ended happily, Otto Wende paid attention to one before he knew how it would end.

James J. Healy, a clerk in Cook County, Illinois, received Diana Johnson's letter on the same day as Wende, and he, too, spread the word.[21] Johnson's story made it into the Polish-language paper associated with the Catholic Church, *Dziennik Chicagoski* (*Chicago Daily News*), where it ran under the headline, "*Szuka Krewnych*," or "Looking for Relatives."[22] Perhaps the immigrant experiences of leaving family behind touched a nerve here as well.

Shoehorned between an announcement for the Chicago Poultry, Cat, Pet Stock Show and predictions for a good corn crop, four other Illinois papers—the *Champaign Daily Gazette*; the *Freeport Journal* and *Daily Journal*, both published in Freeport; and the *Rock Island Argus*—ran a short announcement the next day: "A letter has been received at Chicago from Mrs. Diana Johnson, of Edna, Tex., formerly a slave, asking help in locating her relatives, who were sold away from her before the war."[23] The same announcement appeared in papers that day in Kenosha, Wisconsin; Waterloo, Iowa; and Fremont, Nebraska. There wasn't much information to work with, but it showed that Diana Johnson's decision to take her search to the offices of county clerks was a good one. Like Otto Wende, Healy had sent her appeal, in abbreviated form, to the offices of newspapers in the Chicago area; from there it was carried, likely via telegraph, as far away as Nebraska, perhaps farther.

And, for a few more days, newspapers in Buffalo continued to publish Diana Johnson's letter in full. Perhaps her name was called out from the pulpit and repeated in the pews at Michigan Street Baptist Church and Vine Street African Methodist Episcopal Church, the city's two Black churches.[24] In Chicago, appeals like Diana's went out from the pews of Black churches and were published in the Black press.[25]

Perhaps for people in the small towns in Illinois, Wisconsin, Iowa, and Nebraska, Diana Johnson's story brought slavery from the past into the present. Among their neighbors were people whose stories they didn't know, slavery's survivors who were also looking for someone they had lost.

✦

When Diana Johnson arrived in 1840, Goliad was a sparsely populated frontier town, not much more than a fort and an old Spanish presidio. In 1835, Texan colonists in Goliad, fearing that Mexican forces were fomenting insurrection among their slaves, began a rebellion against Mexico; a year later, Mexican general Santa Anna executed three or four hundred of the defeated rebels on the presidio grounds.[26] The defeat at Goliad, just a few weeks after a similar one at the Alamo in San Antonio, was not as well remembered, but locals likened the men who died there to martyrs. The rebels pushed Santa Anna back a few weeks later and declared their insurgency victorious, but Texas's war with Mexico still boiled.

Johnson came to Goliad as the property of Bill Haden, even though, under Mexican law, slavery had been outlawed. Men like Haden were confident, nonetheless, that their property would be secure there, or they would force the issue. That force came in 1845, when the U.S. annexed Texas. U.S. victory in the war with Mexico that began the next year secured enslavers' rights to ownership of the enslaved people they had force-marched into the state from all over the Upper South. The Bill Hadens kept coming with their human chattel, and by the Civil War, there were 843 enslaved people in Goliad, including Diana Johnson and her children: fourteen-year-old Alexander, five-year-old Maria, four-year-old Edward, and Kate, who was around three.[27] Bill Haden either did not stay long or he died soon after, for no Haden—or Hayden—ever appeared in a census. Neither were there any slaveholders by the name of Johnson to whom he might have sold Diana and from whom she may have derived her last name, leaving open the question: Who "owned" Diana and her children? The record is silent, too, about the children's father or fathers.[28] Lucy was born in September 1864, the last of Diana's children; she was free before she celebrated her first birthday.[29]

That child grew up to be a teacher. Like all teachers in Texas, Lucy had to pass competency and morality tests before she entered the classroom. Then, her determination was tested when the state's new white supremacist leadership, attempting to destroy Black aspirations, starved rural schools like those in Edna of resources.[30] Lucy was still teaching there in 1900 when her mother came for a visit.

It is a testament to Diana Johnson's resourcefulness that she survived the war and kept her five children alive. "They sure were hard times," Martha Patton recalled of the war years in her Federal Writers' Project interview. Formerly enslaved to Christian Susan Lott, a widowed Goliad slaveholder and owner of twenty-three enslaved people, Martha described shortages of food and water, how she and her family made do with the little cornmeal and flour they could get, how all the creeks and wells dried up and they had to tote water for half a mile, how they ignored the dead cows near the watering hole and the grasshoppers that lay on top. "Didn't make us sick, lady," the ninety-one-year-old replied to the interviewer's question about drinking that water, "'twas all we had and the good Lord took care of us."[31]

Johnson had lived in Goliad for twenty years when the wagons carrying food stopped coming, flour and corn reserves dried up along with the wells, and white children, too, felt the pangs of hunger that enslaved children knew well. When there was no food, clothing, or medicine, whites in Goliad depended on enslaved people who wove cloth from the wool salvaged from dead sheep and the patches of cotton they kept near their cabins, brewed a tea by boiling corn shucks that could break a fever, and who knew better than to look to their enslavers when they were hungry.

Enslaved people brought the news that slavery had ended before Union troops arrived in Goliad to enforce General Gordon Granger's emancipation order. Eight years later, in July 1873, Diana Johnson bought her land on Manahuilla Creek, about five miles east of Goliad.

This was an extraordinary accomplishment. Within a decade as a free woman, Diana Johnson had established herself and her family on a homestead where she would answer to no one. Not to a white landowner. Not a husband. The property she bought ensured her family's future together. Her children attended school and learned to read and write. Having arrived as an enslaved child, fifty-one-year-old Diana Johnson was surrounded now by a growing family, living on property she owned in full, in a town that stood at the center of Texas's postwar cattle industry. The work involved in running that property was considerable—protecting the cattle from droughts in the summer and winter ice storms, preparing the stock for spring trail drives, and mending the fences—but, amidst the long days, Diana Johnson surely allowed herself moments to feel contentment and experience joy.

The law under which Diana Johnson bought her property marked the high point of Reconstruction in Texas. During his one term as governor, Edmund Davis, a U.S. Army veteran, oversaw revisions to the state constitution that eradicated the state Black Codes, recognized freed people's basic civil rights, and mandated that all children in the state attend public schools. In 1870, Davis signed into law an act declaring that "every head of a family who has not a homestead" was entitled to purchase 160 acres of land for one dollar an acre; homesteaders were required to have lived on and worked the property for three years, called a "preemption."[32] Under that law, Black Texans like Diana Johnson had access to that hallmark of freedom; just about everywhere else in the postwar South, white lawmakers passed laws that prohibited Black landownership.[33] Joseph Smith and George Washington, two formerly enslaved men from Victoria, Texas, registered land purchases the same year as Johnson, about nine miles east of her property. Smith and Washington built the town of Cologne, where Black residents provided for and protected one another. Proximity to the residents of Cologne gave Diana Johnson peace of mind as the state's brief experiment with racial equality ended abruptly and former Confederates forced their way back into power. Johnson was safe there on her own land—or safer, at least, than she'd ever been before in her life.

The concentration of Black landowners just outside the town turned postwar Goliad into something of a magnet for Black cowboys. Armed and mounted, these men—most of them were men—served as a private army protecting Black Texans. They turned out on election days, lining the streets of Goliad as a show of force and as a warning to anyone who might consider standing between a Black man and the ballot box.[34] Diana was armed with the shotgun she always carried, except, perhaps on Sundays, when she attended services at Fannin Street Methodist Church in town or Minnehulla Baptist, close to her property.[35]

Mostly, there wasn't anything new about the violence or threats of violence that hung over a town like Goliad. The first white Texans who settled there died for the right to be slaveholders, and so did the second wave of settlers. In between, county leaders passed ever harsher ordinances restricting enslaved people's movements and their gatherings, each ordinance indicating the failure of the last one.[36] The appearance of the Ku Klux Klan in South Texas towns in the 1870s marked the latest effort to check the power Black Texans had seized as voters, officeholders, and landowners. What *was* new were the armed Black men and women who stood guard at the church door or who took aim when a stranger approached their property line.

When Diana Johnson sold the last of her property in 1884, it may have been because she was tired of ranching or she saw trouble coming with the work underway on the railroad line connecting Victoria to Goliad.[37] Two weeks later, she bought that plot of land in town and found people who were searching for their families by writing to the papers.

In 1885, Diana placed her advertisement in the paper looking for the family she had last seen a lifetime ago but for whom her love was still strong. Other Black women and men in Goliad wrote for their families, too, including George Washington, one of the original settlers at Cologne. In his ad, Washington helped a neighbor by adding her name to his appeal for word of their families in Virginia.[38] Among the community of freed people in Goliad, Texas, people were either looking for their family or helping others to do so—sometimes both.

Like others we have read about in these pages, it is difficult to know if Diana Johnson found her people.

✦

Diana Johnson survived slavery, the war, and postwar violence. Miraculously, she also survived the 1902 tornado that ripped through the town on a Sunday morning that spring, destroying the Fannin Street Church and killing fifty parishioners inside. Survivors recalled the line of black cones reaching for the ground and a sound "like an explosion." "It just destroyed everything," an old-timer remembered. "The Negroes were having a church service down at their church and the roof collapsed and everyone in there was killed. It was a very bad thing."[39] Among the dead were Diana Johnson's friends and neighbors, people who had been like kin to her when she arrived all those years ago, holding on to the names of her loved ones in North Carolina.

There were fewer doors to knock on in the Black part of town in 1910 when a census enumerator knocked on Diana Johnson's; she likely knew the names of many people who would not be counted that year. Johnson said she was eighty-five and told the enumerator that she was a widow, as were her daughters Lucy and Maria, who lived with their mother on her property. So did her son Eddie. It was the only time that Diana's marriage was ever recorded in extant records; by then, she'd been head of her family for more than forty years.

Diana Johnson died sometime before 1920. There is no record of her death or where she was buried, although surely her burial was attended by her children, who she had kept alive through slavery and the war that ended it and whose safety and independence she'd helped to secure since then. Johnson may have been buried in the Black cemetery in Cologne. Or maybe she was buried on the land she bought in Goliad or outside of town, the 160 acres that is still identified by its original owner, "Abstract #171, D. Johnson, Goliad Preemption." A piece of that land remained in the family for a time. There isn't much there today that Diana Johnson wouldn't recognize, except a modern house at one end and a mobile home park farther down the road. Cattle huddle in the shade of mesquite trees. In her search for family, Diana Johnson had built her children a living monument, a legacy of hope that was a gift from her generation to theirs.

Acknowledgments

I don't recall when I first started thinking about this book, but it was in 2019 when my dear friend Catherine Kerrison encouraged me to write it and introduced me to her (and now my) agent, Howard Morhaim. Howard saw the potential of the project and has been a stalwart advocate of it throughout. Because of Howard, I received the greatest gift I could have asked for in getting to work with Bob Bender. Bob has edited many extraordinary books of history about figures large and small. It has been a profound privilege to work with and learn from him. Bob read the manuscript twice; each time, he coaxed me to keep my eyes on one person's story line and not to crowd the book with names. If readers encounter any crowds in the pages of this book, that's my fault and not Bob's. I am deeply grateful for his generosity and patience. I hope that pulling this book over the finish line has kept him distracted through a disappointing NCAA season at Villanova.

I am thrilled to have the opportunity to offer my thanks to the National Endowment for the Humanities for awarding me a 2023 Public Scholar Award. This support allowed me to complete a draft of the book. I am delighted to thank the family of Robert M. Birmingham for supporting this research. I am grateful to Villanova University for supporting my leave. Special thanks to my friends and department

colleagues Marc Gallicchio and Lynne Hartnett, who championed this work from the beginning, and thanks to Franny Murphy and Vicki Sharpless for all that they do to make our work easier.

Archivists and librarians are history's equivalents of first responders. When the pandemic shut everything down—and afterward when things began reopening, but often with skeleton crews—they cheerfully answered queries, scanned materials, opened access to in-house databases, and in every respect enabled the work to go on. I also had the good fortune and pleasure of traveling to archives, libraries, courthouses, and cemeteries and was reminded of how much more one can learn by talking with locals about the histories of their communities. I would like to thank some of these people here, including: Tim Hodgdon at the Louis Round Wilson Special Collections Library, University of North Carolina at Chapel Hill; Mindy Babarskis at Library of Michigan; Sue Patterson, Volunteer Reference Department at the Yazoo (MS) Library; Marisa Richardson, manager, Bossier Parish (LA) Libraries History Center; Fermand M. Garlington II, university records manager and archival associate, Archives and Special Collections, Noel Memorial Library, Louisiana State University, Shreveport, LA; Melissa McPherson, librarian, Willard Library, Battle Creek, Michigan; Shelley Parks, Goliad Center for Texas History; Lynda Breeding, Goliad County Historical Commission chair; Vickie Quinn, Goliad County district clerk; Sawyer Magnus, assistant archivist, Special Collections and University Archives, Velma K. Waters Library, Texas A&M-Commerce; Laurel Neuman, research specialist, Texas General Land Office. Katherine Vollen and Dennis Edelin at the National Archives and Records Administration, Washington, D.C., helped me to get access to pensions and patiently answered my repeated follow-up queries. Villanova librarian Jutta Seibert helped solve many research mysteries, and, if a reel of microfilm or other source existed in a library, Luisa Cywinski convinced them to lend it to us. Thank you to Margaret Jerrido, archivist at Mother Bethel AME Church, Philadelphia, who opened the archives of the *Christian Recorder* and made it possible for this project to get underway. Margaret is the longest and most resolute friend of the project.

Eric Paul Morningstar, an undergraduate student at Western Michigan University, and Anthony Pandolfino, undergraduate at University of Texas at Austin, went back into archives for me when I realized I'd forgotten things. Jesse Nasta volunteered for the project when he was a graduate student at Northwestern. Thank you to the Villanova graduate students who spent hours reading microfilm to find the advertisements, including Katarina Andersen, Tia Antonelli, Carly Beehler, Kristin Bridges, Chris Byrd, Jenna Cholowinski, Karyna Hlyvynska, Ari Levine, Bonnie Loden, Janis Parker, Hannah Pfeifer, Margaret Strolle, and Jessica Talarico. Some of them continued to work on the project even after they graduated. Daniel Runyon and Michael Fiorelli coded the ads when we had just over one thousand, helping me think about the questions that I should ask. Katarina Andersen conducted research on a few of the book's potential subjects, and her enthusiasm and spirit continue to inspire me. I am very proud of all my former students and grateful for what they taught me.

I am indebted to many friends in history who wrote letters for me, read drafts of grant applications, helped me decipher sources, pointed to the things I needed but couldn't remember, and read drafts of chapters. These include Carole Emberton, Margaret Humphreys, Anne Marshall, Randall Miller, Megan Kate Nelson, Joshua Rothman, Donald Shaffer, Andrew Slap, Diane Miller Sommerville, Yael Sternhell, Amy M. Taylor, and Kidada Williams. I am very lucky to have such generous friends. Lesley Gordon, Anne Sarah Rubin, and Susannah Ural supported me in innumerable ways over the years I spent writing the book and when I wasn't. Special thanks to Lori Ginzberg, who read every word of every chapter and pushed me to think more carefully and write more clearly.

Catherine Kerrison and Signe Peterson Fourmy are the best allies and writing companions I could ask for. The regular meetings of our Writing Accountability Group turned ugly first drafts of chapters into sensible second drafts. And at every step of the way since then, Catherine and Signe have encouraged and supported me in this work. Long live the WAG! Thanks to Joan Koven, Rachel Torrano, and Abby Gaertner, for their enthusiasm and for making the time spent away from the desk at Teeple memorable.

As always, my biggest debt of gratitude goes to those closest to me. Ed Fierros reads everything I write and helps me to see what's important in a project—and in life. He is and always will be what's most important to me, as are our children, Diego, Pablo, and Marisol. It may have been because of Diego and Pablo that my eyes first landed on the advertisements that are the basis of this book. I recall the moment in 2007—Diego was ten and Pablo was eight—when I read Elizabeth Williams's advertisement looking for her four children. Williams, who lived in Marysville, California, had last seen her children in Franklin County, Tennessee, twenty-five years before. "Any information given concerning them," she wrote, "will be very gratefully received by one whose love for her children survives the bitterness and hardships of many long years spent in slavery." Williams's words stuck with me. Since then, our newsfeeds have been filled with stories like Williams's, of children taken from their parents, of separated families' determined efforts to be reunited, of love that endures. We can try but we will fail to understand Elizabeth Williams's pain in losing her children. I wasn't sure this was my book to write. But I do know that it was important to try, because if we don't try to see this history through her eyes, we will be doomed to continue to repeat it.

—Judith Giesberg
Havertown, Pennsylvania
April 2024

Notes

Introduction

1 Ira Berlin, *Generations of Captivity: A History of African-American Slaves* (Cambridge, MA: Harvard University Press, 2003), 8, 245–70.

2 Sarah Debro Interview, *Federal Writers' Project: Slave Narrative Project*, Vol. 11, North Carolina, Part 1, Adams–Hunter, 1936, 253, Manuscript/ Mixed Material, Library of Congress, https://www.loc.gov/item/mesn111/.

3 Walter Johnson, *Soul by Soul: Life Inside the Antebellum Slave Market* (Cambridge, MA: Harvard University Press, 1999), 49–50, 64.

4 Michael Tadman, *Speculators and Slaves: Masters, Traders and Slaves in the Old South* (Madison: University of Wisconsin Press, 1989), 144.

5 John Hope Franklin and Loren Schweninger, *Runaway Slaves: Rebels on the Plantation* (New York: Oxford University Press, 1999), 52, 97–123.

6 Violet Lester to Miss Patsy Patterson, North Carolina, Bullock County, GA, August 23, 1857, Lester Violet, Joseph Allred Papers, 1819–1903, David M. Rubenstein Library, Duke University.

7 Eric Gardner, "Remembered (Black) Readers: Subscribers to the *Christian Recorder*, 1864–1865," *American Literary History* 23, no. 2 (2011): 240–42.

8 Edited by Revs. A. E. P. Albert and Marshall W. Taylor, the *Southwestern* was founded in 1873. James B. Bennett, *Religion and the Rise of Jim Crow in New Orleans* (Princeton, NJ: Princeton University Press, 2005), 47–51. Irvine Garland Penn, *The Afro-American Press, and Its Editors* (1891) (New York: Arno Press, 1969), 223–27.

9 Naro Gillespie, "Lost Friends," *Southwestern Christian Advocate* (New Orleans, LA), December 1, 1881, in *Last Seen: Finding Family After Slavery*,

https://informationwanted.org/items/show/1393. Advertisements in both papers sometimes also appeared as letters to the editor.

10 Isabel Wilkerson, *Warmth of Other Suns: The Epic Story of America's Great Migration* (New York: Random House, 2010), 11.

11 Heather Ann Williams, *Help Me to Find My People: The African American Search for Family Lost in Slavery* (Chapel Hill: University of North Carolina Press, 2012), 192.

12 "After Forty-Four Years," *The Tennessean* (Nashville, TN), September 25, 1903. "A Romance of Slavery," *Butler Weekly Times* (Butler, MO), January 20, 1884.

13 Bessel van der Kolk, *Body Keeps the Score: Brain, Mind, and Body in the Healing of Trauma* (New York: Viking, 2014), 193. Jacek Debiec, "A Sudden and Lasting Separation from a Parent Can Permanently Alter Brain Development," The Conversation, June 21, 2018, https://theconversation.com/a-sudden-and-lasting-separation-from-a-parent-can-permanently-alter-brain-development-98542, accessed October 25, 2021. Rachel Yehuda et al., "Relationship Between Cortisol and Age-Related Memory Impairments in Holocaust Survivors with PTSD," *Psychoneuroendocrinology* 30 (2005): 678–87.

14 Tiya Miles, *All That She Carried: The Journey of Ashley's Sack, a Black Family Keepsake* (New York: Random House, 2021), 126.

15 "Mary Delaney," Information Wanted ad, *Christian Recorder* (Philadelphia, PA), April 17, 1902. Lula Montgomery, "Do You Know Them?," *Richmond Planet* (Richmond, VA), August 20, 1898.

16 Jessie Johnson, Mr. Editor, *Southwestern Christian Advocate*, February 21, 1884, https://informationwanted.org/items/show/2888.

17 Samuel Clemens (Mark Twain), "A True Story, Word for Word as I Heard It," *The Atlantic*, November 1874, 23.

18 John Williams, *Asheville Daily Citizen* (Asheville, NC), December 31, 1892, http://informationwanted.org/items/show/3235. See also Jack Corkley, *Cincinnati Daily Star* (Cincinnati, OH), January 23, 1879, http://informationwanted.org/items/show/3252.

19 Barbara Hochman, *"Uncle Tom's Cabin" and the Reading Revolution: Race, Literacy, Childhood, and Fiction* (Amherst: University of Massachusetts Press, 2011), 152.

20 Saidiya Hartman, "Venus in Two Acts," *Small Axe* 12, no. 2 (June 2008): 14, 4.

CHAPTER ONE **Patience and Clara Bashop**

1 Harriet Beecher Stowe, *Uncle Tom's Cabin* (1852) (New York: Penguin, 1981).

2 Joseph Pulitzer owned both the *World* and the *Dispatch*. "Joseph Pulitzer: American Newspaper Publisher," *Britannica*, https://www.britannica.com /biography/Joseph-Pulitzer, accessed March 25, 2024.

3 "Hunting Her Child: A Former Slave Still in Search of Her Lost Daughter," *St. Louis Post Dispatch* (St. Louis, MO), October 2, 1892, in *Last Seen: Finding Family After Slavery*, http://informationwanted.org/items /show/3140. "Parted in Bondage. A Colored Woman's Patient Search," *San Francisco Chronicle*, October 11, 1892, 2, https://informationwanted .org/items/show/502.

4 "A Thirty Years' Search," New York *World*, October 2, 1892, https:// informationwanted.org/items/show/3142.

5 Walter Johnson, *Soul by Soul: Life Inside the Antebellum Slave Market* (Cambridge, MA: Harvard University Press, 1999), 26–30.

6 Caroline Randall Williams, "You Want a Confederate Monument? My Body Is a Confederate Monument," *New York Times*, June 26, 2020.

7 Edward E. Baptist, *The Half Has Never Been Told: Slavery and the Making of American Capitalism* (New York: Basic Books, 2014), 102–3.

8 "Patience Green and John Williams," *The Appeal: A National Afro-American Newspaper* (Chicago, IL), June 4, 1892, https://informationwanted.org /items/show/2263.

9 "Do You Know Her?," *Richmond Planet* (Richmond, VA), August 10, 1895, https://informationwanted.org/items/show/1032.

10 The first twenty hits in a search in the census for the name Patience and a Virginia birthday around 1847 turned up fifteen "Black" and "Mulatto" women and five white women. 1850–1900 Federal Censuses, Ancestry. com. Ira Berlin, *Many Thousands Gone: The First Two Centuries of Slavery in North America* (Cambridge, MA: Belknap Press of Harvard University Press, 1998), 95, 239–40. Heather Andrea Williams, *Help Me to Find My People: The African American Search for Family Lost in Slavery* (Raleigh: University of North Carolina Press, 2012), 159.

11 "100 Dollars Reward," *Carolina Centinel* (Newbern, NC), June 13, 1818, in *N.C. Runaway Slave Advertisements*, Digital Collections, Library of University of North Carolina, Greensboro, https://dlas.uncg.edu/notices/notice/361/.

12 John W. Burgess, *The Middle Period: 1817–1858* (New York: Charles Scribner's Sons, 1897), 102, 105–6.

13 The latter are marked as "employed" in the 1860 Federal Slave Schedule. "Richd. Christian," 1860 Federal Census—Slave Schedules, Virginia, Charles City, 14–15.

14 Amy Murrell Taylor, *Embattled Freedom: Journeys Through the Civil War's Slave Refugee Camps* (Chapel Hill: University of North Carolina Press, 2018), 20.

15 "Richard Christian," Enlisted as Sergeant in Company D, Virginia 3rd Cavalry Regiment, May 1861, U.S., Civil War Soldier Records and Profiles, 1861–1865, Virginia Regimental Histories Series, U.S. Civil War Soldier Records and Profiles, 1861–1865. "Richd Christian," 1860 Federal Census, Charles City, VA, 28–29. His wife's name appears to be spelled "Matha."

16 *Charles City County: Record of Slaves That Have Escaped to the Enemy During the War* [1861–1863], Digital Collections, Library of Virginia.

17 Tera Hunter, *Bound in Wedlock: Slave and Free Black Marriage in the Nineteenth Century* (Cambridge, MA: Harvard University Press, 2017), 298.

18 Steven Hahn, *A Nation Under Our Feet: Black Political Struggles in the Rural South from Slavery to the Great Migration* (Cambridge, MA: Harvard University Press, 2003), 43n53. Christopher Hager, *Word by Word: Emancipation and the Act of Writing* (Cambridge, MA: Harvard University Press, 2015), 163.

19 Abigail Cooper, "'Away I Goin' to Find My Mamma': Self-Emancipation, Migration, and Kinship in Refugee Camps in the Civil War Era," *Journal of African American History*, 102, no. 4 (October 2017): 449, 461.

20 Hahn, *A Nation Under Our Feet*, 467, 325.

21 Hahn, *A Nation Under Our Feet*, 467.

22 "Former Slaves Join Fortunes," San Francisco *Call*, July 23, 1904, http://informationwanted.org/items/show/3250.

23 "Romantic Meeting," Memphis *Public Ledger*, June 28, 1882, http://informationwanted.org/items/show/3239.

24 "Found Her Aged Mother," *Philadelphia Inquirer*, March 22, 1908, http://informationwanted.org/items/show/3221.

25 "Reunited After Thirty Years," *Evening World*, February 23, 1894, 3, https://informationwanted.org/items/show/4987.

26 Clara Baship, 1900 Federal Census, New York, NY, June 8, 1900, n.p.

27 C. Vann Woodward, "History from Slave Sources," *American Historical Review* 29, no. 2 (April 1974): 472–73.

CHAPTER TWO **The Children of Hagar Outlaw**

1 The short-lived *Journal of Freedom* was published by white northerner Edward P. Brooks. *Journal of Freedom* (Raleigh, NC), Library of Congress, *Chronicling America*, https://chroniclingamerica.loc.gov/lccn/sn88074095/, accessed March 13, 2024.

2 Richard Elliott, Information Wanted, *Tri-Weekly Standard* (Raleigh, NC), May 14, 1868, 3, in *Last Seen: Finding Family After Slavery*, https://informationwanted.org/items/show/1345.

3 Daniel West, *The Freeman* (Indianapolis, IN), June 25, 1892, http://informationwanted.org/items/show/3036.
4 Mr. L. E. Gideon, *Topeka Plaindealer* (Topeka, KS), July 27, 1906, https://informationwanted.org/items/show/3202.
5 Glenn L. Carle, "The First Kansas Colored," *American Heritage* 43, no. 1 (February/March 1992), https://www.americanheritage.com/first-kansas-colored#3, accessed November 2, 2023.
6 Herbert Gutman found that enslaved people retained the names of their first enslavers to give their families a sense of continuity. Roberta Sue Alexander showed that formerly enslaved North Carolinians preferred the surnames of their last enslavers—that is, when they did not change their names altogether. Ira Berlin points out that formerly enslaved in the Lower South often retained the names of their enslavers because "the selective, paternal manumission of slaves" shaped their paths to freedom and encouraged them to seek to retain their connections with the planter class. Herbert Gutman, *The Black Family in Slavery and Freedom, 1750–1925* (New York: Random House, 1976), 230–56. Roberta Sue Alexander, *North Carolina Faces the Freedmen: Race Relations During Presidential Reconstruction, 1865–67* (Durham, NC: Duke University Press, 1985), 665–66. Ira Berlin, *Many Thousands Gone: The First Two Centuries of Slavery in North America* (Cambridge, MA: Belknap Press of Harvard University Press, 1998), 321.
7 Marriage of Primas Heckstall and Cherry Outlaw, Windsor, NC, 1877, North Carolina, Marriage Records, 1741–2011. Cherry Heckstall, 1880 Federal Census: Whites, Bertie, NC; Roll: 953, p. 284C; Enumeration District: 015.
8 Deborah Gray White found that enslaved women had a child on average about every two and half years. Deborah Gray White, *Ar'n't I a Woman? Female Slaves in the Plantation South* (New York: W. W. Norton, 1985), 97–98.
9 Heather Andrea Williams, *Help Me to Find My People: The First Two Centuries of Slavery in North America* (Cambridge, MA: Belknap Press of Harvard University Press, 1998), 50–51.
10 Clara Jones Interview, *Federal Writer's Project: Slave Narrative Project*, Vol. 11, North Carolina, Part 2, Jackson–Yellerday, 1936, 32, Manuscript/Mixed Material, Library of Congress, https://www.loc.gov/item/mesn112/.
11 White, *Ar'n't I a Woman?*, 110.
12 1860 Federal Census—Slave Schedules.
13 Twenty-one-year-old Isodore Outlaw lived near Wake Forest and owned an unnamed 24-year-old enslaved woman who may have been one of Hagar's daughters. Isodore Outlaw, 1850 Federal Census; Davis, Franklin, NC;

Roll: M432_630; 369B; 349. Isodore Outlaw, Franklin County, NC, 1850 Federal Census—Slave Schedules.

14 Rebecca B. Littleton, "Outlaw, David (14 Sept. 1806–22 Oct. 1868)," in *Dictionary of North Carolina Biography*, ed. William S. Powell, Vol. 4, L–O (Chapel Hill: University of North Carolina Press, 1991), 407–8.

15 In 1850, Bertie County's slave population numbered 7,194; by 1860 the total was 8,185. In 1860, thirteen of the county's 408 enslavers owned 70 or more slaves. Enslaved people produced 1,310 bales of cotton, each weighing 400 pounds, in 1850; ten years later the total was 6,672 bales. "Statistics of North Carolina," *The Seventh Census of the United States: 1850. An Appendix, Embracing Notes Upon the Tables of Each of the States, etc.* (Washington, D.C., 1853), 307–8. *Agriculture of the United States in 1860; Compiled from the Original Returns of the Eighth Census* (Washington, D.C., 1864), 104–11.

16 The enslaved population in Duplin County grew from 6,007 in 1850 to 7,124 in 1860. Only seven of Duplin County's 674 enslavers owned 70 or more slaves. *Seventh Census of the United States*: *1850*, 307, 309. *Agriculture of the United States in 1860*, 235.

17 Stephanie McCurry, "The Politics of Yeoman Households in South Carolina," in *Divided Houses: Gender and the Civil War*, ed. Catherine Clinton and Nina Silber (New York: Oxford University Press, 1992), 22–38.

18 David Outlaw to Emily Outlaw, December 10, 1849, 3, Outlaw Family Papers, University of North Carolina (Vol. 1, 104); David Outlaw to Emily Outlaw, January 19, 1849, 3 (Vol. 1, 29).

19 David Outlaw to Emily Outlaw, December 18, 1849 (Vol. 1, 131).

20 Darlene Clark Hine, "Rape and the Inner Lives of Black Women in the Middle West," *Signs* 14, no. 4 (Summer 1989): 912–20.

21 Nell Painter, "Soul Murder and Slavery: Toward a Fully Loaded Cost Accounting," in *Southern History Across the Color Line* (Chapel Hill: University of North Carolina Press, 2002), 38–39.

22 John L. Mckenzie, S.J., *Dictionary of the Bible* (New York: Simon & Schuster, 1995), 330.

23 Annette Gordon-Reed, *The Hemingses of Monticello: An American Family* (New York: W. W. Norton, 2008), 282–83. Rhys Isaac notes that in the King James Bible, Hagar is described as Abraham's "wife," which could be interpreted as broadly synonymous with "woman." Rhys Isaac, "Monticello Stories, Old and New," in *Sally Hemings and Thomas Jefferson: History, Memory, and Civic Culture*, ed. Jan Ellen Lewis and Peter S. Onuf (Charlottesville: University of Virginia Press, 1999), 121–22.

24 Patricia C. Click, *Time Full of Trial: The Roanoke Island Freedom's Colony, 1862–1867* (Chapel Hill: University of North Carolina Press, 2001), 1, 38.

25 General Orders No. 32, J. A. Campbell, Assistant Adjutant General, Raleigh, NC, April 27, 1865, *Official Records of the War of the Rebellion*, Series 1, Vol. 47, Part 3, 331. Lieutenant General John M. Schofield, *Forty-Six Years in the Army* (New York: The Century Company, 1897), 367.

26 Fannie Graves and Annie P. Merrian, March 1865 Monthly Report, *The Freedmen's Record: Organ of the New England Freedmen's Aid Society* (Boston, 1865), 93–94.

27 Major General J. M. Schofield, Raleigh, NC, to Maj. Gen. W. T. Sherman, May 5, 1865, *Official Records of the War of the Rebellion*, Series 1, Vol. 47, Part 1: Reports, Chapter 59, 1895, 39. Amy Murrell Taylor coined the term "freedom-seeking people." Amy Murrell Taylor, *Embattled Freedom: Journeys Through the Civil War's Slave Refugee Camps* (Chapel Hill: University of North Carolina Press, 2018), 2.

28 General Orders No. 32, J. A. Campbell, Assistant Adjutant General, Raleigh, NC, April 27, 1865, *Official Records of the War of the Rebellion*, Series 1, Vol. 47, Part 3, 331.

29 General Orders No. 46, J. A. Campbell, Assistant Adjutant General, Raleigh, NC, May 15, 1865, *Official Records of the War of the Rebellion*, Series 1, Vol. 47, Part 3, 503.

30 Alexander, *North Carolina Faces the Freedmen*, 2–3.

31 Tera Hunter, *Bound in Wedlock: Slave and Free Black Marriage in the Nineteenth Century* (Cambridge, MA: Harvard University Press, 2017), 310.

32 "An Act Concerning Negroes and Persons of Color or of Mixed Blood," *Public Laws of the State of North-Carolina, Passed by the General Assembly, 1865–1866*, https://digital.ncdcr.gov/digital/collection/p249901coll22/id/177322, 99–105.

33 Alexander, *North Carolina Faces the Freedmen*, 44–57.

34 David Outlaw died in October 1868. R. Hargus Taylor, "David Outlaw," in Powell, *Dictionary of North Carolina Biography*, Vol. 4, L–O, 407–8.

35 Eric Foner, *Freedom's Lawmakers: A Directory of Black Officeholders During Reconstruction*, rev. ed. (Baton Rouge: Louisiana State University Press, 1996), 184. Karen Lorene Zipf, *Labor of Innocents: Forced Apprenticeship in North Carolina, 1715–1919* (Baton Rouge: Louisiana State University Press, 2005), 103. J. G. de Roulhac, *Reconstruction in North Carolina* (1906) (New York: Columbia University, 1914), 230.

36 Alexander, *North Carolina Faces the Freedmen*, 9.

37 Thomas Heath to J. A. Campbell, October 9, 1865, Letters Received, quoted in Alexander, *North Carolina Faces the Freedmen*, 9n53.

38 Alexander, *North Carolina Faces the Freedmen*, 71–76.

39 Derek Chang, *Citizens of a Christian Nation: Evangelical Missions and the Problem of Race in the Nineteenth Century* (Philadelphia: University of Pennsylvania Press, 2010), 107, 135–40.

40 "Hagar Outlaw," 30 March 1868 (46), 24 April 1868 (49), May 1868 (64), June 1868 (72), citing Residence, Raleigh, Wake, NC, "United States, Freedmen's Bureau Ration Records, 1865–1872," National Archives and Records Administration (NARA) microfilm publications M1909. Records of the Bureau of Refugees, Freedmen, and Abandoned Lands, 1861–1880, RG 105 (Washington, D.C.: NARA, 1969–1980); Roll 51; FHL microfilm 2,427,056, FamilySearch, https://familysearch.org/ark:/61903/1:1:Q2QL-JX83: 16 March 2018.

41 United States War Department, "The Ration," in *Revised United States Army Regulations of 1861* (Washington, D.C.: Government Printing Office, 1863), 244.

42 Amy Murrell Taylor, *Embattled Freedom: Journeys Through the Civil War's Slave Refugee Camps* (Chapel Hill: University of North Carolina Press, 2018), 142–50.

43 E. Whittlesey to Major General O. O. Howard, First Quarterly Report, Fall 1865, North Carolina Assistant Commissioner, Letters Sent, Vol. 1 (7), July 4, 1865–July 13, 1867, *Freedmen's Bureau Digital Collection, 1865–1872*, U.S. National Archives and Records Administration (NARA), FamilySearch International, and the Smithsonian National Museum of African American History and Culture, https://transcription.si.edu/project/8492, 453–62.

44 E. Whittlesey to O. O. Howard, September 28, 1865, North Carolina Assistant Commissioner, Letters Sent, Vol. 1 (7), July 4, 1865–July 13, 1867, *Freedmen's Bureau Digital Collection, 1865–1872*, U.S. National Archives and Records Administration, FamilySearch International, and the Smithsonian National Museum of African American History and Culture, https://transcription.si.edu/project/8492, 451–52.

45 "Freedmen's Bureau in North Carolina," *Weekly Standard* (Raleigh, NC), May 23, 1866,1.

46 Harriet Jacobs, "Life Among the Contrabands," *The Liberator* (Boston, MA), September 5, 1862, 3.

47 Taylor, *Embattled Freedom*, 76–80. Julie Saville, *Work of Reconstruction: From Slave to Wage Laborer in South Carolina, 1860–1870* (New York: Cambridge University Press, 1994), 109.

48 "Hagar Outlaw," 1870 Federal Census, Raleigh Township, Wake County, NC, July 5, 1870, 103.

49 "D. W. Outlaw," 1880 Federal Census, Raleigh Township, Wake County, NC, June 15, 1880, 51. "David Outlaw," 1900 Federal Census, Raleigh Township, Wake County, NC, June 4, 1900, 6. "David W. Outlaw," 1920

Federal Census, Raleigh Township, Wake County, NC, January 16 and 17, 1920, 22A.

50 Daniel L. Dreisbach, "The 'Vine and Fig Tree' in George Washington's Letters: Reflections on the Biblical Motif in the Literature of the American Founding Era," *Anglican and Episcopal History* 76, no. 3 (September 2007): 299–326.

CHAPTER THREE **Both of Tally Miller's Children**

1 Tally Miller, 1880 Federal Census, Bossier Parish, Louisiana, June 1, 1880, 4.

2 Ta-Nehisi Coates, *Between the World and Me* (New York: Spiegel & Grau, 2015), 127.

3 Tally's son's 1881 Lost Friends letter included the details about the girls' marriages. His name is spelled a number of ways, including "Tigue" (1876 Marriage License), "Tuege" (1880 Census), "Tuague" in the 1881 Lost Friends letter, and "Teague" (1900 Census). Marriage of Tigue Miller and Hannah Miller, Bossier, Louisiana, February 1, 1876, Louisiana Secretary of State's Office; Baton Rouge, LA; Louisiana Marriage Index. Tuege Millen, 1880 Federal Census, Bossier Parish, Louisiana, June 5, 1880, 32. Tuague (Teague) Miller to "Dear Editor," Lost Friends, *Southwestern Christian Advocate* (New Orleans, LA), September 15, 1881, https://informationwanted.org/items/show/5014. Teague Miller, 1900 Federal Census, Bossier Parish, Louisiana, June 4, 1900, 32.

4 Edward Baptist, *Half Has Never Been Told: Slavery and the Making of American Capitalism* (New York: Basic Books, 2014), 103.

5 Walter Edgar, *South Carolina: A History* (Columbia: University of South Carolina Press, 1998), 270–77.

6 In 1850, Bossier Parish's slave population numbered 4,455, and the white population was 2,507; in 1860, slaves numbered 8,000, and whites were 3,348. No free Blacks were identified on either census. Paulina Pickett was one of only ten planters in the county who owned 100 or more slaves in 1860. "Statistics of Louisiana," *The Seventh Census of the United States: 1850. An Appendix, Embracing Notes Upon the Tables of Each of the States, etc.* (Washington, D.C., 1853), 473. *Agriculture of the United States in 1860; Compiled from the Original Returns of the Eighth Census* (Washington, D.C., 1864), 189–91.

7 Estimates are based on enslaved people described in the 1830 Federal Census and who could not be found in 1840; some may have escaped or died. James B. Pickett, 1830 Federal Census, Chester County, SC, 346–7. James B. Picket [*sic*], 1840 Federal Census, Chester County, SC, 49–50.

James B. Pickett, 1830 Federal Census, Fairfield County, SC, 374. State of South Carolina, County of Chester, Probate of estate of James B. Picket(t), deceased, *South Carolina, U.S., Wills and Probate Records, 1670–1980*, July 21, 1843, 697, 711.

8 Newspapers referred to her as "Pauline." "Died," Obituary of Mrs. Pauline Pickett, *Evening Journal* (Shreveport, LA), June 6, 1899, 5. "An Early Settler Gone," Obituary of Mrs. Pauline Pickett, *The Times* (Shreveport, LA), June 7, 1899, 9.

9 Jesse Williams, 1830 Federal Census, Chester County, SC, 300. Jesse Williams, 1840 Federal Census, Chester County, SC, 319.

10 Larry E. Hudson Jr., *To Have and to Hold: Slave Work and Family Life in Antebellum South Carolina* (Athens: University of Georgia Press, 1997), 142.

11 Harriet A. Jacobs, *Incidents in the Life of a Slave Girl, Written by Herself* (1861), ed. Jean Fagan Yellin (Cambridge, MA: Harvard University Press, 1987), 77.

12 Tera Hunter, *Bound in Wedlock: Slave and Free Black Marriage in the Nineteenth Century* (Cambridge, MA: Harvard University Press, 2017), 20.

13 Jesse Williams, 1850 Federal Slave Schedule, Chester County, SC, October 29, 1850, n.p.

14 Edward E. Baptist, *The Half Has Never Been Told: Slavery and the Making of American Capitalism* (New York: Basic Books, 2014), 24. For Tally Miller, that man on the horse might have been the "Col. Williamson" he mentions in his letter. Richard Williamson, 1850 Federal Census, Natchitoches County, LA, November 12, 1850, n.p.

15 Northrup might have been referring to a bobcat when he said tiger. Solomon Northrup, *Twelve Years a Slave: A Citizen of New York, Kidnapped in Washington City in 1841 and Rescued in 1853, From a Cotton Plantation Near the Red River in Louisiana* (1853) (Vancouver, BC: Sapling Books, 2014), 59.

16 Alan L. Olmstead and Paul W. Rhode, "Wait a Cotton Pickin' Minute!": A New View of Slave Productivity," April 2007, 7, http://faculty.econ.ucdavis.edu/faculty/alolmstead/Working_Papers/Cotton_Pickin.pdf, accessed March 18, 2021.

17 Frederick Law Olmsted, November 1853, *The Papers of Frederick Law Olmstead*, vol. 2, *Slavery and the South, 1852–1857*, ed. Charles E. Beveridge and Charles Capen McLaughlin (Baltimore: Johns Hopkins University Press, 1981), 221.

18 Northrup, *Twelve Years a Slave*, 61.

19 Carin Peller-Semmens, "Unreconstructed: Slavery and Emancipation on Louisiana's Red River, 1820–1880" (PhD diss., University of Sussex, 2016), 48.

20 In Natchitoches, Caddo, Bossier, Rapides, and DeSoto Parishes, between 1830 and 1840, the slave population increased 125 percent, and the total white population, in relation to slave, from 40 percent in 1830 to 39 percent in 1840. From 1840 to 1850, the enslaved population grew 67 percent. Peller-Semmens, "Unreconstructed," 46.

21 In the 1855 divorce settlement, Paulina Pickett received nine Red River plantations—Orchard, Hurricane Bluff, Gold Point, Willow Chute, Chalk Level, Rough and Ready, Red Chute, Kain Point, and Winston—plus additional Louisiana properties, including in New Orleans, and a few thousand acres in Arkansas. Pickett also "received" 339 enslaved people; among them were Tally and Mahala Miller and their children. James and Paulina Gilmer, Deed of Conveyance, State of Louisiana, Parish of Bossier, Book 4, Clerk of Bossier Parish, October 4, 1855, 105–33.

22 Paulina and James's daughter, Sarah, died in 1855. Sarah Pickett, 1850 Federal Census, Bossier Parish, LA, November 13, 1850, 591. "Died," *The South Western* (Shreveport, LA), June 13, 1855, 3.

23 In the deed of conveyance transferring property to her son, Paulina DeGraffenreid Pickett indicated the family groups to which enslaved people belonged, including Tally, Mahala, and their five sons. Paulina Pickett to James Pickett, Deed of Conveyance, State of Louisiana, Parish of Bossier, Book 4, Clerk of Bossier Parish, February 6, 1857, 247–49. Paulina Pickett to John Pickett, Deed of Conveyance, State of Louisiana, Parish of Bossier, Book 5, Clerk of Bossier Parish, January 24, 1860, 239–40.

24 "Let the Friends of Union and Liberty," *New Orleans Tribune*, December 8, 1864.

25 John H. Ransdell to Gov. Thomas Moore, 24 May 1863, quoted in Ted Tunnell, *Crucible of Reconstruction: War, Radicalism and Race in Louisiana* (Baton Rouge: Louisiana State University Press, 1984), 51–52n3. (The 1863 date is most likely an error, as the campaign occurred in 1864.)

26 Rev. Thomas Conway to General Oliver Otis Howard, July 18, 1865. Records of the Bureau of Refugees, Freedmen, and Abandoned Lands, War Records Division, National Archives and Records Administration (NARA), Washington, D.C., Louisiana Records, CDXLVII, RG 105, Box 262, quoted in Howard White, *The Freedmen's Bureau in Louisiana* (Baton Rouge: Louisiana State University Press, 1970), 20n9. Testimony of Henry Adams, *Report and Testimony of the Select Committee of the United States Senate to Investigate the Causes of the Removal of the Negroes from the Southern States to the Northern States*, Part 2 (Washington, D.C., 1880), 190–91.

27 "Constable's Sale," *The Times* (Shreveport, LA), May 15, 1877, 4. "River Plantation for Rent," *The Times*, December 13, 1883, 4.

28 Pauline Pickett, 1870 Federal Census, McMinnville, Warren County, TN, June 22, 1870, 6.

29 J. B. Pickett, 1880 Federal Census, Shreveport, Caddo Parish, LA, June 7, 1880, 12. Untitled Obituary for James Pickett, *The Times*, November 2, 1880, 4.

30 Eric Foner, *Reconstruction: America's Unfinished Revolution, 1863–1877* (New York: Harper & Row, 1988), 263, 437.

31 Matthew Christensen, "The 1868 St. Landry Massacre: Reconstruction's Deadliest Episode of Violence" (MA thesis, University of Wisconsin–Milwaukee, 2012), UMW Digital Commons, https://dc.uwm.edu/etd/190, 60–63.

32 Nikole Hannah-Jones, "It Is Time for Reparations," *New York Times Magazine*, June 24, 2020.

33 In 1860, there were 331,726 enslaved people, 18,647 free Blacks, and 357,629 whites living in the state. In 1870, Black Louisianans numbered 364,210 and whites were 362,065. Francis A. Walker, *A Compendium of the Ninth Census* (June 1, 1870) (Washington, D.C.: Government Printing Office, 1872), 8–17.

34 Henry Adams and other ex-USCT created "the Council" or "Committee" in Caddo Parish. Nell Painter, *Exodusters: Black Migration to Kansas After Reconstruction* (New York: Alfred A. Knopf, 1977), 76.

35 "Matrimony," *Official Journal of the Proceedings of the Convention, for Framing a Constitution for the State of Louisiana* (New Orleans: J. B. Roudanez & Co., 1867), 16, https://archive.org/details/officialjournal000loui/page/16/mode/2up.

36 John H. Winters, *The Civil War in Louisiana* (Baton Rouge: Louisiana State University Press, 1963), 234, 211, 427. *Commercial Directory of the City of Shreveport for the Year of 1875* (1875) (Shreveport, LA: Shreveport Times Print, 1975), 7.

37 Painter, *Exodusters*, 102–3. Testimony of Henry Adams, *Report and Testimony of the Select Committee of the United States Senate to Investigate the Causes of the Removal of the Negroes from the Southern States to the Northern States*, Part 2, June 1, 1880, 46th Congress, 2nd Session, S.Rpt. 693 Part 1, Washington, D.C., 1880, xi.

38 James B. Pickett to Tolly [*sic*] Miller, Shad Johnson, Oliver Cromwell, and Teague Miller, Deed of Conveyance, State of Louisiana, Parish of Bossier, Book 11, Clerk of Bossier Parish, February 21, 1879, 204–5.

39 "Death of Hon. H. W. Ogden," *Bossier Banner* (Bossier, LA), July 27, 1905.

40 Willow Chute went first to John A. Haynes, whose land was seized and sold at a sheriff's auction to H. W. Ogden. *James B. Pickett v. John H.*

Haynes, Judicial District Court, State of Louisiana, Parish of Bossier, Clerk of Bossier Parish, October 17, 1878, Book 11, 86–89.

41 "Ogden, Henry Warren (1842–1905)," *Biographical Directory of the United States Congress*, https://bioguideretro.congress.gov/Home/MemberDetails?memIndex=O000044, accessed June 28, 2021.

42 Testimony of Henry Adams, xi.

43 Tally Miller, "Lost Friends," *Southwestern Christian Advocate* (New Orleans, LA), February 7, 1884, February 14, 1884, February 21, 1884.

44 Tuague [*sic*] Miller, "Lost Friends," *Southwestern Christian Advocate*, September 15, 1881, https://informationwanted.org/items/show/5014.

45 Then they had agreed to pay more than $15,000 for those acres; a decade later his widow and son sold the land for $1,763. Shed Johnson, Oliver Cromwell, Teague Miller, and Mahala Miller to Joseph Boisseau, Deed of Conveyance, State of Louisiana, Parish of Bossier, Book 15, Clerk of Bossier Parish, December 2, 1889, 130.

46 Nathan Cardon, "'Less Than Mayhem': Louisiana's Convict Lease, 1865–1901," *Louisiana History: The Journal of the Louisiana Historical Association* 58, no. 4 (2017): 417–41.

47 Rosetta Miller, Fannie Anderson, and Milkey Miller to the Texas Company, Deed of Conveyance, State of Louisiana, Parish of Bossier, Book 51, Clerk of Bossier Parish, November 19, 1919, 341.

48 "List of Jurors for November Special Term of District Court, 1874," *Bossier Banner*, Bellevue, Bossier Parish, LA, October 17, 1874, 4. Henry Adams described his experience serving on a Caddo Parish jury in 1873: "I saw little colored boys in there for stealing a can of oysters. I seen little girls in there for stealing such things as thimbles, scissors, & c.; and [there] was several colored men in prison, and only two white men were put in jail for crimes they had committed." Testimony of Henry Adams, 180.

CHAPTER FOUR **I Was the Boy**

1 Britton Richardson, *Tri-Weekly Standard* (Raleigh, NC), November 26, 1867, in *Last Seen: Finding Family After Slavery*, http://informationwanted.org/items/show/3328. Priscilla Stark, *Alexandria Gazette* (Alexandria, VA), August 10, 1864, http://informationwanted.org/items/show/2696. Mrs. E. Wilson, *The Appeal* (Chicago, IL), January 4, 1891, http://informationwanted.org/items/show/2217. Rachel Raider, *Christian Recorder* (Philadelphia, PA), November 9, 1882, http://informationwanted.org/items/show/731.

2 Robert H. Pantell, "The Child Witness in the Courtroom," *Pediatrics* 139, no. 3 (March 2017), https://pediatrics.aappublications.org/content

/pediatrics/early/2017/02/16/peds.2016-4008.full.pdf. Bessel A. van der Kolk, M.D., *The Body Keeps the Score: Brain, Mind, and Body in the Healing of Trauma* (New York: Penguin, 2014), 193–95.

3 Karen Sanchez-Eppler, "'Remember Dear, When Yankees Came Through Here, I Was Only 10 Years Old': Valuing the Enslaved Child of the WPA Slave Narratives," in *Child Slavery Before and After Emancipation*, ed. Anne Mae Duane (Cambridge, UK: Cambridge University Press, 2017), 30.

4 Edward E. Baptist, *The Half Has Never Been Told: Slavery and the Making of American Capitalism* (New York: Basic Books, 2014), 106.

5 Michael Tadman, "The Interregional Slave Trade in the History and Myth-Making of the U.S. South," in *The Chattel Principle: Internal Slave Trades in the Americas*, ed. Walter Johnson (New Haven, CT: Yale University Press, 2004), 131.

6 Erik J. Hofstee, "The Great Divide: Aspects of the Social History of the Middle Passage in the Trans-Atlantic Slave Trade" (PhD diss., Michigan State University, 2001), 65.

7 Sanchez-Eppler, "Valuing the Enslaved Child of the WPA Slave Narratives," 42.

8 Bruin ran regular advertisements in the papers for his auctions. "Bruin and Jones Slave Auction," *Alexandria Gazette*, January 29, 1844, 1.

9 Joseph Brewen [*sic*], 1850 Federal Census, Fairfax County, VA, July 27, 1850, 111(a). Lisa Kraus, "Archaeology of the Bruin Slave Jail" (PhD diss., University of Texas at Austin, 2009), 49–54.

10 Joseph Bruin, 1860 Federal Census, Fairfax County, VA, October 23, 1860, 64–65.

11 In 1848, Bruin purchased several enslaved people captured aboard the *Pearl* when they tried to escape; abolitionists worked to purchase and free the captives. And in 1850, abolitionists interceded on behalf of a woman named Emily Russell who was to be sold into sex slavery. Kraus, "Archaeology of the Bruin Slave Jail," 54–67.

12 Kraus, "Archaeology of the Bruin Slave Jail," 62.

13 Harriet Beecher Stowe, *The Key to Uncle Tom's Cabin: Presenting the Original Facts and Documents Upon Which the Story Is Founded* (London: Clarke, Beeton, and Co., 1853), 7, American Antiquarian Society, Sabin Americana, Gale Document Number GALE|CY0110407121.

14 Harriet Beecher Stowe, *Uncle Tom's Cabin* (1852) (New York: Penguin, 1981), 17–18.

15 Stowe, *The Key to Uncle Tom's Cabin*, 322.

16 Stowe, *The Key to Uncle Tom's Cabin*, 314.

17 Nell Painter, "Soul Murder and Slavery: Toward a Fully Loaded Cost Accounting," *Southern History Across the Color Line* (Chapel Hill: University of North Carolina Press, 2002), 16.

18 The town of Leesburg had a population of 1,691 in 1850. The population of Loudon County in 1850 was 15,081 whites, 1,357 free Blacks, 5,641 enslaved. "Population of Such Cities, Towns, Townships, Hundreds & c.," 1850 Federal Census: Compendium of the Seventh Census, Part 6, 324, 363.

19 Charlotte Stuart, *The Freeman* (Indianapolis, IN), October 15, 1892, https://informationwanted.org/items/show/3046. Charles Stewart, *Southern Republican* (Demopolis, AL), December 21, 1870, https://informationwanted.org/items/show/3170. Allison Washington, *Southwestern Christian Advocate* (New Orleans, LA), November 22, 1883, https://informationwanted.org/items/show/2377. Lucinda Lowery, *The Colored Tennessean* (Nashville, TN), October 14, 1865, https://informationwanted.org/items/show/915.

20 Catharine Mason, *Christian Recorder*, April 7, 1866, https://informationwanted.org/items/show/133. Henry and Virginia Thompson, *Christian Recorder*, May 19, 1866, https://informationwanted.org/items/show/2. Catherine Rhodes, *Christian Recorder*, September 14, 1867, https://informationwanted.org/items/show/278.

21 Some survivors recalled that women and children were not chained, and others remembered that they were; "the children who were able to walk; and following them came mothers with their infants and young children in their arms." John Brown, *Slave Life in Georgia: A Narrative of the Life, Sufferings, and Escape of John Brown, a Fugitive Slave, Now in England*, ed. L. A. Chamerovzow (London, 1855), 16. Sella Martin, "Narrative," in *Slave Testimony: Two Centuries of Letters, Speeches, Interviews, and Autobiographies*, ed. John W. Blassingame (Baton Rouge: Louisiana State University Press, 1977), 704–5.

22 John P. Parker and Frank M. Gregg, *His Promised Land: The Autobiography of John P. Parker, Former Slave and Conductor on the Underground Railroad*, ed. Stuart Seely Sprague (New York: W. W. Norton, 1996), 27–29.

23 Parker and Gregg, *His Promised Land*, 27–29.

24 Brenda Stevenson, *Life in Black and White: Family and Community in the Slave South* (New York: Oxford University Press, 1996), 183.

25 Harriet Martineau, *Retrospect of Western Travel*, Vol. 2 (London: Saunders and Otley, 1838), 85–86.

26 "An Act to Provide for an Exchange of Lands with the Indians Residing in Any of the States or Territories, and for Their Removal West of the River Mississippi," *A Century of Lawmaking for a New Nation: U.S. Congressional Documents and Debates, 1774–1875*, 21st Congress, 1st Session, Chapter 148, May 28, 1830, 411–12

27 "XVIII Floddenfield," WPA Interviews, Pickett Folder, *Families of Vaughan, MS*, ed. Claude Pepper (Yazoo Library Association, 1936), 23–25.

28 William Faulkner, *Absalom, Absalom!* (1936) (New York: Vintage, 1990), 293.

29 James Cobb found that the infant death rate among enslaved people in the Delta in 1850 was more than twice the rate of whites. James C. Cobb, *The Most Southern Place on Earth: The Mississippi Delta and the Roots of Regional Identity* (New York: Oxford University Press, 1992), 22, 339n63.

30 J. D. B. DeBow, *A Compendium of the Seventh (1850) Census*, Statistical View of the United States, Part VI: Statistical Detail of Cities, Towns, Counties, etc. (Washington, D.C., 1854), 260, 264. Joseph C. G. Kennedy, *Population of the United States in 1860; Compiled from the Original Returns of the Eighth Census*, State of Mississippi (Washington, D.C., 1864), 264–73. Mississippi law requiring them to pay an annual fee and carry a license kept the population of free Blacks small. Charles Sydnor, "The Free Negro in Mississippi Before the Civil War," *American Historical Review* 32, no. 4 (July 1927): 769–70.

31 Joe Clinton Interview, Marvell, AR, Federal Writers' Project of the Works Progress Administration, George P. Rawick, ed., *The American Slave: A Composite Autobiography*, Vol. 8, Arkansas Narratives, Part 2 (Westport, CT: Greenwood Publishing, 1972), 32.

32 Delia Hill Interview, St. Louis, MO, August 12, 1937, Federal Writers' Project of the Works Progress Administration, George P. Rawick, ed., *The American Slave: A Composite Autobiography*, Vol. 11, Missouri Narratives (Westport, CT: Greenwood Publishing, 1972), 181.

33 Wilma King, *Stolen Childhood: Slave Youth in Nineteenth-Century America* (Bloomington: Indiana University Press, 1995), 46–55. Steven Mintz, *Huck's Raft: A History of American Childhood* (Cambridge, MA: Harvard University Press, 2004), 107–8.

34 Lemuel P. Conner's Record, Slave Testimony Before the Examination Committee, Second Creek, Adams County, Mississippi, September 1861, in Winthrop Jordan, *Tumult and Silence at Second Creek: An Inquiry into a Civil War Slave Conspiracy* (Baton Rouge: Louisiana State University Press, 1995), 279, 281, 274.

35 Vernon Lane Wharton, *The Negro in Mississippi, 1865–1890* (Chapel Hill: University of North Carolina Press, 1947), 17, 31.

36 Anonymous interview notes, Pickett File, Yazoo Library Association, 3.

37 Stephanie McCurry points out that Brigadier General Lorenzo Thomas's activities in the Mississippi Valley blurred the lines between recruitment and impressment. Stephanie McCurry, *Women's War: Fighting and Surviving the American Civil War* (Cambridge, MA: Harvard University Press, 2019), 97–98.

38 According to the 1860 Federal Census, there were 436,631 slaves in Mississippi. Wharton estimated that by the end of the war half of the

state's enslaved people had freed themselves. *Population of the United States in 1860*, 270. Wharton, *The Negro in Mississippi*, 13, 26.

39 John Eaton, *Grant, Lincoln, and the Freedmen: Reminiscences of the Civil War* (New York: Longmans, Green, and Co., 1907), 2–3.

40 Henry and Ann appear together in the 1880 Federal Census, and Henry names Ann as his first wife in his 1891 pension application. Henry and Ann Tibbs, 1880 Federal Census, Issaquena County, MS, June 24, 1880, 20. Pension application for Henry Tibbs, Corporal, U.S. Colored Light Infantry, Battery D, Bolivar, MS, January 6, 1891, National Archives and Records Administration (NARA), RG 15, Pension Application No. 983208, 3, 2.

41 McCurry, *Women's War*, 84.

42 Henry Tibbs, *Compiled Military Service Records of Volunteer Union Soldiers Who Served with the United States Colored Troops: Artillery Organizations*, Card No. 300398, NARA, RG 94, Roll 0293, 7.

43 Bruce Tap, *The Fort Pillow Massacre: North, South, and the Status of African Americans in the Civil War Era* (New York: Routledge, 2014), 52n11.

44 Wharton, *The Negro in Mississippi*, 28. Amy Murrell Taylor, *Embattled Freedom: Journeys Through the Civil War's Slave Refugee Camps* (Chapel Hill: University of North Carolina Press, 2018), 112–16.

45 Thavolia Glymph, *The Women's Fight: The Civil War's Battles for Home, Freedom, and Nation* (Chapel Hill: University of North Carolina Press, 2020), 242–43. John Eaton witnessed "indescribable" suffering as freezing women and children clung to the outside of trains making their way slowly toward Memphis. Eaton, *Grant, Lincoln, and the Freedmen*, 30.

46 John Cimprich, *Fort Pillow, A Civil War Massacre, and Public Memory* (Baton Rouge: Louisiana State University Press, 2005), 70–85. John Cimprich and Robert C. Mainfort Jr., "Fort Pillow Revisited: New Evidence About an Old Controversy," *Civil War History* 28, no. 4 (1982): 296n11.

47 Testimony of Thomas Adison, Private, Company C, 6th United States Heavy Artillery, in F. Wade and D. W. Gooch, *Reports of the Committee on the Conduct of the War: Fort Pillow Massacre. Returned Prisoners.* Testimony Before the Senate, 38th Congress, 1st Session, Rep. Com. 63, May 5, 1864, 20.

48 Henry Tibbs, *Compiled Military Service Records*. Henry Tibbs's Pension Application, 10.

49 "An Act to Confer Civil Rights on Freedmen," November 25, 1865, and "An Act to Regulate the Relation of Master and Apprentice," November 22, 1865, *Laws of the State of Mississippi* (Jackson: J. J. Shannon & Co., 1866), 82–86, 86–90.

50 Joseph Logsdon, introduction to *Yazoo; or, On the Picket Line of Freedom in the South*, by Albert T. Morgan (1884) (Columbia: University of South Carolina Press, 2000), xl.

51 African Americans were 71 percent of the county's total population in 1870, 12,395 of 17,279. Francis A. Walker, *A Compendium of the Ninth Census (June 1, 1870)* (Washington, D.C., 1872), 64–65.

52 According to *Mapping Occupation*, there were 385 USCT in Yazoo in June 1865. In October their numbers reached 954, then dwindled to 751 in November before the men were pulled out entirely. A small company of troops arrived again in the summer of 1867 and remained there for a couple of months. Greg Downs and Scott Nesbitt, *Mapping Occupation*, http://mappingoccupation.org/, accessed October 1, 2021.

53 In 1865, the Freedmen's Bureau leased to the state's approximately 437,303 freed people 59,280 acres of land confiscated from slaveholders. James Wilford Garner, *Reconstruction in Mississippi* (Gloucester, MA: Peter Smith, 1964), 257.

54 Micajah Pickett to President Andrew Johnson, Applications for Pardon Submitted to President Andrew Johnson by Former Confederates, Amnesty Papers, Compiled 1865–1867, NARA, RG 94, July 13, 1865. Micajah Pickett Agreement with Parties of Freedmen, No. 78, June 19, 1865, Records of the Assistant Commissioner for the State of Mississippi, Bureau of Refugees, Freedmen, and Abandoned Lands, 1863–1869, M826, No. 43. M. Pickett, Wildwood Plantation, Yazoo County, Mississippi Records of the Field Offices for the State of Mississippi, Bureau of Refugees, Freedmen, and Abandoned Lands, 1865–1872, Subordinate Field Offices, Yazoo City (Subcommissioner), Register of Plantation Census in Yazoo County, Vol. 329, M1907, No. 65, 69–75.

55 Morgan, *Yazoo*, 38–42.

56 Morgan, *Yazoo*, 181–87.

57 Dennis Mitchell, *A New History of Mississippi* (Jackson: University Press of Mississippi, 2014), 174–80. Eric Foner, *Freedom Lawmakers: A Directory of Black Officeholders During Reconstruction*, rev. ed. (Baton Rouge: Louisiana State University Press, 1996), xiv, 29–30, 180–81.

58 These men were W. H. Foote, James M. Dixon, Walter Boyd, and James G. Patterson. Eric Foner counted 226 Black officeholders in the state before 1875, at least 59 of whom were formerly enslaved. Foner, *Freedom Lawmakers*, 76, 131–32, 88, 219, 76, 63–64, 23, 167. Logsdon, introduction to *Yazoo*, xliii. Garner, *Reconstruction in Mississippi*, 269.

59 Logsdon, introduction to *Yazoo*, xliv.

60 The number of Black churches more than doubled from 105 in 1865 to 283 in 1870, and the number of Mississippians of color employed as preachers increased from just 73 after the war to 262. Testimony of Senator Blanch Bruce, "The Mississippi Election," *Congressional Record*, 44th Congress, 2nd Session, March 31, 1876, 2102–3.

61 Wharton, *The Negro in Mississippi*, 175.
62 Henry Tibbs, *Southwestern Christian Advocate*, December 11, 1879, http://informationwanted.org/items/show/1400.
63 Morgan, *Yazoo*, 232.
64 Thomas McAfee, *Southwestern Christian Advocate*, September 9, 1886, http://informationwanted.org/items/show/1943.
65 Algernon S. Tebbs, 4th Texas Infantry, Company A, 1863, U.S. Confederate Soldiers Compiled Service Records. A. Sidney Tebbs, Application for Presidential Pardon, June 25, 1866, Applications for Pardons Submitted to President Andrew Johnson by Former Confederates, Amnesty Papers, NARA, RG 94. Marriage Record for Algernon Sidney Tebbs and Miss Tillie F. Paxton, Platte City, MO, May 8, 1868, Missouri, U.S., Marriage Records, 1805–2002. Algernon Sidney Tebbs, d. August 18, 1872, Findagrave.com, https://www.findagrave.com/memorial/158696647/algernon-sidney-tebbs.
66 Horace Augustus, Certificate of Death, Alexandria, VA, September 30, 1916. Hannah (Au)Gustus, 1870 Federal Census, Alexandria County, VA, August 29, 1870, 33.
67 Algernon S. Tebbs, Private, Company A, 4th Texas Infantry, Confederate States of America, Compiled Service Records of Confederate Soldiers Who Served in Organizations from the State of Texas, NARA, RG 109, Texas, Roll 0292.
68 Henry Tibbs, 1880 Federal Census, Issaquena County, MS, June 24, 1880, 20. In 1871, Henry wrote to Governor Alcorn requesting a job, noting that he had for three months served as provost marshal of Brookhaven, MS, a town about one hundred miles south of Yazoo. Henry J. Tibbs to Mississippi Governor James L. Alcorn, January 17, 1871, Mississippi Department of Archives and History, *The Civil War and Reconstruction Era Governors of Mississippi*, https://cwrgm.org/item/mdah_786-972-02-09.
69 Logsdon, introduction to *Yazoo*, xlv–xlvi.
70 Logsdon, introduction to *Yazoo*, xlvi.
71 Henry and Ann appear as one of many tenants on the Moorland Plantation. Henry Tibbs, 1880 Federal Census, Issaquena County, MS, June 24, 1880, 20. In 1900, Tibbs was described as a "farmer" and Louisa a "farm laborer"; as in 1880, Tibbs did not own property. Henry Tibbs, 1900 Federal Census, Bolivar County, MS, June 3, 1900, 21.
72 Henry Tibbs's Physical Examination, September 9, 1891, Henry Tibbs's Pension Application, 9. Frank W. Rawles, Special Examiner, to Commissioner of Pensions, June 20, 1893. Henry Tibbs's Pension Application, 68, 72–73.

73 The *New York Times* published an August 1884 story about an investigation of fake agents in Vicksburg. "Bogus Pension Claim Agents. How They Have Swindled Poor People in Mississippi," *New York Times*, August 7, 1884. The *Washington Post* said that Black claimants were "easier victims for designing lawyers" than whites. "Bogus Pension Claims," *Washington Post*, July 22, 1883, 5.

CHAPTER FIVE The Andersons of Mineola, Texas

1 Wood County Historical Commission, *Images of America: Wood County* (Charleston, SC: Arcadia Publishing, 2004), 7.
2 *International & Great Northern Railroad, Lone Star Route* (Woodward, Tiernan & Hale, 1878), David Rumsey Historical Map Collection, https://www.davidrumsey.com/luna/servlet/detail/RUMSEY~8~1~22085~770067?qvq=q%3AGreat%20Northern%20railroad%3Bsort%3Apub_list_no_initialsort%2Cpub_date%2Cpub_list_no%2Cseries_no%3Blc%3ARUMSEY~8~1&mi=20&trs=41, accessed March 16, 2024. *Texas and Pacific Railway Company, Map of Texas*, 1878, David Rumsey Historical Map Collection, https://www.davidrumsey.com/luna/servlet/detail/RUMSEY~8~1~22069~760038:State-Of-Texas-?sort=Pub_Date%2CPub_List_No_InitialSort&qvq=q:Pub_List_No%3D%273254.000%27%22%20;sort:Pub_Date%2CPub_List_No_InitialSort,lc:RUMSEY~8~1&mi=2&trs=3, accessed March 16, 2024.
3 Carl Moneyhon, *Texas After the Civil War: The Struggle for Reconstruction* (College Station: Texas A&M University Press, 2004), 61.
4 From 1875 to 1900, 50 percent of prisoners in Texas were Black, although only 25 percent of the state's population was African American. Lawrence Rice, *The Negroes of Texas, 1874–1900* (Baton Rouge: Louisiana State University Press, 1971), 246–47.
5 White prisoners cut three-quarters of a cord. Testimony of Willie Donahue and of D. C. Williams, *Testimony re: Treatment of Convicts at Wood Camp in Mineola. Taken Before Superintendent and Assistant Superintendent, 1879*, Records Relating to the Penitentiary: An Inventory of the State Archives Records Relating to the Penitentiary, 1846–1921, Texas State Archives, Austin, Box 022-11, Folders 10–12, 2–3, 18. Assistant Superintendent, Report on Treatment of Convicts at Mineola Camp, July 1879, Records Relating to the Penitentiary: An Inventory of the State Archives Records Relating to the Penitentiary, 1846–1921, Texas State Archives, Austin, Box 022-9, Folders 17, 2.

More than 50 percent of the prisoners working in railroad construction in Texas died every two years. Rice, *The Negroes of Texas*, 249.

6 According to location metadata in the Last Seen archive, 745 ads/letters (as of December 17, 2021) were placed either by people searching from Texas or for people they suspected might be there. Five hundred twenty-nine appeared in the *Southwestern Christian Advocate*. Mrs. Ann Carter, Lost Friends letter, *Southwestern Christian Advocate* (New Orleans, LA), February 23, 1888, in *Last Seen: Finding Family After Slavery*, http://informationwanted.org/items/show/3992. E. W. Carter, Lost Friends letter, *Southwestern Christian Advocate*, February 23, 1888, http://informationwanted.org/items/show/3994. Ann Carter, Lost Friends letter, *Southwestern Christian Advocate*, May 3, 1888, http://informationwanted.org/items/show/4078.

7 Lucy Mead, *Richmond Planet* (Richmond, VA), October 19, 1895, https://informationwanted.org/items/show/1036.

8 Moneyhon, *Texas After the Civil War*, 84.

9 Randolph Campbell, *Grass-Roots Reconstruction in Texas, 1865–1880* (Baton Rouge: Louisiana State University Press, 1998), 109.

10 William A. Blair, *The Record of Murders and Outrages: Racial Violence and the Fight over the Truth at the Dawn of Reconstruction* (Chapel Hill: University of North Carolina Press, 2021), 123.

11 Lucy Meade [*sic*], 1870 Federal Census, Garden Valley, Smith County, TX, August 4, 1870, 16. Lucy Meed [*sic*], 1880 Federal Census, Precinct No. 2, Wood County, TX, June 9, 1880, 25. Lucy Mead appeared in both the 1880 and 1900 Federal Census as a widow. In 1900, she lived with her son, Sandy, a widower, and his two children, three-year-old George and two-year-old Sandy. Sandy Anderson, 1900 Federal Census, Precinct No. 2, Wood County, TX, June 5, 1900, 18.

A John Anderson appeared in the 1880 Federal Census in Mineola. He was forty years old, roughly the same age as Henry, but the enumerator indicated that he had been born in Virginia. This John Anderson lived alone. John Anderson, 1880 Federal Census, Precinct No. 1, Wood County, TX, June 1, 1880, 2.

12 Henry and Susan Anderson, 1870 Federal Census, Garden Valley, Smith County, TX, August 4, 1870, 16. Henry and Susan Anderson, Federal 1880 Census, Precinct No. 2, Wood County, TX, June 9, 1880, 25.

13 "An Act Establishing a General Apprentice Law," *An Act to Establish a Code of Criminal Procedure for the State of Texas*, Eleventh Legislature of the State of Texas, August 26, 1866.

14 Tera Hunter, *Bound in Wedlock: Slave and Free Black Marriage in the Nineteenth Century* (Cambridge, MA: Harvard University Press, 2017), 234–35.

15 Blair, *The Record of Murders and Outrages*, 113. James Smallwood, "Emancipation and the Black Family: A Case Study in Texas," *Social Science Quarterly* 57, no. 4 (March 1977): 856. Moneyhon found that by 1880,

73 to 75 percent of Black households in Texas "consisted of a husband, wife, and children, with no other members." Moneyhon, *Texas After the Civil War*, 169, 102. Hunter, *Bound in Wedlock*, 298.

16 Susan Anderson, *The Freeman* (Indianapolis, IN), March 3, 1894, https://informationwanted.org/items/show/3077.

17 Henry and Susan Anderson appear in the 1870 Federal Census in Smith County, just south of Wood County. By 1880, the couple was living in Wood County, where they would remain thereafter. Susan and Henry Anderson, 1870 Federal Census, Smith County, TX, August 6, 1870, 40. Henry and Susan Anderson, 1880 Federal Census, Precinct No. 2, Wood County, TX, June 9, 1880, 25.

18 Lucy Burruss, 1850 Federal Census, Louisa County, VA, July 31, 1850, n.p. John L. Burruss, 1850 Federal Slave Schedule, Louisa County, VA, July 31, 1850, n.p.

19 Susan Anderson, *The Freeman*, March 3, 1894, https://informationwanted.org/items/show/3077.

20 Sandy Anderson to "Editor of the PLANET," *Richmond Planet*, July 28, 1894, https://informationwanted.org/items/show/3112.

21 This may have been the Henry Burruss who lived in Louisa County in 1870 with his wife, Clara, and their four children. Henry Burruss, 1870 Federal Census, Northern District, Louisa County, VA, July 13, 1870, 63.

22 Sandy Anderson, Agent, "From Texas," *Richmond Planet*, August 11, 1894. Two notices appeared in the Indianapolis *Freeman* on September 29, 1894. The first was a copy of Sandy Anderson's July 28, 1894, letter to the "Editor of the PLANET," cited above, and the second appeared under the heading "Found Her Relatives." "Editor of the PLANET" and "Found Her Relatives," *The Freeman*, September 29, 1894, https://informationwanted.org/items/show/3112.

23 Emma Lou Thornbrough, "American Negro Newspapers, 1880–1914," *Business History Review* 40, no. 4 (1966): 480, 475–76. *The Freeman*, January 10, 1914, quoted in Thornbrough, "American Negro Newspapers," 476n29.

24 Ann Field Alexander, *Race Man: The Rise and Fall of the "Fighting Editor," John Mitchell, Jr.* (Charlottesville: University of Virginia Press, 2002), 28–37.

25 John Anderson, "Lost Relatives," *Richmond Planet*, December 8, 1894, https://informationwanted.org/items/show/4732. Henry Anderson, "Lost Relatives," *The Freeman*, December 7, 1895, https://informationwanted.org/items/show/3246.

26 Wood County, TX, Index to Marriages, 1879–1979 (Reel 1632002); Marriage Records, 1879–1935 (Reel 1632007, Vol. D), Wood County, TX, Records, Special Collections, Velma K. Waters Library, Texas A&M-Commerce, n.p.

27 Sandy Anderson, 1900 Federal Census, Precinct No. 2, Wood County, TX, July 5, 1900, 18.
28 Their children were Mary, John, Cornelia ("Carnelia"), Samuel ("Lemule"), Louisa, and Alexene. John D. Anderson, 1850 Slave Schedule, Dublin, Somerset County, MD, August 24–25, 1850, n.p. John D. Anderson, 1850 Federal Census, Dublin, Somerset County, MD, August 26, 1850, n.p.
29 In another letter, Henry identified Adam Lankford as his stepfather. Henry Anderson, "Lost Relatives," *Richmond Planet*, January 26, 1896.
30 John D. Anderson, 1850 Federal Slave Schedule, Dublin, Somerset County, MD, August 24–25, 1850, n.p.
31 John D. Anderson, 1850 Federal Census, Dublin, Somerset County, MD, August 25, 1850, n.p.
32 Free Black Marylanders stayed close or sought to close the distance between themselves and their enslaved family members. Barbara Jeanne Fields, *Slavery and Freedom on the Middle Ground: Maryland During the Nineteenth Century* (New Haven, CT: Yale University Press, 1985), 24–33.
33 Orphans' Court Notice, *Baltimore Sun*, March 31, 1854, 3.
34 John Anderson, "Information Wanted," *Richmond Planet*, December 8, 1894, https://informationwanted.org/items/show/4732.
35 Henry Anderson, "Lost Relatives," *Richmond Planet*, January 26, 1896.
36 Henry Anderson, "Found His Relatives," *The Freeman*, April 23, 1896.
37 Emphasis in the original. Felix Haywood Interview, San Antonio, TX, June 6, 1938, Federal Writers' Project Interviews (FWP Interviews) of the Works Progress Administration, ed. George P. Rawick, *The American Slave: A Composite Autobiography*, Supplement, Series 2, Vol. 5, Texas Narratives, Part 4 (Westport, CT: Greenwood Press, 1979), 1690.
38 Baumgartner found that three-quarters of fugitive slaves caught in Texas between 1837 and 1861 were headed to Mexico and 8 percent to Indian Territory (Oklahoma). Alice Baumgartner, *South to Freedom: Runaway Slaves to Mexico and the Road to the Civil War* (New York: Basic Books, 2020), 165–82. Alwyn Barr, *Black Texans: A History of African Americans in Texas, 1528–1995* (Norman: University of Oklahoma Press, 1996), 29.
39 Charles W. Ramsdell, "The Natural Limits of Slavery Expansion," *Southwestern Historical Quarterly* 33 no. 2 (October 1929): 97.
40 Walter Johnson, *River of Dark Dreams: Slavery and Empire in the Cotton Kingdom* (Cambridge, MA: Belknap Press of Harvard University Press, 2017), 330–65.
41 Henry and Susan Anderson, 1880 Federal Census, Precinct No. 2, Wood County, TX, 25. Henry and Susan Anderson, 1900 Federal Census, Wood County, TX, 19.
42 Barr, *Black Texans*, 17.

43 Frederick Law Olmsted, *A Journey Through Texas; or, A Saddle-Trip on the Southwestern Frontier* (New York: Dix, Edwards, & Co, 1857), 66, 123.
44 Olmsted, *A Journey Through Texas*, 92.
45 Randolph B. Campbell, *Empire of Slavery: The Peculiar Institution in Texas, 1821–1865* (Baton Rouge: Louisiana State University Press, 1989), 185–226.
46 Lu Lee Interview, Dallas, TX, April 5, 1938, Federal Writers' Project of the Works Progress Administration, George P. Rawick, ed. *The American Slave: A Composite Autobiography*, Supplement, Series 2, Vol. 6, Texas Narratives, Part 5 (Westport, CT: Greenwood Press, 1979), 2300–2301.
47 Randolph B. Campbell, *Gone to Texas: A History of the Lone Star State* (New York: Oxford University Press, 2003), 255–59.
48 According to Barr, 47 enslaved Texans enlisted in the USCT. Barr, *Black Texans*, 37.
49 Campbell, *Gone to Texas*, 259–60.
50 Dale Baum estimates that 51,000 enslaved people were taken to Texas during the war. Dale Baum, "Slaves Taken to Texas for Safekeeping During the Civil War," in *The Fate of Texas: The Civil War and the Lone Star State*, ed. Charles D. Grear (Fayetteville: University of Arkansas Press, 2008), 88.
51 Smith Austin Interview, Hill Country, TX, District No. 8, July 19, 1937, Federal Writers' Project of the Works Progress Administration, George P. Rawick, ed. *The American Slave: A Composite Autobiography*, Supplement, Series 2, Vol. 2, Texas Narratives, Part 1 (Westport, CT: Greenwood Press, 1979), 133–34.
52 Felix Haywood Interview, FWP Interviews, 1691–92.
53 Campbell, *Empire of Slavery*, 249.
54 Barr estimates 250,000. Barr, *Black Texans*, 36. Baum estimates 240,099 in 1864. Baum, "Slaves Taken to Texas," 89. William L. Richter estimates there were 400,000 in 1865. William L. Richter, *The Army in Texas During Reconstruction, 1865–1870* (College Station: Texas A&M University Press, 1987), 33n5.
55 Felix Haywood Interview, FWP Interviews, 1692.
56 Richter, *The Army in Texas*, 16. Twenty-seven thousand USCT troops occupied the state in 1865, half of the total Union forces in the state. David Work, "United States Colored Troops in Texas During Reconstruction, 1865–1867," *Southwestern Historical Quarterly* 109, no. 3 (January 2006): 340.
57 Felix Haywood Interview, FWP Interviews, 1692.
58 Major General Philip H. Sheridan to Major General John A. Rawlins, October 1, 1866, New Orleans, *Executive Documents Printed by Order of the House of Representatives During the Second Session of the Fortieth Congress,*

1867–'68, Vol. 7 (Washington, D.C.: Government Printing Office, 1868), 32. Major General Philip H. Sheridan to Major General John A. Rawlins, "Report on Operations in Texas and on the Rio Grande," November 14, 1866, New Orleans, *The War of the Rebellion: The Official Records of the Union and Confederate Armies*, Series 1, Vol. 48, Part 1, Reports, Section 1, 301–2.

59 Only 5,000 troops were in Texas February 1866, and nearly all of them were on the border. Moneyhon, *Texas After the Civil War*, 37.

60 "Colored Conference," *Tri-Weekly Herald* (Marshall, TX), July 5, 1879, 2.

61 Rice, *The Negroes of Texas*, 203.

62 Nell Painter, *Exodusters: Black Migration to Kansas After Reconstruction* (New York: Alfred A. Knopf, 1977), 137.

63 "Reasons for and Against the Negro Exodus: Frederick Douglass Gives His Views in Opposition—A Reply by Prof. Greener," *New York Times*, September 13, 1879.

64 "Colored Conference," 2.

65 The Brookses had three children in 1880, one who was school-aged. Pinkney and Bettie Brooks, 1880 Federal Census, Precinct No. 2, Wood County, TX, June 2, 1880, 6.

66 St. Paul Missionary Baptist Church website, http://www.stpaulbaptistmineola.org/church-history.html, accessed March 27, 2022.

67 East Chapel Christian Methodist Episcopal Church was founded in 1872. East Chapel Christian Methodist Episcopal Church website, https://www.eastchapelcmechurch.org/aboutus, accessed April 4, 2022. Sandy Anderson reported on the work of ME reverends. Sandy Anderson, "Mineola, Wood Co., Tex., October 13, 1894," *Richmond Planet*, October 20, 1894.

68 Wood County Historical Commission, *Images of America*, 98. Moneyhon, *Texas After the Civil War*, 59, 168.

69 Lucy Mead, "Do You Know Them," *Richmond Planet*, October 19, 1895, https://informationwanted.org/items/show/1036.

70 Sandy Anderson for Sallie Gatewood, "Wanted," *Richmond Planet*, October 25, 1902, https://informationwanted.org/items/show/2814.

71 "Texas Wants One Million Emigrants Annually for Twenty Years," the company-produced timetable map announced. *International & Great Northern R.R.*, 1878.

72 According to the 2020 Federal Census, Mineola's population is 4,823. A poverty rate of 22 percent was derived from the United States Census Bureau, 2019 American Community Survey 5-Year Estimates, U.S. Census Bureau, American Community Survey Office, December 10, 2020, https://www.texas-demographics.com/mineola-demographics, accessed March 29, 2022.

73 Henry and Susan Anderson, 1900 Federal Census, Precinct No. 2, Wood County, TX, July 9, 1900, 19. Sandy Anderson (and "Lucy M."), 1900 Federal Census, Precinct No. 2, Wood County, TX, July 5, 1900, 18. Ann Carter, 1900 Federal Census, Mineola, Wood County, TX, June 6, 1900, 6. Susan Anderson, 1910 Federal Census, Precinct No. 2 (Mineola), Wood County, TX, April, n.d., 1910, 4.

74 Donald R. Walker, *Penology for Profit: A History of the Texas Prison System, 1867–1912* (College Station: Texas A&M University Press, 1988), 188.

CHAPTER SIX **Looking for Lias**

1 George and Beverly appear in the 1890 Montclair Township Directory. *Baldwin's Directory of the Oranges and Townships of Essex County* (Orange, NJ: F. W. & J. H. Baldwin, 1889), 73–74. George Tibbs, New Jersey State Census, 1905, Town of Montclair, NJ, June 10, 1905, 14. Beverly Tibbs, 1900 Federal Census, Worcester City, MA, June 7, 1900, 7. Beverly appears as a porter in *Worcester Directory* 1900, Fred. A. Mann & Company, Worcester Historical Museum, 485.

2 Carrie Allen McCray, *Freedom's Child: The Life of a Confederate General's Black Daughter* (Chapel Hill, NC: Algonquin Books, 1998), 136.

3 Carole Emberton, *To Walk About in Freedom: The Long Emancipation of Priscilla Joyner* (New York: W. W. Norton, 2022), xix.

4 Howard Thurman quoted in James Grossman, *Land of Hope: Chicago, Black Southerners, and the Great Migration* (Chicago: University of Chicago Press, 1991), 19.

5 Jack Temple Kirby, "The Southern Exodus, 1910–1960: A Primer for Historians," *Journal of Southern History* 49, no. 4 (November 1993): 1.

6 Moore F. and Lucy B. Carter, 1850 Federal Census, Turners District, Fauquier County, VA, July 31, 1850, n.p. Moore F. and Lucy B. Carter, 1860 Federal Census, 9th Magisterial District, Fauquier County, VA, June 16, 1860, 11.

7 Historian Stephanie Jones-Rogers contrasts examples of male enslavers giving children away with female enslavers who either kept the children or sold them. Stephanie E. Jones-Rogers, *They Were Her Property: White Women as Slave Owners in the American South* (New Haven, CT: Yale University Press, 2019), 135–36.

8 Samuel J. Tebbs, 1850 Federal Census, Turners District, Fauquier County, VA, October 3, 1850, 324. Samuel J. Tebbs, 1850 U.S. Federal Slave Schedule, Turners District, Fauquier County, VA, October 3, 1850, 95–96. S. J. Tebbs, 1860 U.S. Federal Slave Schedule, N.E. District, Fauquier County, VA, July 5, 1860, 22.

9 Richard J. Hinton, *John Brown and His Men; with Some Account of the Roads They Traveled to Reach Harper's Ferry* (New York: Funk & Wagnalls Company, 1894), 310–11.

10 William Blair, *Virginia's Private War: Feeding Body and Soul in the Confederacy, 1861–1865* (New York: Oxford University Press, 2000), 123.

11 Emberton, *To Walk About in Freedom*, 36.

12 Ida Powell Dulany Diary, November 28, 1864, quoted in Kathi Ann Brown, Walter Nicklin, and John T. Toler, *250 Years in Fauquier County: A Virginia Story* (Fairfax, VA: George Mason University Press, 2008), 98–99.

13 Brown et al., *250 Years in Fauquier County*, 89–92. Thavolia Glymph, *The Women's Fight: The Civil War's Battles for Home, Freedom, and Nation* (Chapel Hill: University of North Carolina Press, 2020), 113.

14 Lucy Tibbs (39 yrs) + male child (5 yrs), "List of Indigent Freedmen in L'Ouverture Hospital recommended for transfer to Freedmans Village, Va.," L'Ouverture Hospital, Alexandria, VA, Records of the Field Offices for the State of Virginia, Bureau of Refugees, Freedmen, and Abandoned Lands, 1865–1872, National Archives and Records Administration (NARA), Washington, D.C., NARA Series Number: M1913, NARA Reel No. 43, RG 105, October 7, 1866. Lucy Tibbs & Son, "Names of Persons to Whom Shoes Have Been Issued at L'Ouverture Hospital," Reel No. 54, November 29, 1866. Amy Murrell Taylor, *Embattled Freedom: Journeys Through the Civil War's Slave Refugee Camps* (Chapel Hill: University of North Carolina Press, 2018), 160.

15 Harriet Jacobs to L. M. Child, Alexandria, VA, March 18, 1863, *The Harriet Jacobs Family Papers*, Jean Fagin Yellin et al., eds, Vol. 2 (Chapel Hill: University of North Carolina Press, 2008), 469.

16 Harriet Jacobs, quoted in "Fair for Disabled Colored Soldiers at Alexandria, VA," *The Liberator* (Boston, MA), January 12, 1865, Jacobs Family Papers, Vol. 2, 610.

17 The July 17, 1862, Militia Act stipulated that Black soldiers would earn less than whites and not be paid bounties. Although the March 3, 1863, Enrollment Act allowed drafted men to hire a substitute for $300, military officials later clarified that there would be no interracial substitutions. The policy seems to have been universally ignored. Militia Act, July 17, 1862. Enrollment Act, March 3, 1863. James B. Fry, Circular No. 53, July 20, 1863, *Official Records of the War of the Rebellion*, Series 3, Vol. 3, 548. The U.S. Congress approved equal pay for USCT troops on June 15, 1864. Chap. CXXIV, Statutes at Large, Treaties, and Proclamations of the United States, Vol. 13 (Boston, 1866), 126–30.

18 George "Tabes," 6th USCT, Company F, Compiled Military Service Records of Volunteer Union Soldiers Who Served with the United States Colored Troops, NARA, RG 94, 4.

19 James McPherson, *Battle Cry of Freedom: The Civil War Era* (New York: Oxford University Press, 2003), 819.

20 James M. Paradis, *Strike the Blow for Freedom: The 6th United States Colored Infantry in the Civil War* (Shippensburg, PA: White Mane Books, 1998), 82–83.

21 Invalid Pension Application for George Tibbs, Private, 6th USCT, Company F, Montclair, NJ, April 21, 1898, Pension Application No. 965735, in Julia A. Tibbs, Widow's Pension Application, Montclair, NJ, April 11, 1924, Pension Application No. 1122973, NARA, RG 15, 18.

22 Anonymous, "Bought and Sold," *Christian Recorder* (Philadelphia, PA), February 20, 1864, 1.

23 According to Paradis, the 6th was made up of soldiers with the following birthplaces: Pennsylvania (36 percent), Delaware (16 percent), Maryland (15 percent), and Virginia (12 percent); the remaining 21 percent hailed from many places, including Washington, D.C., New Jersey, New York, Canada, Jamaica, and Great Britain. Paradis, *Strike the Blow for Freedom*, 35, 159–63.

24 Asher died of typhoid in Wilmington, NC. Jeremiah Asher to Abraham Lincoln, Philadelphia, PA, September 7, 1863, in *To Address You as My Friend: African Americans' Letters to Abraham Lincoln*, ed. Jonathan W. White (Chapel Hill: University of North Carolina Press, 2021), 186–87. Don Sailer, "Asher, Jeremiah W.," *House Divided: The Civil War Research Engine at Dickinson College*, https://hd.housedivided.dickinson.edu/node/32518, accessed July 22, 2022.

25 "The Colored Republican Meeting," *Montclair Times* (Montclair, NJ), September 20, 1902, 4.

26 George Tibbs, Invalid Pension Application, 18.

27 Adam (60 years), Lucy (55 years), George (28 years), and Beverly (13 years) Tibbs, 1870 Federal Census, Scott Township, Fauquier County, VA, August 19, 1870, 96.

28 Mose [Moore] F. Carter, 1870 Federal Census, Third Township, Warren County, VA, August 3, 1870, 39.

29 Frank Marten to Joe Perkins, Esq., Claiborne County, MS, n.d., 1873, Fluvanna Historical Society Collections, Palmyra, VA.

30 Eugene M. Scheel, *The Civil War in Fauquier County, Virginia* (Warrenton, VA: Fauquier Bank, 1985), 94–95.

31 By 1900, there were 26 Black churches in Fauquier County. Brown, *250 Years in Fauquier County*, 122.

32 Richard Lowe, "Local Black Leaders During Reconstruction in Virginia," *Virginia Magazine of History and Biography* 103, no. 2 (April 1995): 181–206. J. Tivis Wicker, "Virginia's Legitimization Act of 1866," *Virginia Magazine of History and Biography* 86, no. 3 (July 1978): 339–44.

33 Eric Foner, *Reconstruction: America's Unfinished Revolution, 1863–1877* (New York: Harper & Row, 1988), 592–93.

34 Brendan Wolfe, "Danville Riot (1883), *Encyclopedia of Virginia*, https://encyclopediavirginia.org/entries/danville-riot-1883/, accessed August 16, 2022. "The Danville Riot," Richmond *Dispatch*, November 4, 1883, 2.

35 Ida Powell Dulany, *In the Shadow of the Enemy: The Civil War Journal of Ida Powell Dulany* (Knoxville: University of Tennessee Press, 2009), December 1864, 177–80. Jones-Rogers, *They Were Her Property*, 175–76.

36 Mary Taylor placed the couple's home in Willisville. Deposition of Mary Taylor, April 14, 1925, Julia Tibbs Widow's Pension Application, Deposition H, 25.

37 Elias Tibbs, d. June 3, 1877, Virginia Death Registers, 1853–1911, Library of Virginia, Richmond, VA.

Bronchitis causes the lungs and airways to become inflamed. Upper respiratory infections are the leading cause of death of children in the developing world, particularly children with underlying conditions or who are exposed to airborne pollutants. American children who die of this condition are likely to be Black and male. Michel Garenne, Caroline Ronsmans, and Harry Campbell, "The Magnitude of Mortality from Acute Respiratory Infections in Children Under 5 Years in Developing Countries," *World Health Statistics Quarterly* 45 (1992): 45.

38 Ida Tibbs, b. June 1875, Orange, VA, Library of Virginia State Archive, Births, Marriages, and Deaths, 1853–1900. Witnesses on behalf of Julia Tibbs's pension application testified that Ellen died in 1887. Chief of Special Examination Division, Special Examination Division, January 17, 1925, Julia A. Tibbs Widow's Pension Application.

39 Emberton, *To Walk About in Freedom*, 130.

40 Henry S. Little et al., Senate Joint Resolution No. 1, State of New Jersey, February 19–20, 1868.

41 Association for the Study of African American Life and History, "The Negro in New Jersey," *Negro History Bulletin* 5, no. 3 (December 1941): 59, 70.

42 *Souvenir Program: Dr. Booker T. Washington's Tour of New Jersey, September 7th, 8th, 9th, 10th, 1914*, Compiled by W. P. Burrell, 1914, New Jersey State Publications Digital Library, 35–36.

43 Booker T. Washington, "Cotton States and International Exposition Speech," Atlanta, GA, 1895.

44 Julia Tibbs, Julia Tibbs's Widow's Pension Application, January 31, 1925, Deposition A, 6–10.

45 The *Montclair Times* claimed that the man charged people 25 cents for the use of his ladder. "North-Western Weather: The Commerce of the Metropolis Paralyzed by a Fair Specimen of a Dakota Snow Storm," *Montclair Times*, March 17, 1888, 3.

46 Henry Whittemore, *History of Montclair Township, New Jersey; Including the History of Families Who Have Been Identified with Its' {sic} Growth and Prosperity* (New York: The Suburban Publishing Company, 1894), 105.

47 "Mr. George Tibbs and Mrs. Julia Stevens," Personal, *Montclair Times*, April 14, 1888, 3.

48 Death of James Crane, *Montclair Times*, December 30, 1882, 3.

49 Four Tibbses appear in the 1890 Montclair City Directory, including Beverly and George and also Stephen and Charles. George and Julia lived on Orange Road and Beverly on Glenridge Avenue. *Baldwin's Directory of the Oranges and Townships of Essex County* (Orange, NJ: F. W. & J. H. Baldwin, 1889), 73–74. George and Julia first appear on 19 Cross Street in 1908. *Directory of Montclair, Bloomfield, Caldwell, Essex Fells, Glen Ridge, and Verona* (Newark, NJ: The Price & Lee Company, Publishers, 1908), 207. Union Baptist was located on Bloomfield Avenue. Whittemore, *History of Montclair Township*, 105. Today, the church is located at Midland Avenue. Union Baptist Church of Montclair website, https://www.ubcmontclair.org/, accessed July 10, 2022.

50 Julia Tibbs Deposition, 5.

51 In 1905 and 1910, two Virginia-born female tenants lived with them and worked as laundresses; their husbands and sons worked as servants. George Tibbs, 1905 New Jersey State Census, Essex County, Town of Montclair, June 10, 1905, 14. George Tibbs, 1910 Federal Census, Essex County, NJ, April 23, 1910, 8.

52 Carrie Allen McCray, *Freedom's Child: The Life of a Confederate General's Black Daughter* (Chapel Hill, NC: Algonquin Books, 1998), 148.

53 George Tibbs's Invalid Pension Application, 115.

54 Edward Ayers, *The Promise of the New South: Life After Reconstruction* (New York: Oxford University Press, 1992), 52. Maxine N. Lurie and Richard Veit, *New Jersey: A History of the Garden State* (New Brunswick, NJ: Rutgers University Press, 2012), 205–6.

55 "Competing with a Circus: The New Jersey Republican League Has a Meeting," *New York Times*, August 16, 1888, 4.

56 "Delegates to Asbury Park," *Montclair Times*, August 11, 1888, 2. In 1902, George was elected vice president of Montclair's Colored Republican Club. "Colored Republican Meeting," *Montclair Times*, September 20, 1902, 4.

57 W. E. Burghardt Dubois [*sic*], "The Republicans and the Black Voter," *The Nation*, June 5, 1920, 757.

58 In her deposition in support of Julia's pension application, Alice claimed that she and Beverly were married in 1888. To further complicate matters, an 1890 Essex County, NJ, birth record indicates that Alice Young gave birth to a baby girl whose father was Beverly Tibbs. By 1900, Beverly Tibbs was living in Worcester with his wife of seven years, Mary. Deposition of Alice Tibbs, Worcester, MA, August 28, 1925, Julia Tibbs's Widow's Pension Application, Deposition A, 3–4. Beverly Tibbs, 1900 Federal Census, Worcester City, County of Worcester, MA, June 7, 1900, n.p. Beverly Tibbs, 1910 Federal Census, Worcester City, County of Worcester, MA, April 22, 1910, n.p. Beverly Tibbs and Alice Young, Marriage Registration, NJ, August 19, 1915, No. 34384.

59 Deposition of Alice Tibbs, Julia Tibbs's Application for a Widow's Pension, August 26, 1925, Deposition A, 4.

60 Deposition of Lessie [*sic*] Irvine, Julia Tibbs's Application for a Widow's Pension, Montclair, NJ, February 9, 1925, Deposition F, 19.

61 McCray, *Freedom's Child*, 136.

62 Grossman, *Land of Hope*, 68, 74.

63 Mia Bay, *Traveling Black: A Story of Race and Resistance* (Cambridge, MA: Harvard University Press, 2021), 63.

64 Private Elias Tibbs, Company H, 1st U.S.C.I., Compiled Military Service Records of Volunteer Union Soldiers Who Served with the United States Colored Troops, NARA, RG 94, M1819, Roll No. 0015, 12.

65 The island was renamed Theodore Roosevelt Island. C. R. Gibbs, *Black, Copper, and Bright: The District of Columbia's Black Civil War Regiment* (Silver Spring, MD: Three Dimensional Publishing, 2002), 147. William Dobak, *Freedom by the Sword: The U.S. Colored Troops, 1862–1867* (Washington, D.C.: The Center for Military History, 2011), 314.

66 Dobak, *Freedom by the Sword*, 317.

67 Du Bois quoted in David Levering Lewis, *W. E. B. Du Bois: A Biography, 1868–1963* (New York: Henry Holt, 2009), 380.

68 Brandi Clay Brimmer, *Claiming Union Widowhood: Race, Respectability, and Poverty in the Post-Emancipation South* (Durham, NC: Duke University Press, 2020), 215.

69 Beverly died in 1939; he and Alice had no children. After her husband's death, Alice returned to Montclair, living just a couple of miles from where Julia and George had once lived. Beverly Tibbs, Worcester, 1939, *Index to Deaths in Massachusetts, 1936–1940*, U.S., Death Index, 1901–1980, Vol. 95, 213. Alice Tibbs, "wid. Beverly," *Montclair, New Jersey, City Directory* (Price & Lee Co., 1955), 448.

CHAPTER SEVEN Emeline and Julia

1 Octavia Ethrington, "Do You Know Them?," *Richmond Planet* (Richmond, VA), January 11, 1896, in *Last Seen: Finding Family After Slavery*, https://informationwanted.org/items/show/1039. Mrs. Eannie [Fannie] R. Roly, "Can You Help Her?," Information Wanted, *Huntsville Gazette* (Huntsville, AL), July 31, 1886, https://informationwanted.org/items/show/3462.

2 "Personalities," *Sunday Morning Call* (Battle Creek, MI), December 14, 1884, Courtesy of Willard Library, Battle Creek, MI.

3 Untitled, *Battle Creek Daily Moon* (Battle Creek, MI), November 18, 1885, Courtesy of Willard Library, Battle Creek, MI. "After Forty-One Years: Meeting of Two Sisters Who Last Saw Each Other in Slavery," *Sunday Morning Call*, November 22, 1885, Courtesy of Willard Library, Battle Creek, MI. The *Moon* claimed the women had been separated thirty-five years.

4 In 1850, the couple had two children, three-year-old Aurena and one-year-old Rebecca. A third child appears in the 1860 Census, three-year-old Joseph. Born in Canada, Joseph likely died sometime before he turned thirteen, as he disappears from the record. In both censuses, their household included Kentucky-born men whose relationship to them was unclear. In 1880, Joseph and Emeline "Skippworth" lived with their daughters, nineteen-year-old Frances and sixteen-year-old Jennie. Carrie "Skiperth" appears only in a county death record, next to the names of her parents. She was fifteen when she died of typhoid pneumonia. Joseph and Emeline Skipworth, 1850 Federal Census, Emmett Township, Calhoun County, MI, August 23, 1850. Joseph and Emeline Skipworth, 1860 Federal Census, City of Battle Creek, Calhoun County, MI, June 9, 1860, 71. Joseph and Emeline Skippworth [*sic*], 1880 Census, Fifth Ward, City of Battle Creek, Calhoun County, MI, June 18, 1880, 33. Carrie Skiperth [*sic*], d. May 24, 1880, Death Records, Michigan Department of Community Health, Division for Vital Records and Health Statistics, Lansing, MI; U.S. Death Records, 1867–1952, September 24, 1881, 130.

5 Untitled, *Battle Creek Daily Moon*, November 18, 1885.

6 "After Forty-One Years," *Sunday Morning Call*, November 22, 1885.

7 "After Forty-One Years," *Sunday Morning Call*, November 22, 1885.

8 A study of freedom-seeking people in five states found that only 19 percent of suspected runaways were female. John Hope Franklin and Loren Schweninger, *Runaway Slaves: Rebels on the Plantation* (New York: Oxford University Press, 1999), 212, 64. Anne Marshall estimated that 5,000 enslaved people escaped Kentucky every year. Anne E. Marshall, *Creating a Confederate Kentucky: The Lost Cause and Civil War Memory in a Border State* (Chapel Hill: University of North Carolina Press, 2013), 13.

9 Isaiah and Julia Lyons had three children in their household in 1860: nineteen-year-old Henry, eight-year-old Harriet (both of whom were born in Kentucky), and Walter, a seven-month-old boy born in Ohio. Isaiah and Julia Lyons, 1860 Federal Census, Troy, Miami County, OH, June 8, 1860, 47.

10 Henry Bibb, *Narrative of the Life and Adventures of Henry Bibb, An American Slave, Written by Himself* (New York, 1846). Ezra Greenspan, *William Wells Brown: An African American Life* (New York: W. W. Norton, 2014). Carver Clark Gayton, "A Re-Introduction to Lewis Clarke, Harriett Beecher Stowe's Forgotten Hero," in Lewis Garrard Clarke, *Narrative of the Sufferings of Lewis Clarke, During a Captivity of More than Twenty-Five Years* (1845) (Seattle: University of Washington Press, 2012). Lewis Hayden in: Stephen Kantrowitz, *More than Freedom: Fighting for Black Citizenship in a White Republic, 1829–1889* (New York: Penguin, 2012).

11 "Out of Bondage: A Reminiscence of the Underground Railroad. How Perry Sanford Escaped Slavery. Thrilling Experiences on the Way to Michigan," *Sunday Morning Call*, August 3, 1884, Courtesy of Willard Library, Battle Creek, MI.

12 "After Forty-One Years," *Sunday Morning Call*, November 22, 1885.

13 According to the 1840 Census, John R. Stephens owned three female slaves, ages 10 to 23 years; perhaps among them was Julia and/or Emeline. One female slave on the inventory appears old enough—36 to 54 years—to have had teenage children. Jesse Petty, Catherine's husband, owned three female slaves, ages 10 to 23 years, that same year, although any of John Stephens's slaves would have been part of Catherine's dowry. In 1850, Emeline was likely the 21-year-old female marked as "Fugitive from the state." John R. Stephens, 1840 Federal Census, Kenton, KY. Jesse Petty, 1840 Federal Census, Kenton, KY. Death Record for Carrie Skiperth [*sic*], May 24, 1880, Return of Deaths, Calhoun County, Battle Creek Department of Community Health, Division for Vital Records and Health Statistics, Lansing, MI.

14 Julia was consistently identified with an "M" for "mulatto" on the census schedules. In 1870, she was a live-in domestic in the household of a Black (marked with a "B") man named Henry Banks with her children: 29-year-old Henry Vickers and 10-year-old Walter, eight-year-old Arthur, and five-year-old Elisa Lyons. All three of the younger children were attending school. Julia Lyons, 1870 Federal Census, Troy, Miami County, OH, June 7, 1870, 51.

15 Abram White, *Southwestern Christian Advocate* (New Orleans, LA), September 9, 1885, https://informationwanted.org/items/show/2392.

16 Sarah Ann Lewis, *Southwestern Christian Advocate*, September 21, 1882, https://informationwanted.org/items/show/1813.

17 Jesse Petty spelled his wife's name "Catharine" in his will; elsewhere it is "Catherine." Last Will and Testament of Jesse Petty, July 13, 1833. Probated in Kenton County Court, KY, September 15, 1845, Wills and Probate Records, Index to Order Books (Probate Matters), 1840–1962.

18 Stephanie E. Jones-Rogers, *They Were Her Property: White Women as Slave Owners in the American South* (New Haven, CT: Yale University Press, 2019), 31–37. Catherine did not remain a widow for long; she married sometime before the 1850 Census. James Huston, 1850 Federal Census, Kenton County, KY, September 23, 1850, 102.

19 "After Forty-One Years," *Sunday Morning Call*, November 22, 1885.

20 "$25 Reward," *Weekly Standard* (Raleigh, NC), October 12, 1852, *Freedom on the Move*, https://database.freedomonthemove.org/advertisements/8c33206f-e3a4-4b49-aa8a-e8b656542a8f. "Fifteen Dollars Reward," *Carolina Sentinel* (New Bern, NC), March 2, 1827, *Freedom on the Move*, https://database.freedomonthemove.org/advertisements/498a0507-e402-4230-bd5e-127e216a2bc2. Runaway slave ad looking for Littleton, *Tennessee Republican Banner* (Nashville, TN), October 1, 1841, and April 18, 1842, quoted in Franklin and Schweninger, *Runaway Slaves*, 63–65, 656n39.

21 By comparison, *Freedom on the Move* includes more than 30,000 (32,254 as of May 22, 2024) "Runaway Slave" advertisements placed before 1865. https://app.freedomonthemove.org/.

22 William Robinson, *The Liberator* (Boston, MA), March 2, 1849, https://informationwanted.org/items/show/3298. John A. Murry, *Provincial Freeman and Weekly Advertiser* (Windsor/Toronto/Chatham, Canada West), March 1, 1856, https://informationwanted.org/items/show/1140. Ellen Nettleton, *Provincial Freeman and Weekly Advertiser*, November 10, 1855, https://informationwanted.org/items/show/1138.

23 Eric Foner estimates that 1,000–5,000 people escaped every year between 1830 and 1860. Eric Foner, *Gateway to Freedom: The Hidden History of the Underground Railroad* (New York: W. W. Norton, 2015), 4.

24 Berenice Bryant Lowe, *Tales of Battle Creek* (Albert L. and Louisa B. Miller Foundation, Inc., 1976), 19–20.

25 Federal government policy aimed to relocate the Potawatomi and Ottawa north to present-day Wisconsin and Minnesota. Elizabeth Neumeyer, "Michigan Indians Battle Against Removal," *Michigan History* 4 (1971): 275. About the Pottawatomi, Lowe concludes, "It is surprising that the local Indians gave up their favorite spots with meekness." Lowe, *Tales of Battle Creek*, 30–31. Neumeyer's study, on the other hand, determined that only 651 Indigenous people, most of them likely Potawatomi and the rest perhaps Ottawa and Chippewa, had left the state by 1850. Neumeyer, "Michigan Indians Battle Against Removal," 278.

26 Steven Hahn, *The Political Worlds of Slavery and Freedom* (Cambridge, MA: Harvard University Press, 2009), 31–32.

27 According to the 1840 Federal Census, there were 10,599 people living in Calhoun County, excluding Native Americans. Twenty-three were free people of color. In 1850, the total population of the county was 19,162; 207 were free people of color. The free Black population of Cass County, located to the south and west of Calhoun, on the Ohio border, grew even more rapidly. The total non-Indigenous population of Cass County in 1840 was 5,710; this included eight free people of color. By 1850, Cass County's non-Indigenous population had grown to 10,907, of which 389 were free people of color. Compendium of the 1840 Federal Census, 92–94. Compendium of the 1850 Federal Census, 254.

28 Lowe, *Tales of Battle Creek*, 36–37. Bruce A. Rubenstein and Lawrence E. Ziewacz, *Michigan: A History of the Great Lakes State*, 5th ed. (Hoboken, NJ: Wiley-Blackwell, 2014), 91–92.

29 "Out of Bondage," *Sunday Morning Call*, August 3, 1884.

30 The white population grew by 10,000. The total non-Indigenous population of Calhoun County was 29,180. Compendium of the 1860 Federal Census, 231, 233.

31 The modern church is located at 364 West Van Buren. Gerda Gallop and Sonya Bernard, "Since the 1850s, Black Churches in Battle Creek Have Been Helping People and Fighting Battles," *Battle Creek Enquirer* (Battle Creek, MI), January 28, 1996, 1A and 5A. Frank Brown, "The Vision Made Real: The History of Mt. Zion AME Church," in *A Brief History of 34 Black Churches in Battle Creek, 1849–1998: One Hundred Forty-Nine Years of Progress* (Battle Creek, MI: Willard Public Library, 1998), n.p.

32 According to Lowe, by 1860 the two grammar schools were located on Green and Champion Streets; the secondary school was located at the corner of Champion and McCamly Streets. Lowe, *Tales of Battle Creek*, 100.

33 "Sojourner Truth Dead." *Nightly Moon* (Battle Creek, MI), November 26, 1883. Nell Irvin Painter, *Sojourner Truth: A Life, A Symbol* (New York: W. W. Norton, 1996), 254.

34 "Sojourner Truth Dead," *The Citizen* (Battle Creek, MI), December 1, 1883.

35 Olive Gilbert and Frances W. Titus, "A Memorial Chapter Giving the Particulars of Her Last Sickness and Death," in *Narrative of Sojourner Truth; a Bondswoman of Olden Time, Emancipated by the New York Legislature in the Early Part of the Present Century; with a History of Her Labors and Correspondence Drawn from Her "Book of Life"; Also, a Memorial Chapter, Giving the Particulars of Her Last Sickness and Death* (Battle Creek, MI: Review and Herald Office, 1884), 10.

36 Joseph Skipworth, d. November 20, 1881, Michigan Deaths and Burials, 1800–1995. Joseph Skiperth [*sic*], d. 20 November 1881. Burial: Oak Hill Cemetery, Battle Creek, Calhoun County, MI. Plot: Lot 809E, Rt 3. Findagrave.com.

37 A notable exception occurred on March 6, 1863. When the U.S. government began drafting white men into the army, whites attacked African Americans and destroyed Black-owned property in Detroit, as was the case in other Northern cities. The *Detroit Free Press* called it "the bloodiest day that ever dawned upon Detroit." "A Bloody Riot," *Detroit Free Press*, March 7, 1863, 1. Paul Finkelman, "Michigan," *Oxford African American Studies Center*, 2006, https://doi-org.ezp1.villanova.edu/10.1093/acref/9780195301731.013.44887, accessed March 8, 2023.

38 June Baber Woodson, "The Negro in Detroit to 1900," *Negro History Bulletin* 22, no. 5 (January 1959): 90–91.

39 In the 1884 Battle Creek directory Emeline was listed as a widowed laundress living with her daughter Frances on Pittee Street. Her occupation does not appear in the 1886 directory, and she and Frances lived at 2 Pittee Street. Emeline and Frances L. Skiperth [*sic*], 3 Pittee Street, Battle Creek, MI, City Directory, 1884, U.S. City Directories, 1822–1995, 176. Emeline and Frances L. Skiperth [*sic*], 2 Pittee Street, Battle Creek, MI, City Directory, 1886, U.S. City Directories, 1822–1995, 196.

40 Aurena married a stonemason named John Henderson. Rebecca married Alexander Dixon; in 1880 they had two daughters, Luttie and Carrie, who lived close enough to visit their grandmother. Frances lived with and cared for her mother until Emeline died. Then she married an engineer named James Mack and settled in Battle Creek for a time. John and "Irena" Henderson, 1880 Federal Census, Fifth Ward, City of Battle Creek, Calhoun County, MI, June 3, 1880, 5. Alexander and Rebecca Dixon, 1880 Federal Census, First Ward, Battle Creek, Calhoun County, MI, June 7, 1880, 13. Frances died on May 1937 in Robbins, Cook County, IL, Illinois Deaths and Stillbirths Index, 1916–1947.

41 "Personalities," *Sunday Morning Call*, December 14, 1884.

42 The total number of enslaved people in the state in 1850 was 210,751; of those, 96 were recorded as "fugitives." By 1860, the enslaved population totaled 225,483; 119 were "fugitives." James C. Klotter and Craig Thompson Friend, *A New History of Kentucky* (Lexington: University of Kentucky Press, 2018), 161.

43 "After Forty-One Years," *Sunday Morning Call*, November 22, 1885. Julia appears as "Judy" in Stephens's will; she is named alongside a man named Dennis, likely her uncle. Last Will and Testament of John R. Stephens, Kentucky, U.S., Wills and Probate Records, 1774–1989, April 26, 1857.

44 Marriage License for Isaiah Lyons and Julia "Vakers" [*sic*], September 24, 1859, Ohio, County Marriages, 1789–2016, Marriage records 1854–1862, Vol. G, image 217 of 325.

45 No death certificate or record could be found for Isaiah Lyons; he no longer appears in the census after 1860. In his 1897 affidavit in support of Julia's application for a mother's pension, Isaiah's brother Walter Lyons stated that Isaiah died around 1867. Affidavit of William H. Lyons, September 9, 1897, Mother's Pension Claim of Julia Lyons, Mother of Henry Vickers, 5th USCT, Company D, Application No. 615.751, NARA, RG 15.

46 Vickers, Henry, Co. D., 5th US Colored Infantry, Compiled Military Service Records of Volunteer Union Soldiers, M1820. Affidavit of A. J. Johnson in support of Henry Vickers, 5th USCT Company D, Declaration for an Original Invalid Pension, Application No. 727.401, December 31, 1889, NARA, RG 15. William Dobak, *Freedom by the Sword: The U.S. Colored Troops, 1862–1867* (Washington, D.C.: The Center for Military History, 2011), 312, 368, 405.

47 The Black population of Miami County, Ohio, in 1860 was 800, and whites numbered 29,157. By 1870, the numbers were 1,049 and 31,691, respectively. 1860 Census Compendium, 369, 365. 1860 Census Compendium, 82, 83.

48 Mrs. Elizabeth Smith searching for her sister, *Christian Recorder* (Philadelphia, PA), March 17, 1887, https://informationwanted.org/items/show/853. Mrs. Anna M. Cox searching for her brother Thomas Henry Burrah, *Southwestern Christian Advocate*, September 9, 1884, https://informationwanted.org/files/show/2794. George Green searching for his son Samuel Allen, *Southwestern Christian Advocate*, May 21, 1885, https://informationwanted.org/files/show/2674.

49 Affidavit of Julia Lyons, March 7, 1898, Julia Lyons's Dependent Mother's Pension Application, No. 615.751.

50 Records show addresses in Detroit, Chicago, and Cleveland, as well as in Troy, Ohio. In both the 1880 and 1900 Census, Walter was living with his mother in Troy. In 1880, Julia's occupation was listed as "washerwoman." Her household included two sons, two daughters, and a granddaughter: twenty-one-year-old Walter and 15-year-old Ella [Eliza] Lyons and 40-year-old Henry Vickers, 27-year-old Harriet Vickers, and nine-year-old Ida Clark. Marriage License for Walter S. Lyons and Maud Singleton, December 28, 1910, No. 71567, Ohio, U.S., County Marriage Records, 1774–1993. Death Certificate for Walter S. Lyons, Cleveland, OH, Certificates of Death, 1908–1953, November 8, 1912. Julia Lyons, 1880 Census, Troy, Miami County, MI, June 12, 1880, 29. Julia Lyons, 1900 Census, Elm Street, Troy, Miami County, OH, June 16, 1900, 25.

51 "After Forty-One Years," *Sunday Morning Call*, November 22, 1885.

52 David Blight, *Race and Reunion: The Civil War in American Memory* (Cambridge, MA: Belknap Press of Harvard University Press, 2001), 233.

53 Blight, *Race and Reunion*, 237.

54 Wilbur H. Siebert, *The Underground Railroad from Slavery to Freedom: A Comprehensive History* (New York and London: Macmillan Company, 1898). When Siebert began collecting Underground Railroad reminiscences in the 1890s, popular interest in Underground Railroad stories had been building for some time, fed by local initiatives like Battle Creek's.

55 Foner, *Gateway to Freedom*, 12–14.

56 "Out of Bondage," *Sunday Morning Call*, August 3, 1884.

57 Berenice Bryant Lowe estimated Sanford was 20 years old when he escaped slavery. Sanford worked at Nichols & Shepard Company, a foundry that made plows and thrashers. Perry Sanford, 1880 Federal Census, Battle Creek, Calhoun County, MI, June 2, 1880, 3. Perry Sanford, 1900 Federal Census, Battle Creek, Calhoun County, MI, n.d., n.p. Lowe, *Tales of Battle Creek*, 64.

58 "Moonlight," *Battle Creek Daily Moon*, March 7, 1887.

59 Julia died sometime between the administration of the 1900 Federal Census and 1910 when William married Maud Singleton. Julia and William Lyons, 1900 Federal Census, Troy City, Miami County, OH, June 16, 1900, 25. Marriage License for Walter S. Lyons and Maud Singleton, December 28, 1910.

60 Untitled, *Battle Creek Daily Moon*, November 18, 1885.

CHAPTER EIGHT **Henry Saffold's Chain of Evidence**

1 Hubbard O. M. Poe and W. E. Craighill, "The Engineers with General Sherman's Army," *Professional Memoirs, Corps of Engineers, United States Army, and Engineer* 6, no. 27 (May/June 1914): 389.

2 Henry Saffold to Hon. H. H. Carlton, Washington, D.C., May 8, 1888, in Invalid Pension Application for Henry Saffold, Corporal, 135th United States Colored Troops, Company E, Penfield, GA, Pension Application No. 570818, National Archives and Records Administration (NARA), RG 15.

3 Henry Saffold, *Morning News* (Savannah, GA), August 4 and 5, 1888, in *Last Seen: Finding Family After Slavery*, https://informationwanted.org/items/show/3578.

4 Henry Saffold, *Savannah Tribune* (Savannah, GA), November 17 and 24, 1888.

5 Brandi Clay Brimmer, *Claiming Union Widowhood: Race, Respectability, and Poverty in the Post-Emancipation South* (Durham, NC: Duke University Press, 2020), 69.

6 Henry's birthplace was listed once as Athens, Clark County, GA, but other documents indicate that he was born in Morgan County. Henry Saffold, Declaration for an Increase of Pension, Maxeys, Oglethorpe County, GA, February 4, 1905, 15. Affidavit of Henry Saffold Pension application, Maxeys, Oglethorpe County, GA, August 25, 1904, 29.

7 Henry Saffold to Gen. John C. Black, Commissioner, Washington, D.C., Saffold Pension File, May 30, 1888. Even so, Henry continued to appear in the census as Nelson.

8 Arthur Hood to Scott Harrison, Secretary of State, Millegeville, GA, November 7, 1851. File II, Reference Services, RG 4-2-46, Georgia Archives. There were 73 enslaved people on his Buckhead, Georgia, plantation in 1860 and another 22 in Greene. Thomas P. Saffold, 1860 Federal Slave Schedule, Buckhead, Morgan County, GA, August 24, 1860, 91. T. P. Saffold, 1860 Federal Slave Schedule, Greene County, GA, August 10, 1860, 67.

9 Sarah Reid hailed from Eatonville. If Dinah was part of Sarah Reid's dowry, then she came to Buckhead sometime around 1854, when Thomas married Sarah. Or her enslaver may have been the James Reid, Sarah's cousin, who lived in Buckhead and who counted 71 enslaved people as his property. James S. Reid, 1860 Federal Slave Schedule, Buckhead District, Morgan County, GA, August 24, 1860. Henry Nelson (Saffold), 1870 Federal Census, Madison, Morgan County, GA, July 26, 1870, 183.

10 Thomas P. Saffold, 1860 Federal Census, Buckhead District, Morgan County, GA, August 24, 1860, 989.

11 Joseph E. Brown, "Special Message of Gov. Joseph E. Brown, to the Legislature of Georgia," Milledgeville, GA, November 7, 1860, in *Secession Debated: Georgia's Showdown in 1860*, ed. William W. Freehling and Craig M. Simpson (New York: Oxford University Press, 1992), xii. Alexander H. Stephens, "Unionist Speech, Wednesday Evening, November 14," Milledgeville, GA, November 14, 1860, in Freehling and Simpson, *Secession Debated*, 70–71. "Georgia Secession," January 29, 1861, The Avalon Project, Yale University. Republic of Georgia, "Ordinance of Secession, Passed Jan'ry 19, with the Names of the Signers. An Ordinance to Dissolve the Union Between the State of Georgia and Other States United with Her Under a Compact of Government," Augusta, GA, January 19, 1861, Library of Congress.

12 Thomas P. Saffold to President Andrew Johnson, Confederate Amnesty Papers, NARA, RG 94, August 25, 1865, 1.

Thomas enlisted for six months on August 4, 1863. His absence in November 1864 is a mystery that is not explained in the family history. Thomas P. Saffold, Company B, 9th Georgia Infantry (State Guards), August 4, 1863, Civil War Service Records, Compiled Service Records of Confederate Soldiers Who Served in Organizations from the State of Georgia, NARA, RG 109.

13 Anne Sarah Rubin, *Through the Heart of Dixie: Sherman's March and American Memory* (Chapel Hill: University of North Carolina Press, 2017), 10.

14 Enslaved people in southeastern Georgia fled to occupying U.S. troops on the Sea Islands beginning in spring 1862. It remained exceedingly dangerous for those in the interior of the state to self-emancipate until the arrival of Sherman's men. Clarence L. Mohr, "Before Sherman: Georgia Blacks and the Union War Effort, 1861–1864," *Journal of Southern History* 45, no. 3 (August 1979): 336, 332.

15 Major General Henry W. Slocum, who commanded the left wing, estimated that at least 14,000 enslaved people followed the two wings to Savannah. Report of Major General Henry W. Slocum, Headquarters Left Wing, Army of Georgia, Savannah, GA, No. 49, January 9, 1865, *Official Records of the War of the Rebellion*, Series 1, Vol. 44 (Washington, D.C.: Government Printing Office, 1893), 159.

16 "Special Field Orders No. 120," November 9, 1864, *Memoirs of General William T. Sherman*, Vol. 2 (New York: D. Appleton and Company, 1875), Hathi Trust, 176.

17 Karen Bell Cook, *Claiming Freedom: Race, Kinship, and Land in Nineteenth-Century Georgia* (Columbia: University of South Carolina Press, 2018), 34–36.

18 Clarence Mohr, "Black Troops in Civil War Georgia," *New Georgia Encyclopedia*, July 17, 2020, https://www.georgiaencyclopedia.org/articles/history-archaeology/black-troops-in-civil-war-georgia, accessed March 23, 2023.

19 "Special Field Orders No. 120," *Memoirs of General William T. Sherman*, 176.

20 Henry Saffold to Hon. H. H. Carlton, May 8, 1888, Saffold Pension File. "Carlton, Henry Hull, 1835–1905," History, Art and Archives, U.S. House of Representatives, https://history.house.gov/People/Listing/C/CARLTON,-Henry-Hull-(C000155)/, accessed May 3, 2023.

21 Dolly Lunt Burge, *A Woman's Wartime Journal: An Account of the Passage over Georgia's Plantation of Sherman's Army on the March to the Sea* (New York: The Century Co., 1918), 24–25.

22 Ottis Edwin Guinn Sr. and Suellen Clopton Blanton, "A Tempest in the Briar Patch," *The Clopton Chronicles*, https://homepages.rootsweb.com/~clopton/briar.htm, accessed March 23, 2023.

23 "Your Wife S. Sal" [Sarah] to Thomas, Buckhead, GA, November 5, 1863, in Guinn and Blanton, "A Tempest in the Briar Patch."

24 Thomas P. Saffold, 1860 Federal Census, Buckhead, Morgan County, GA, August 24, 1860, 989.

25 First Lieutenant Charles W. Wills, 2nd Illinois Cavalry, to Mary Emily Wills, December 1, 1864, *Army Life of an Illinois Soldier* (1906), ed. Mary E. Kellogg (Carbondale and Edwardsville: Southern Illinois University Press, 1996), 330.

26 Charles D. Kerr, "From Atlanta to Raleigh," *Glimpses of the Nation's Struggle: A Series of Papers Read Before the Minnesota Commandery of the Military Order of the Loyal Legion United States* (St. Paul, MN: St. Paul Book and Stationery Co., 1887), 215–16. A similar incident occurred six days earlier. Chaplain John J. Hight, *History of the Fifty-Eighth Regiment of Indiana Vols*, ed. Gilbert R. Stormont (Princeton, NJ: Press of the Clarion, 1895), 426–27, 431–32.

27 Solomon Gardner Deposition, October 2, 1913, Solomon Gardner (now known as Solomon Monroe), Private, 135th United States Colored Troops, Company E, Augusta, GA, Pension Application No. 1173324, NARA, RG 15, Deposition A, 7–9.

28 Rubin, *Through the Heart of Dixie*, 90–91.

29 Sherman, *Memoirs*, 55. Congress equalized pay for Black and white soldiers on June 15, 1864. Army Appropriations Act, June 15, 1864, U.S. Statutes at Large, Vol. 13 (1864–1865), 38th Congress, 1st Session, 129–30.

30 Gardner Deposition, October 2, 1913, Gardner Pension File, 7.

31 Henry Suffold [*sic*], Corporal, Company E, 135th United States Colored Troops, Compiled Military Service Records of Volunteer Union Soldiers Who Served the United States Colored Troops: 56th–138th USCT Infantry, 1864–1866, NARA, RG 94.

32 Gardner Deposition, October 2, 1913, Gardner Pension File, 8.

33 Recruiters and surgeons were under orders not to reject Black recruits, particularly as the army expected to put them to work at hard labor. Leslie Schwalm, *Medicine, Science, and Making Race in Civil War America* (Chapel Hill: University of North Carolina Press, 2023), 14–15.

34 An online regimental history offers an incomplete list of the men in the 135th USCT, indicating some of the March 28, 1865, promotions. Soldiers from North Carolina in the 135th U.S. Colored Infantry, https://www.ncgenweb.us/ncusct/usct135y.htm, accessed April 2, 2023.

35 Henry used the term "tetter" that he'd heard from an army doctor. The term "tetter" can be found in contemporary homeopathic manuals describing a number of rashes, including some that appeared regularly or annually. A. E. Small, A.M., M.D., *Manual of Homeopathic Practice, for the Use of Families and Private Individuals* (New York: William Radde, 1869), 802–5.

36 Small, *Manual of Homeopathic Practice*, 803–5.

37 Affidavit of Dinah Saffold, March 9, 1888, Saffold Pension File, 13–14.

38 The measure was a tepid acceptance of emancipation, at best. Sidney Andrews, *The South Since the War: As Shown by Fourteen Weeks of Travel*

and Observation in Georgia and the Carolinas (Boston: Ticknor and Fields, 1866), 239, 241.

39 According to the 1860 Federal Census, the total population of enslaved people in Georgia was 462,108, and whites numbered 1,037,286. The free Black population was 3,500. Joseph C. G. Kennedy, *Population of the United States in 1860; Compiled from the Original Returns of the Eighth Census* (Washington, D.C.: Government Printing Office, 1864), 65–71.

40 Andrews, *The South Since the War*, 377.

41 Paul A. Cimbala, *Under the Guardianship of the Nation: The Freedmen's Bureau and the Reconstruction of Georgia, 1865–1870* (Athens: University of Georgia Press, 1997), 93–98.

42 Allison Dorsey, "'The Great Cry of Our People Is Land!': Black Settlement and Community Development on Ossabaw Island, Georgia, 1865–1900," *African American Life in the Georgia Lowcountry: The Atlantic World and the Gullah Geechee* (Athens: University of Georgia Press, 2010), 224–52.

43 W. E. B. Du Bois found that Black farmers owned more than one million acres of land in Georgia in 1891, assessed at a value of $3.9 million. W. E. B. Du Bois, "The Negro Landholder of Georgia," *Bulletin of the United States Bureau of Labor* 35, no. 6 (July 1901): 665.

44 John F. Stover, "Georgia Railroads During the Reconstruction Years," *Railroad History* 134 (Spring 1976): 37–38.

45 Mildred Thompson, *Reconstruction in Georgia: Economic, Social, Political, 1865–1872* (New York: Columbia University Press, 1915), 310.

46 Frank Magwood Interview, *Federal Writers' Project: Slave Narrative Project*, Vol. 11, North Carolina, Part 2, Jackson–Yellerday, 1941, 93–94, Manuscript/Mixed Material, Library of Congress, https://www.loc.gov/resource/mesn.112/?sp=97&st=image&r=-0.605,0.263,2.21,0.769,0. Hilliard Yellerday Interview, Raleigh, NC, *Federal Writers' Project: Slave Narrative Project*, Vol. 11, North Carolina, Part 2, Jackson–Yellerday, 1941, 436 Manuscript/Mixed Material, Library of Congress, https://www.loc.gov/resource/mesn.112/?sp=436.

47 Andrews, *The South Since the War*, 382.

48 Edmund L. Drago, "Georgia's First Black Voter Registrars During Reconstruction," *Georgia Historical Quarterly* 78, no. 4 (Winter 1994): 763–66.

49 Henry Saffold, Election District 28, Georgia, U.S., Returns of Qualified Voters and Reconstruction Oath Book, 1867–1869, June 28, 1867.

50 Saffold, Confederate Amnesty Papers, 1.

51 Edmund L. Drago, *Black Politicians and Reconstruction in Georgia: A Splendid Failure* (Baton Rouge: Louisiana State University Press, 1982), 48–58. Cimbala, *Under the Guardianship of the Nation*, 219.

52 Georgia's legislature ratified a new constitution that disfranchised Black men in 1908. Clarence Bacote, "Some Aspects of Negro Life in Georgia, 1880–1908," *Journal of Negro History* 43, no. 3 (July 1958): 186.
53 Drago, *Black Politicians and Reconstruction in Georgia*, 76–78, 84–86.
54 By 1875, there were more than 926 people incarcerated at the state penitentiary; 805 were Black men and 30 were Black women. In 1876, the governor granted a charter to a prison camp in Scull Shoals, Greene County, where Dinah and Henry lived. In 1881 the state senate issued a report that revealed the cruelties committed in prison camps. A. Elizabeth Taylor, "The Origin and Development of the Convict Lease System in Georgia," *Georgia Historical Quarterly* 26, no. 2 (June 1942): 118, 120.
55 Drago, *Black Politicians and Reconstruction in Georgia*, 67. Thaddeus Brockett Rice, *History of Greene County, Georgia, 1786–1886*, ed. Carolyn White Williams (Macon, GA: The J. W. Burke Company, 1961), 426–27.
56 The Black population of Greene County in 1880 was 18,165, an increase of 4,000 in ten years. The white population totaled 3,765, or 100 fewer than had lived there at the last census. Bureau of the Census, Department of the Interior, Compendium of the Tenth Census, Part 1 (Washington, D.C.: Government Printing Office, 1885), Table XXIII, 342.
57 E. Merton Coulter, "Scull Shoals: An Extinct Georgia Manufacturing and Farming Community," *Georgia Historical Quarterly* 48, no. 1 (March 1964): 33–63.
58 Coulter, "Scull Shoals," 44–56.
59 Henry and Dinah Nelson (Saffold), 1880 Federal Census, Scull Shoals, Greene County, GA, June 22, 1880, 13.
60 Dan and Sandy Reed [*sic*] and Henry and Dinah Nelson (Saffold), 1900 Federal Census, Scull Shoals, June 2, 1900, n.p.
61 J. M. Colclough to Honorable John Black, Commissioner of Pensions, March 10, 1887, Saffold Pension File. Saffold named two of them in an 1898 Pension Bureau questionnaire: Nathan was born 1884 and Mamie in 1886. Questionnaire, May 5, 1898, Saffold Pension File.
62 Affidavit of John M. Colclough, April 17, 1886, Saffold Pension File, 18. Affidavit of John M.Colclough, May 18, 1888, Saffold Pension File, 19. Affidavit of Dinah Saffold, March 9, 1888, Saffold Pension File. Affidavit of R. L. McWhorter, March 9, 1888, Saffold Pension File, 16.
63 "A Raid on the Treasury," Savannah *Morning News*, December 23, 1886, 1, Georgia Historic Newspapers. "Proposed Pension Laws," Savannah *Morning News*, October 12, 1887, Georgia Historic Newspapers.
64 "An Ex-Slave's Pension," *Savannah Tribune*, February 5, 1887, Georgia Historic Newspapers. No title, *Savannah Tribune*, July 21, 1888, Georgia Historic Newspapers.

65 He paid a lawyer $10 to prepare the application, money he borrowed either from Joel Thornton, the white owner of the shop where he bought provisions, or John Colclough, the justice of the peace, notary public, and postmaster in Penfield who helped Henry with the application. J. M. Colclough to Honorable John Black, Commissioner of Pensions, March 10, 1887, Saffold Pension File. John Colclough, 1900 Census, Militia District 148, Penfield, GA, June 18, 1900, 10. "Record Is Broken," *Macon Telegraph* (Macon, GA), October 5, 1911.

66 Henry Saffold to Hon. H. H. Carlton, May 8, 1888, Saffold Pension File.

67 Brimmer, *Claiming Union Widowhood*, 61–66.

68 Donald R. Shaffer, *After the Glory: The Struggles of Black Civil War Veterans* (Lawrence: University Press of Kansas, 2004), 156.

69 "Additional Evidence," Bureau of Pensions, February 25, 1899, Saffold Pension File.

70 The study was based on a sample of 331 companies. Larry M. Logue and Peter Blanck, *Race, Ethnicity, and Disability: Veterans and Benefits in Post–Civil War America* (New York: Cambridge University Press, 2010), 57, 47, 160–61.

71 Reverend Wm. H. Heard, "The True Condition of the Negro in America," *Christian Recorder* (Philadelphia, PA), October 10, 1889.

72 "*Savannah Morning News* (Savannah) 1868–1887," Library of Congress: Chronicling America, https://www.loc.gov/item/sn82015137/. "Col. J. H. Estill Dead," *New York Times*, November 10, 1907, 9

73 John M. Matthews, "Black Newspapermen and the Black Community in Georgia, 1890–1930," *Georgia Historical Quarterly* 68, no. 3 (Fall 1984): 360–65.

74 According to Matthews, there were 12 Black newspapers operating in the state in 1890 and 29 in 1899. Matthews, "Black Newspapermen and the Black Community in Georgia," 350n1.

75 Stephen Bookhart, March 11, 1889, Saffold Pension File. Written statement of Joshua Hull, October 29, 1889, Saffold Pension File. Affidavit of Joshua Hull, December 16, 1889, Saffold Pension File. Affidavit of Jasper Hayes, June 29, 1889, Saffold Pension File. Affidavit of Brutus Butler, May [day unknown], 1889, Saffold Pension File.

76 Brutus Butler Pension Application, December 17, 1892. E. H. [Nichol?] M.D., May 17, 1893, Physician's Report, Butler Pension File.

77 Drs. C. M Paine, R. E. Hinman, and R. R. Kine [?], Fulton County, GA, Surgeon's Certificate, Saffold Pension File, August 18, 1897.

78 Logue and Blanck, *Race, Ethnicity, and Disability*, 28, 63. Drs. T. M. Askin, J. B. Rudolph, and P. J. Duchett, Gainesville, Georgia, Saffold Pension File, March 3, 1903. Drs. T. M. Askin, J. B. Rudolph, and P. J. Duchett, Gainesville, Georgia, Surgeon's Certificate, Saffold Pension File, November 2, 1904.

A 2017 study of the Veterans Administration found that non-Hispanic Blacks are more likely to be rejected when filing for disabilities related to PTSD than other veterans. Black veterans' rejection rate was 12 percent higher. It is hardly reassuring to note that this is an improvement from the 25 percent difference in physician rejection rates for Black versus white Civil War veterans over the period 1890–1907. No wonder, as Richard Brookshire of the Black Veterans Project has pointed out, the study was buried. Quill Lawrence, "Black Veterans Are Less Likely to Be Approved for Benefits, According to VA Documents," *All Things Considered*, National Public Radio, March 24, 2023, https://www.npr.org/2023/03/24/1165977590/black-veterans-are-less-likely-to-be-approved-for-benefits-according-to-va-docum, accessed May 3, 2023). Black Veterans Project, https://www.blackveteransproject.org/. Logue and Blanck, *Race, Ethnicity, and Disability*, 71.

79 Henry Saffold, Declaration for Increase of Pension, Saffold Pension File, Maxeys, Oglethorpe County, GA, February 4, 1905.

80 Savannah *Morning News*, March 20, 1890, 5.

81 "Georgia Negroes Barred," *New York Times*, October 9, 1908.

82 Dr. L. D. Durham, Application for Reimbursement, Saffold Pension File, August 1, 1911, 3.

83 Dr. L. D. Durham, Application for Reimbursement, 3. Receipt, Office of S. D. Durham, Maxeys, GA, September 13, 1911.

84 "Savannah Ours" and "Sherman's Christmas Present," *New York Times*, December 26, 1864, 1, 4.

85 Brimmer, *Claiming Union Widowhood*, 62.

86 See Wilson Thompson's list of servicemen with whom he had served in Company H, 43rd USCT; Lewis Smith's roll call of men from Company F, 66th USCT, where Smith had served as drummer boy; and Charles Grant's various lists of men from Company H, 24th USCT. Wilson Thompson, *Christian Recorder*, February 13, 1890, https://informationwanted.org/items/show/1108. Lewis Smith, *National Tribune* (Washington, D.C.), August 29, 1901, https://informationwanted.org/items/show/2786. Charles W. Grant, *National Tribune*, April 11, 1907, https://informationwanted.org/items/show/2827.

CHAPTER NINE **Husbands and Wives**

1 Anne Humphreys, "*Enoch Arden*, the Fatal Return, and the Silence of Annie," *Victorian Poetry* 30, no. 3/4 (Autumn/Winter 1992): 331.

2 "*Enoch Arden*: Tennyson's New Poem," *Godey's Lady's Book*, February 1865.

3 "Enoch Is Out," *Jackson Daily Citizen* (Jackson, MI), April 22, 1891, 1. More than 40 percent of the dead in the U.S. Army were unidentified; the number was higher in the Confederacy. Drew Gilpin Faust, *This Republic of Suffering: Death and the American Civil War* (New York: Alfred A. Knopf, 2008), 102.

4 "The Latest Enoch Arden," *New York Times*, November 11, 1876, 4. "The Enoch Arden Business," *Weston Democrat* (Weston, WV), December 11, 1876, 1. "Will the Enoch Arden Business Never End," *New York Herald*, September 14, 1882, 6.

5 Untitled, *Ukiah Republican Press* (Ukiah, CA), November 8, 1878, 3. Untitled, reprinted in *New York Tribune*, July 23, 1875, 4. "A Colored Enoch Arden," *Redwood Gazette* (Redwood Falls, MN), January 24, 1878, 2.

6 "Matrimonial Romances," *St. Louis Globe-Democrat* (St. Louis, MO), January 23, 1885. "Sold into Slavery," *Wilson Advance* (Wilson, NC), May 2, 1884.

7 Ulrich B. Phillips, *American Negro Slavery: A Survey of the Supply, Employment and Control of Negro Labor as Determined by the Plantation Regime* (New York: D. Appleton and Company, 1918), Project Gutenberg, e-book, 2004, 460.

8 Robert Anderson and Ida Pryor, "Romantic Lives of Slave Couple," *Staunton Daily Leader* (Staunton, VA), January 9, 1905. Wesley Torrey, "Romantic Meeting," Memphis *Public Ledger*, June 28, 1882.

9 Tera Hunter, *Bound in Wedlock: Slave and Free Black Marriage in the Nineteenth Century* (Cambridge, MA: Harvard University Press, 2017), 29, 26.

10 James Dogans, Private, Company K, 43rd USCT, June 28, 1864, *Civil War Service Records, Compiled Military Service Records of Volunteer Union Soldiers Who Served with the United States Colored Troops: Infantry Organizations*, National Archives and Records Administration (NARA), RG 109.

11 Steven V. Ash, *Middle Tennessee Society Transformed, 1860–1870: War and Peace in the Upper South* (Knoxville: University of Tennessee Press, 2006), 107–9.

12 Amy Murrell Taylor, *Embattled Freedom: Journeys Through the Civil War's Slave Refugee Camps* (Chapel Hill: University of North Carolina Press, 2018), 80–81.

13 William Dobak, *Freedom by the Sword: The U.S. Colored Troops, 1862–1867* (Washington, D.C.: The Center for Military History, 2011), 362–65, 443–46.

14 James Dogans, 1870 Federal Census, Pottstown, Montgomery County, PA, July 14, 1870, 21.

15 Pottstown's white population numbered 4,096 in 1870. Forty miles away, Philadelphia's Black population was 22,147, out of a total population of

651,854. Francis A. Walker, *A Compendium of the Ninth Census* (Washington, D.C., 1872), 319, 320, 86, 87. The *Dispatch* reported on news in Montgomery and Berks Counties.

16 Bethel African Methodist Episcopal Church was founded in 1871. Paul Chancellor, *A History of Pottstown, Pennsylvania*, Historical Society of Pottstown (Pottstown, PA: Feroe Press, 1953), 63.

17 "State News," *Pittsburgh Commercial*, August 5, 1871, 1.

18 Laura Spicer, quoted in Lucy Chase to family, Gordonsville, VA, 1869, Henry L. Swint, *Dear Ones at Home: Letters from Contraband Camps* (Nashville, TN: Vanderbilt University Press, 1966), 242–43.

19 It was not uncommon for more than one woman to file a claim for a widow's pension when a USCT veteran died. Brandi Clay Brimmer, *Claiming Union Widowhood: Race, Respectability, and Poverty in the Post-Emancipation South* (Durham, NC: Duke University Press, 2020), 63.

20 John and Peggie Walker, 1870 Federal Census, 8th District, Nashville, Davidson County, TN, July 28, 1870, 7.

21 Peggy [*sic*] Patterson, 1880 Federal Census, Nashville, Davidson County, TN, June 3, 1880, 7. Peggie and John's son, Miles Walker, and his wife, Amanda, lived next door, along with their six children. In 1870, Miles still went by the last name Patterson, though his mother adopted Walker. Ten years later, the situation was reversed.

22 Henry Adams, *Southwestern Christian Advocate* (New Orleans, LA), June 20, 1878, in *Last Seen: Finding Family After Slavery*, https://informationwanted.org/items/show/1188. Daniel Sherman, *Southwestern Christian Advocate*, April 22, 1880, https://informationwanted.org/items/show/1371.

23 E. M. and Eliza Patterson, 1850 Federal Census, Civil District No. 9, Davidson County, TN, October 4, 1850, n.p. Marriage Certificate of E. M. Patterson and Eliza W. White, Williamson, TN, October 29, 1924, Tennessee State Library and Archives, Nashville, Tennessee State Marriages, 1780–2002.

According to his passport application, Patterson's first name was Everard. Everard M Patterson, U.S. Passport Application, March 2, 1857, NARA, Passport Applications, 1795–1905, Roll 60, Volume Roll 060, 19 Feb 1857–04 Apr 1857.

24 Walter T. Durham, *Volunteer Forty-Niners: Tennesseans and the California Gold Rush* (Nashville, TN: Vanderbilt University Press, 1997), 35.

25 In December 1849, the California legislature approved a constitution that outlawed slavery, but a loophole allowed enslavers like Patterson to come to California with their enslaved people. Rudolph M. Lapp, *Blacks in Gold Rush California* (New Haven, CT: Yale University Press, 1977), 130.

26 In his diary of the journey, a member of the company, Madison Berryman Moorman, refers to the two men as "Walker and John, col'd." Walker is sometimes rendered "Bl'k Walker." There were two other Black man in their company, J. M. Morrow and Dick Rapier. Madison Berryman Moorman, Nashville, TN, April 27, 1860, in *The Journal of Berryman Moorman, 1850–1852*, ed. Irene D. Paden and Louis Parks Barnes (San Francisco Historical Society, 1948), 1, 57, 30. There is no trace of these three Black men alongside the rest of the company in 1860. Everett [Everard] M. Patterson, 1860 Federal Census, Cosumnes River, El Dorado, CA, October 5, 1860, 47.

There were 240 African Americans living in Sacramento County in 1850; 195 were men and 45 were women. Clarence Caeser, "Historical Demographics of Sacramento's Black Community, 1848–1900," *California History* 75, no. 3 (Fall 1996): 200–206.

27 Stacey L. Smith, "Remaking Slavery in a Free State: Masters and Slaves in Gold Rush California," *Pacific Historical Review* 80, no. 1 (February 2011): 53.

28 *Berryman Moorman Journal*, May 1, 1850, 43; May 30, 1850, 16; June 24, 1850, 29; July 26, 1850, 53; July 30–31, 1850, 55–57; September 7, 1850, 79–81.

29 *Berryman Moorman Journal*, June 24, 1850, 30–31.

30 Quoted in Lapp, *Blacks in Gold Rush California*, 12–13, 14.

31 Durham, *Volunteer Forty-Niners*, 165. Patterson put his name forward as postmaster in Sacramento. *Republican Banner and Nashville Whig*, March 14, 1853, 2. Smith, "Remaking Slavery in a Free State," 31.

32 Lapp, *Blacks in Gold Rush California*, 133.

33 "Dark Deeds," *Daily Alta California* (San Francisco, CA), May 29, 1850.

34 Patterson owned 18 enslaved people between the ages of 20 months and 50 years; 14 were men. At least nine of these would have been prime candidates for U.S. Army impressment and recruitment. E. M. Patterson, 1860 Federal Slave Schedule, Davidson County, TN, n.d., 40.

35 Ash, *Middle Tennessee Society Transformed*, 83.

36 James McPherson, *Battle Cry of Freedom: The Civil War Era* (New York: Oxford University Press, 2003), 580–83. Dr. Everard Meade Patterson, d. January 3, 1863, in F. T. Hambrech and J. L. Koste, *Biographical Register of Physicians Who Served the Confederacy in a Medical Capacity* (undated), Findagrave.com, accessed August 7, 2023, https://www.findagrave.com/memorial/115968729/everard-meade-patterson?_gl=1*9pzekk*_gcl_au*MTc4ODkoODAyMi4xNjg3MjY5NTY2.

37 Ash, *Middle Tennessee Society Transformed*, 128–32. Eric Foner, *Reconstruction: America's Unfinished Revolution, 1863–1877* (New York: Harper & Row, 1988), 43–45.

38 Walker lived at No. 114 P Street between 4th and 5th; in 1869, both churches were located on Seventh Street. The Historical Marker Database, https://www.hmdb.org/m.asp?m=4327. Clarence Caeser, "The Historical Demographics of Sacramento's Black Community, 1848–1900," *California History* 75, no. 3 (Fall 1996): 213.

39 Hannah Rosen, *Terror in the Heart of Freedom: Citizenship, Sexual Violence, and the Meaning of Race in the Postemancipation South* (Chapel Hill: University of North Carolina Press, 2009), 61–83.

40 Rosen, *Terror in the Heart*, 259n71.

41 "Their Ultimatum," *Republican Banner* (Nashville, TN), April 30, 1874, 4. Aderson Bellegarde Francois, "Speak to Your Dead, Write to Your Dead: David Galloway, Malinda Brandon, and a Story of American Reconstruction," *Georgetown Law Journal* 111, no. 1 (October 2022): 31–93.

42 "Chapter 1: Of Husband and Wife; Title IV: Of Rights in the Domestic Relations," *Compilation of the Statute Laws of the State of Tennessee, Session of 1870–'71*, ed. Seymour D. Thompson and Thomas M. Steger (St. Louis: W. J. Gilbert, 1873), 2437 (interracial marriage ban); 2447a (automatic marriage for freed people); 2436, 2438, and 2446 (bigamy).

43 Hunter, *Bound in Wedlock*, 219.

44 For instance, Allen Melton was convicted of bigamy when he married a woman without divorcing the woman to whom he had been married in slavery, even though he was not aware that that first marriage had any legal bearing. *State v. Melton*, N.C, 26 S.E. 933 (1897), accessed from *Court Listener* (July 17, 2023), https://www.courtlistener.com/opinion/3930882/state-v-melton/.

45 Untitled, *Bucyrus Journal* (Crawford County, OH), September 16, 1881.

46 Marriage License for John Cantrell and Cornelia Shute, Sumner County, TN, Nashville, May 1866, TN, U.S., Marriage Records, 1780–2002. Cordelia Cantrell, 1900 Federal Census, Princeton City, Gibson County, IN, June 25, 1900, 34.

47 Peggy [*sic*] and Edmund Patterson, 1880 Federal Census, Sixth Ward, Nashville, Davidson County, TN, June 3, 1880, 7.

48 Willie Ann Grey to Husband, Salvisa, KY, April 7, 1866, quoted in Dorothy Sterling, ed., *We Are Your Sisters: Black Women in the Nineteenth Century* (New York: W. W. Norton, 1984), 316.

49 Turner's birth date and place were recorded variously as 1845, 1830, and 1827 and South Carolina, Louisiana, and Alabama. Her 1882 death certificate records her age as fifty-five years and her birthplace as Alabama. Araminta Turner, 1870 Federal Census, Philadelphia, PA, July 8, 1870, 83. Araminta Turner, 1880 Federal Census, Philadelphia, PA, June 7, 1880, 15. Araminta Turner, Coroner's Certificate, Philadelphia, PA, d. October 31, 1882.

50 Anderson Clements, 1850 Federal Slave Schedule, Mobile, AL, December 28, 1850, n.p.

51 Jno (1), John R (2), William (11), H (6), James (6), A (1), Robt (10), Oliver (1), Saml (2), James (12), Chas (3), David (5), Jos (4), Benj Turner (3), 1850 Federal Slave Schedule, Mobile, AL.

52 Randolph B. Campbell, *An Empire for Slavery: The Peculiar Institution in Texas, 1821–65* (Baton Rouge: Louisiana State University Press, 1989), 244–45.

53 Kate Stone, "Elysian Fields," Lamar County, TX, August 1863, 237, and July 7, 1863, *Brokenburn: The Journal of Kate Stone, 1861–1868*, ed. John Q. Anderson (Baton Rouge: Louisiana State University Press, 1955), 237, 223.

54 Ash, *Middle Tennessee Society Transformed*, 112–13, 132–36.

55 Lucy Chase to Dear Ones, March 4, 1863, and July 1, 1864, *Dear Ones at Home*, 53–54, 123–24.

56 Lucy Chase to Dear Ones, April 1, 1863, *Dear Ones at Home*, 68.

57 Taylor, *Embattled Freedom*, 162. Thavolia Glymph, *The Women's Fight: The Civil War's Battles for Home, Freedom, and Nation* (Chapel Hill: University of North Carolina Press, 2020), 191.

58 "Circular," Pennsylvania Abolition Society's Committee on Employment, Pennsylvania Abolition Society Papers, Historical Society of Pennsylvania, Philadelphia, 1865.

59 Anonymous to Pennsylvania Abolition Society, n.d., in Sterling, *We Are Your Sisters*, 255.

60 Glymph, *The Women's Fight*, 192.

61 The Miller children were 20, 15, 12, and eight years old. Andrew and Henrietta Miller, 1870 Federal Census, Philadelphia, PA, July 8, 1870, 83.

62 Judith Giesberg, *Army at Home: Women and the Civil War on the Northern Home Front* (Chapel Hill: University of North Carolina Press, 2009), 105–15.

63 In 1860, Philadelphia's Black population numbered 22,185 (of 565,529 total, or 3.9 percent); twenty years later it was 31,699 (of 847,170, or 3.7 percent). W. E. B. Du Bois, *The Philadelphia Negro: A Social Study* (Philadelphia: University of Pennsylvania Press, 1899), 47.

64 Andrew Diemer, "Reconstructing Philadelphia: African Americans and Politics in the Post–Civil War North," *Pennsylvania Magazine of History and Biography* 133, no. 1 (January 2009): 55–56.

65 Du Bois, *The Philadelphia Negro*, 53–57.

66 "Ex-Slaves Married: Two Old Darkies United After a Separation of Twenty-Five Years," *Courier-Journal* (Louisville, KY), January 17, 1894, https://informationwanted.org/items/show/3359.

67 "After Many Years: Reunion of a Colored Man and His Wife," *Cincinnati Enquirer* (Cincinnati, OH), August 17, 1880, https://informationwanted.org/items/show/3238.

68 Hunter, *Bound in Wedlock*, 14, 31–34.

69 Allen and Rebecca Cuthbert, 1880 Federal Census, Philadelphia, PA, June 7, 1880, 18. Allen was 76, and Rebecca was 68. Araminta Turner's age was listed as 50 (she was actually 53), and her birthplace was mistakenly recorded as Louisiana. A widow, Araminta is identified as the cook. Also in the household were 40-year-old chambermaid Sarah Coppick (white); 25-year-old waitress Helen Hamlin; and 21-year-old gardener S. L. Marshall (Black).

70 Deborah Gray White, *Ar'n't I a Woman? Female Slaves in the Plantation South* (New York: W. W. Norton, 1985), 132.

71 Lou Davis, *Southwestern Christian Advocate*, April 10, 1884. Lou Davis, *Southwestern Christian Advocate*, April 17, 1884. Lou Davis, *Southwestern Christian Advocate*, February 7, 1884.

72 The court confirmed the legality of slave marriages, like Lavinia's, and it ruled that she was a widow and could inherit her deceased husband's property. *Holmes v. Johnson*, 42 Pa. 159 (1862).

73 Araminta Turner, Return of Death in the City of Philadelphia, Cemetery Records (1882), Philadelphia, PA, October 31, 1882. Burial at Olive Cemetery, November 3, 1882. "Philadelphia Matters," *Christian Recorder* (Philadelphia, PA), September 12, 1878.

74 "Woman at Home," *Christian Recorder*, June 8, 1861. Weaver was a fan of Tennyson and quoted from *Enoch Arden* in the pages of the newspaper. "A Dear Baby Song," *Christian Recorder*, August 20, 1864.

75 Charles Chesnutt, "The Wife of His Youth," *Atlantic Monthly*, July 1898.

CHAPTER TEN **Diana Johnson's Hope**

1 In the ads she sent to the papers, her name was spelled variously as "Dianah," "Dianna," and "Diana." The last spelling was most frequent, appearing in the census, tax, and land records.

2 "Lost Friends," *Southwestern Christian Advocate* (New Orleans, LA), July 15, 1885, in *Last Seen: Finding Family After Slavery*, https://informationwanted.org/items/show/2448; September 3, 1885, https://informationwanted.org/items/show/2447; December 13, 1894, https://informationwanted.org/items/show/4956; January 28, 1897, https://informationwanted.org/items/show/4974. "Information Wanted, *Christian Recorder* (Philadelphia, PA), February 17, 1898, https://informationwanted.org/items/show/448.

3 "Echo of Slavery," *Buffalo Evening News* (Buffalo, NY), January 16, 1900, 9, https://informationwanted.org/items/show/4962; "Former Slave Writes

to Clerk," *Buffalo Enquirer* (Buffalo, NY), January 16, 1900, 1, https://informationwanted.org/items/show/4967; "Reminder of Slavery," *Buffalo Review* (Buffalo, NY), January 17, 1900, 6, https://informationwanted.org/items/show/4966; "Szuka krewnych (Looking for Relatives)," *Dziennik Chicagoski* (Chicago Daily News), January 17, 1900; "News Facts in Outline," *Freeport Journal-Standard* (Freeport, IL), January 18, 1900, 3, https://informationwanted.org/items/show/4965; *Rock Island Argus* (Rock Island, IL), January 18, 1900, 4; *Champaign Daily Gazette* (Champaign, IL), January 18, 1900, 7; *Courier* (Waterloo, IA), January 18, 1900, 2; *Kenosha Evening News* (Kenosha, WI), January 18, 1900, 8; *Fremont Semi-Weekly Herald* (Fremont, NE), January 19, 1900, 3.

4 "Reminder of Slavery," *Buffalo Review*, January 17, 1900, 6.

5 Nina Silber, *The Romance of Reunion: Northerners and the South, 1865–1900* (Chapel Hill: University of North Carolina Press, 1997), 178–85.

6 "Former Slave's Letter: Mrs. Diana Johnson of Texas Asks That Her Relatives Communicate with Her," *Buffalo Weekly Express* (Buffalo, NY), January 18, 1900, 2.

7 George Hellard appeared on the 1820 Federal Census as an owner of three enslaved people: one female and male, between the ages of 14 and 25, and a boy under age 14. George Hellard, 1820 Federal Census, Battalion 3 or Forks of the Yadkin, Rowan, NC, August 7, 1820, 392–93. In 1830, he owned six enslaved people, including one woman between 24 and 25 years old and five children, under 10 years old. George Hellard, 1830 Federal Census, Rowan County, NC, n.d., n.p. George could not be found in 1840, but Catherine Hellard appeared in the county in 1840 as the owner of one enslaved person, a woman aged 36 to 54. Catherine Hellard, 1840 Federal Census, Rowan County, NC, n.d., 5.

8 An enumerator recorded Diana's age in 1900 as 72. In 1910, it was 85. Diana Johnson, 1900 Federal Census, Goliad Precinct 1, Goliad, TX, June 8, 1900, 6. Dianah [*sic*] Johnson, 1910 Federal Census, Goliad, TX, May 27, 1910, 18. In 1900, Lucy was listed as living with her mother in Goliad in June, although the letters were addressed from Edna in January.

9 Maria and William Billups had one child; she appears as Anna/Fanny, born in 1868. Maria's sister, Lucy, lived with the couple in 1880. Mariah [*sic*] Billups, 1880 Federal Census, Precinct 1, Goliad, TX, June 1, 1880, 4. Kate and her husband, Sam Ware, had 12 children in 1900: Dianah E, b. 1871; Laticia, b. 1874; twin brothers, Collumbus and A.A., b. 1876; Lucy J., b. 1878; Sammir, b. 1882; Godfrey, b. 1885; Clifford, b. 1887; Arminta, b. 1889; Fannie L., b. 1891; Katie, b. 1895; and Pauline, b. 1897. They had one granddaughter in 1900. Kate and Samuel Ware, 1880 Federal Census, Beeville Precinct 1, Bee County, TX, June 1, 1880, 24. Kate

and Samuel Ware, 1900 Federal Census, Precinct 1, Goliad County, TX, June 1, 1880, 22–23. Alexander and Louisa Johnson's children were Eddie, b. 1882, and Lillian Gray, b. 1879; they had two grandchildren. Alexander Johnson, 1900 Federal Census, Precinct 1, Goliad County, TX, June 25, 1900, 10. Edward, or Eddie, lived with his mother and sisters Lucy and Maria in 1910. Dianah Johnson, 1910 Federal Census, Precinct 1, Goliad Town, Goliad County, TX, May 27, 1910, 18. In 1920, Edward and Maria Billups still lived in Goliad, but there was no sign of their mother, Diana, who would have turned 94 that year. Maria Billups and Edward Johnson, 1920 Federal Census, Goliad Town, Precinct 1, January 24 and 26, 1920, 10A. "Edna, TX," Brownson Malsch, Texas State Historical Association, *Handbook of Texas History*, September 21, 2023, https://www.tshaonline.org/handbook/entries/edna-tx, accessed October 14, 2023.

10 Sara R. Massey, "After Emancipation: Cologne, Texas," in *African Americans in South Texas History*, ed. Bruce A. Glasrud (College Station: Texas A&M University Press, 2011), 90, 93.

11 Eighty-five-year-old Diana told the census enumerator in 1910 that she'd attended school that year. Dianah [*sic*] Johnson, 1910 Federal Census, Goliad, Goliad County, TX, May 27, 1910, 18.

12 The city council authorized the building of a public ferry from San Patricio Street in 1866 and another one on Commercial Street in 1870. Jakie L. Pruett and Everett B. Cole, *History and Heritage of Goliad County* (Austin, TX: Eakin Publications, 1983), 212.

Among Diana Johnson's Goliad neighbors, various freed people placed advertisements in the papers: Amanda Jane Prince, *Southwestern Christian Advocate*, September 10, 1885, https://informationwanted.org/items/show/2399; Adam Coleman, *Southwestern Christian Advocate*, February 28, 1889, https://informationwanted.org/items/show/4312; Nelly Gladney, *Southwestern Christian Advocate*, April 17, 1879, https://informationwanted.org/items/show/1307; Adeline Williams, *Southwestern Christian Advocate*, February 28, 1879, https://informationwanted.org/items/show/1174; Charlotte Butler, *Southwestern Christian Advocate*, September 11, 1884, December 4, 1884, and February 28, 1889, https://informationwanted.org/items/show/4313; Martha Lott, *Southwestern Christian Advocate*, September 13, 1877, https://informationwanted.org/items/show/1200.

13 The census of 1900 registered the following numbers: Buffalo: 1,698 African Americans of 352,387 total. Chicago: 30,150 African Americans of 1,698,575 total. Goliad County: 1,806 African Americans of 8,310 total. New York City's Black population that year was 60,666. *Compendium of 1900 Census*, cxix (Chicago), cxx (Buffalo), cxxi (New York City), and 558 (Goliad County).

14 Affidavit of Diana Johnson, File 47, Abstract 171, Goliad Preemption, Goliad Land Records, Goliad County Courthouse, Diana Johnson, 160 acres, Act of August 12, 1870, July 8, 1873. Affidavit of Diana Johnson to apply for a title, File 47, Abstract 171, August 24, 1876.

Today, that land is still identified the way the clerk recorded it that day: "File #47, Abstract 171, D. Johnson, Goliad Preemption."

15 Diana Johnson Deed, Goliad County Deeds, General Land Office of Texas, Austin, No. 61, Vol. 6, Filed August 9, 1877, Filed September 3, 1881, Recorded September 6, 1881. Affidavit of Diana Johnson attesting to the sale of property to Samuel Ware, September 3, 1881, Goliad Land Records, Goliad County Courthouse.

16 Affidavit of David A. Claiborne attesting to the sale of property to Dianna [*sic*] Johnson, "Lot No. three (3) in Stoddard's addition," March 26, 1884, Goliad Land Records, Goliad County Courthouse.

17 "Echo of Slavery," *Buffalo Evening News*, January 16, 1900, 9, https://informationwanted.org/items/show/4962. "Slavery Days. Texas Woman Tells a Story of the Breaking Up of Her Family—Letter to County Clerk Wende," *Buffalo Commercial Advertiser* (Buffalo, NY), January 16, 1900, 9, https://informationwanted.org/items/show/3642. "Former Slave Writes to Clerk," *Buffalo Enquirer*, January 16, 1900, 1, https://informationwanted.org/items/show/4967.

18 Otto H. Wende lived with his widowed mother, Mary. Otto Wende, 1900 Federal Census, Alden, Erie County, NY, n.d., 7. "Otto H. Wende Dies Following an Operation," *Buffalo Courier Express* (Buffalo, NY), December 26, 1926, 29. "Otto H. Wende Dead," *Buffalo Times* (Buffalo, NY), December 26, 1926, 43.

19 Ruth-Ann Harris and Donald M. Jacobs, *The Search for Missing Friends: Irish Immigration Advertisements Placed in the Boston* Pilot (Boston: New England Historic Genealogical Society, 1989), Vol. 1, ix–x.

20 Maxine Seller, "The Education of Immigrant Children in Buffalo, New York, 1890–1916," *New York History* 57, no. 2 (April 1976): 184.

21 The Cook County Courthouse was the subject of a corruption investigation in 1906, but James Healy was cleared of all charges. "Hear of Safe Loot During Linn Regime," *Inter-Ocean* (Chicago, IL), January 22, 1906, 3. "Clerk Aids Healy in Graft Inquiry," *Inter-Ocean*, January 23, 1906, 3.

22 "Szuka krewnych" (Looking for Relatives), *Dziennik Chicagoski* (*Chicago Daily News*), January 17, 1900, https://informationwanted.org/items/show/4972. About *Dziennik Chicagoski*, Chicago, IL, 1890–1971, Library of Congress, Chronicling America, https://chroniclingamerica.loc.gov/lccn/sn83045747/, accessed October 14, 2023.

23 Untitled, *Rock Island Argus*, January 18, 1900, https://informationwanted.org/items/show/4973.

24 Lillian Serece Williams, *Strangers in the Land of Promise: The Creation of an African American Community, Buffalo, New York, 1900–1940* (Bloomington: Indiana University Press, 1999), 12.

25 Clara Bashop (Chapter 1) and Beverly Tibbs (Chapter 6) placed ads in Black newspapers in Chicago.

26 Randolph B. Campbell, *An Empire for Slavery: The Peculiar Institution in Texas, 1821–65* (Baton Rouge: Louisiana State University Press, 1989), 41.

27 Population of the United States, Compendium of the 1860 Census, 480. On the 1870 Federal Census, Diana's children are Alexander, Edward, Catherine, Lucy, and Maria (Billups). Catherine was 13 at the time, indicating a birth date of around 1857. There are no further records of Catherine, but in all remaining censuses, Kate (and sometimes Katie) appears to be about the same age. Diana Johnson, 1870 Federal Census, Goliad, TX. Kate Ware, 1880 Federal Census, Beeville, Bee County, TX, June 1, 1880, 23.

28 Enumerators consistently marked Diana as "Black" and her children as "mulatto." Maria's death certificate said her father was a man named Dick Jones. In the census, Alex said his father was Mexican. Mrs. Maria Billups, Certificate of Death, Goliad, Goliad County, TX, January 26, 1923. Alex Johnson, 1910 Federal Census, Beeville, Bee County, TX, April 28, 1910, 12A.

29 Lucy H. Johnson, 1900 Federal Census, Precinct 1, Goliad County, TX, June 8, 1900; here Lucy's birthday is listed as September 1864. Diana (and her daughter Lucy) appears as a widow on the 1910 census. Dianah [*sic*] Johnson, 1910 Federal Census, Goliad, Goliad County, TX, May 27, 1910, 18.

30 Carl H. Moneyhon, *Texas After the Civil War: The Struggle of Reconstruction* (College Station: Texas A&M University Press, 2004), 146–50, 202.

31 Martha Patton Interview, *Federal Writers' Project: Slave Narrative Project*, Vol. 16, Texas, Part 3, Lewis–Ryles, 1941, 175, Manuscript/Mixed Material, Library of Congress, https://www.loc.gov/item/mesn163/. Christian L. Lott, 1850 Federal Census, Goliad County, TX, September 17, 1850, n.p. C. S. Lott, 1860 Federal Slave Schedule, Goliad County, TX, July 18, 1860, 24. C. S. Lott, 1860 Federal Census, Goliad County, TX, July 18, 1860, 3.

32 "Article 3455: An Act to Regulate the Disposal of the Public Lands of the State of Texas," August 1, 1870, *Early Laws of Texas: General Laws from 1836 to 1879*, Vol. 3, 30–31. Pruett and Cole, *History and Heritage of Goliad County*, 85.

Freed people in South Carolina and Florida purchased uninhabited/uncultivated property via a similar program. Eric Foner, *Reconstruction: America's Unfinished Revolution, 1863–1877* (New York: Harper & Row, 1988), 374–75, 375n53.

33 Alwyn Barr found that, despite restrictions that came after the 1870 measure, around 30 percent of Black Texans still owned some land early in the twentieth century. Alwyn Barr, introduction to *Black Cowboys of Texas*, ed. Sara R. Massey (College Station: Texas A&M University Press, 2004), 13.

34 The account of armed Black men lining the streets of Goliad on election day 1872 has been told variously, with one account claiming that the men were part of the State Police and others identifying the men as "Black cowhands." Pruett and Cole, *History and Heritage of Goliad County*, 27. Craig H. Roell, "Goliad County," Texas State Historical Association, 1952 (updated: October 27, 2020), https://www.tshaonline.org/handbook/entries/goliad-county.

35 Fannin Street Church was founded in 1872. Pruett and Cole, *History and Heritage of Goliad County*, 78. Minnehulla was founded around 1870, according to the application filed at the Texas Historical Commission for a historical marker. J. A. White Family Goliad Center of Texas History Archives, Goliad Historical Association, Goliad Public Library, Goliad, TX.

36 In 1856, for instance, the board passed ordinances punishing enslaved people with 50 lashes for appearing in town without a pass, prohibiting the assembly of "more than four negroes," and banning enslaved people from visiting town. Minutes of the Board of the Corporation of Goliad, 1869–1895, in Pruett and Cole, *History and Heritage of Goliad County*, 211–12.

37 Pruett and Cole, *History and Heritage of Goliad County*, 54.

38 George Washington, *Southwestern Christian Advocate*, June 12, 1884, https://informationwanted.org/items/show/2514.

39 Death estimates varied in the storm's aftermath. The *Houston Daily Post* reported a total of 72. The *El Paso Herald* put the number at 90. Most of the dead were Black. "Southwestern Texas Cyclone," *Houston Daily Post* (Houston, TX), May 19, 1902, 1. "Texas Town Wiped Out," *El Paso Herald* (El Paso, TX), May 19, 1902, 1. Pruett and Cole, *History and Heritage of Goliad County*, 39.

Index